THE MYSTICAL AS POLITICAL

The Mystical
AS POLITICAL

———

Democracy and Non-Radical Orthodoxy

ARISTOTLE PAPANIKOLAOU

———

University of Notre Dame Press
Notre Dame, Indiana

University of Notre Dame Press
Notre Dame, Indiana 46556
www.undpress.nd.edu
All Rights Reserved

Manufactured in the United States of America
Copyright © 2012 by University of Notre Dame Press
Reprinted in 2014

Library of Congress Cataloging-in-Publication Data

Papanikolaou, Aristotle.
The mystical as political : democracy and non-radical Orthodoxy /
by Aristotle Papanikolaou.
p.   cm.
Includes bibliographical references (p.   ) and index.
ISBN 978-0-268-03896-0 (pbk.) — ISBN 978-0-268-08995-5 (web pdf)
1. Christianity and politics—Orthodox Eastern Church. 2. Political theology.
3. Deification (Christianity) 4. Orthodox Eastern Church—Doctrines.   I. Title.
BX335.P34   2012
261.7—dc23
2012024903

To Byron and Alexander

My Boys

The fear of the Lord is twofold. The first type is produced in us from threats of punishment, and from it arise in proper order self-control, patience, hope in God, and detachment, from which comes love. The second is coupled with love itself and constantly produces reverence in the soul, lest through the familiarity of love it become presumptuous of God. Perfect love casts out the first fear from the soul which by possessing it no longer fears punishment.

—Maximus the Confessor,
The Four Hundred Chapters on Love

As the grandson of Carpatho-Russian immigrants to the United States, I cannot imagine my life in any other society, and I feel extremely grateful for my personal destiny. But as an Orthodox Christian . . . I cannot imagine a way of life more insidious to Christian Orthodoxy and more potentially dangerous to human being and life.

—Thomas Hopko, Former Dean of St. Vladimir's
Orthodox Theological Seminary

Contents

Acknowledgments

I want first to thank John Witte Jr. and Frank Alexander, co-founding directors of the Center for the Study of Law and Religion at Emory University, for inviting me to be a senior fellow of the center, and to participate in the Christian Jurisprudence II project. This book is the fruit of that participation in every sense of the word, because it could not have been realized without the thoughtful and charitable engagement among the Christian lawyers, theologians, philosophers, historians, and ethicists that took place over a five-year period. I am grateful for what I learned from these colleagues and for the bonds that were formed with them. I also thank John and Frank for including the Orthodox voice in this project. As I indicate in this book, the Orthodox voice in matters of law and politics is severely underdeveloped, and the Christian Jurisprudence II project offered the opportunity to fill this gap. I was moved by their insistent belief that the wider Christian discussion on jurisprudence itself needed the Orthodox contribution.

This project was supported by a generous grant from the Alonzo L. McDonald Family Agape Foundation to the Center for the Study of Law and Religion at Emory University. I wish to thank especially Ambassador Alonzo L. McDonald, Peter McDonald, and the other McDonald Agape Foundation trustees. I very much admire their support of the production of intellectual ideas whose impact is not always tangible and never immediate. The opinions in this publication are my own and do not necessarily reflect the views of the foundation or the center. I am also grateful to Fordham University for a Faculty Fellowship, which enabled me to make significant progress on this project. I would also like to thank the E. Rhodes and Leona B. Carpenter

Foundation for a grant that allowed me the opportunity to conduct the research that has shaped the chapter on the relation between truth-telling and political forgiveness.

In addition to my colleagues who participated in the Christian Jurisprudence II project, I thank David Hollenbach, S.J., and Charles T. Mathewes, whose incisive insights made this a better book. They, of course, are not to blame for whatever is lacking in these pages. I would also be remiss if I did not thank my two graduate-student assistants at Fordham, Nathaniel Wood and Matthew Baker, without whose help I would not have been able to finish the manuscript. Readers of this book should be on the lookout in the near future for Nathaniel Wood's work on the political theologies of Russian sophiology and radical Orthodoxy, which will offer an exhaustive and rigorous Orthodox contribution to political theology.

I thank my wife, Dena, for her constant support, patience, and understanding as I was writing this book, especially during its last stages. I dedicate this book to my beautiful boys, (Lord) Byron and Alexander (the Great), who are simply a daily source of joy for me. In the presence of Dena, Byron, and Alexander, I feel gifted.

Introduction

The Christian theological notion of *theosis,* usually translated as deification, is not intuitively associated with political theology.[1] In fact, some might argue that *theosis* gets in the way of a Christian political theology, as it focuses attention on the individual striving for a mystical, nonhistorical, world-denying union with God. The monk escapes to the desert to avoid the messy realities of politics, which distract attention away from the acquisition of the divine light. Supporting this view of the apolitical nature of deification is the fact that the Christian tradition most associated with this idea, the Orthodox Christian tradition, has never really been known for its political theology, except for what some interpret as the Eusebian glorification of the Christian emperor and the Christian empire—pejoratively labeled "Christendom."

If one were to analyze more closely all that is implied in the Christian theological notion of *theosis,* however, one would more clearly see that *theosis* has everything to do with politics: the mystical is the political. Admittedly, the association between *theosis* and politics is not self-evident. The problem could be with the word "deification," as it conjures up images of individual striving toward some sort of superhuman, godlike transformation. If there was one thing that deification was not meant to signify, it was the human transformation into Zeus.

1

As a result of the misunderstanding that surrounds the word "deification," I prefer a less literal translation for *theosis:* divine-human communion. First, divine-human communion reminds us that *theosis* is primarily a relational category. The human transformation that it signifies results from a relationship with God. This relationship, however, is not one of distance but of progressive union with the life of God that does not obliterate the difference between God and the human. It does not allow this difference to preclude communion; instead, this difference is the precondition for such a communion. Above all, *theosis* asserts that the human was created for such a communion with God.

One cannot stop there: to assert that the human is created for communion with God is to make a statement about the structure of creation itself. Although creation is ontologically other than the uncreated, it was created with the capacity of presencing the uncreated. Although existing as the not-God, creation is not the enemy of God, even when immersed in sin; nor is it in competition with God. It exists with the eternal capacity for transformation, which is nothing other than the presencing of the divine in its very materiality. This capacity to embody the divine is what contemporary Orthodox theologians refer to as the sacramentality of creation. To assert that creation was created for communion with God is to simultaneously claim that creation already exists in and through the divine, that the divine is latently present within the material creation at its core.

The emphasis, thus, is on divine-*human* communion, because the burden to figure out how to tap the latent divine presence within creation ultimately depends on humans. Divine-human communion is not meant in any way to denigrate nonhuman materiality—quite the contrary. It is simply meant to emphasize how communion with the divine, for which all of creation is destined, depends on how humans relate to God. *Theosis* simply asserts that the thriving of creation is proportionate to the degree in which humans commune with the divine.

The sacramentality of creation is, then, not reached through acts of magic, but through an ascetics of divine-human communion—a performance of ascetical practices that opens one up to communing with the life of God that is in and around creation, and communicated definitively in Jesus Christ. One way to see Christian asceticism is as a tradition of thinking on the kinds of practices one needs to perform so as to make oneself available to God's love, which is always on offer. The point of the practices is not to earn or to merit communion with God—which, if one thinks about it, doesn't really make sense—but to remove what gets in the way of experiencing what is readily available.

In the end, the Christian ascetical tradition took very seriously the command to love God with "all your heart, and with all your soul, and with all your strength, and with all your mind; and your neighbor as yourself" (Lk 10:27). It also realized the paradoxical nature of the command—one cannot will to love. Asceticism is a tradition of thinking on how to fulfill this commandment, which *is theosis*. Divine-human communion *is* to love God with all of one's heart, soul, strength, and mind, that is, singularly, and to love neighbor as self. To exist in this way is to exist in communion with God. And yet the realization of that love requires work—one must learn how to love. Reflecting on the Christian obligation to love, Christian ethics has typically either debated what love is or how loves are to be ordered. For example, Christian ethics has considered the question of whether Christians have an obligation to love all equally or if one is obliged to love family before friends, and so on. An ascetics of divine-human communion is concerned not so much with discerning whom one is obliged to love over whom, but with what gets in the way of love. For example, it makes little sense to tell a woman addicted to crack, whose first impulse after giving birth is to get high rather than embrace her baby, that she is obliged to love her child. The most that such an obligation can point to is what is possible for her as a mother. False ego-constructions, repressed losses, destructive practices that lead to addictions (vices), together with the simple fear of not mattering, often get in the way of loving the people we say we love. It is simply difficult for humans to love their family members—siblings, parents, children—let alone their friends and neighbors. An ascetics of divine-human communion is meant to be a performance of practices that

move the human toward fulfilling the command she is obliged to fulfill. To be created for communion with God, then, is to be called to
learn how to love. An ascetics of divine-human communion is the
performance of practices aimed at moving one toward the acquisition
of the virtue of love. It is not a formula but more like an artistic
tradition that passes on time-tested practices.

If the Christian calling is to learn how to love, then an ascetics of
divine-human communion cannot be confined either to the monastery or to the church—the whole world is the field in which this
ascetics must be played out. And if this learning how to love goes beyond family or other Christians, and includes the neighbor, who may
also be the stranger, then politics cannot be irrelevant to an ascetics
of divine-human communion. In fact, insofar as politics can be construed as an engagement with the neighbor/stranger, then politics
must be considered as one of the many practices within an ascetics of
divine-human communion.[2] The political community is not the antithesis to the desert but one of the many deserts in which the Christian must combat the demons that attempt to block the learning of
love. In no other field is the temptation to demonize the neighbor
more compelling or more seemingly justifiable than in the field of
politics; in no other space than in the political, then, is the Christian
more challenged to fulfill the commandment to love.

This book, then, is an attempt to draw out the implications for a
political theology of the Christian claim that humans were created for
communion with God. It will do so by deducing what the principle of
divine-human communion implies for a Christian political theology.
If Christians affirm the principle of divine-human communion, then,
to be consistent, what kind of political community must they support and advocate? It will also look at concrete Christian practices of
divine-human communion to see the form of political community
these practices are shaping. Again, Christians do not engage in practices of divine-human communion only in the church, even if the
church is the fullness of the realization of all these practices can make
available; Christians engage in these practices no matter where they
are, and so by performing these practices, they are not simply affect-
ing their bodies, their families, or their church communities, but,

potentially, the political spaces they inevitably inhabit. If truly performing an ascetics of divine-human communion, what form of political community are these practices shaping?

Two trends prompt this book. First, the fall of Communism in the traditional Orthodox countries has revealed an unpreparedness on the part of Orthodox Christianity to deal with questions of political theology in a way that is consistent with its core axiom: the principle of divine-human communion. Second, recent Christian political theology, some of it evoking the notion of "deification," has been critical of liberal democracy, implying a mutual incompatibility between a Christian worldview and that of modern liberal democracy. I will engage both these recent trajectories within Christian political theology in attempting to discern a political theology based on the principle of divine-human communion.

I will begin by surveying the role that the principle of divine-human communion has played in the formation of Christian political theology in the tradition that has consistently affirmed this principle as the core of Christian thought—the Orthodox tradition. It is really a remarkable fact, given both its long history and the interruptions in this history through Ottoman and Communist conquests, both of which decimated the intellectual tradition of Orthodox Christianity, that Orthodox thought past and present has consistently affirmed this principle of divine-human communion as the beginning and end of Christian thought. And while nothing on the scale of a *City of God* was produced in Orthodox Christianity, the writings on political theology that do exist within this tradition reflect the guiding influence of this principle. From Eusebius of Caesarea to Sergius Bulgakov, one can discern an attempt to construct a political theology that is grounded in the affirmation of the presence of the divine in creation. The political logic of divine-human communion does not necessarily lead to the same result, as Eusebius defended a Christian empire, while Bulgakov advocated for an American-style form of democracy. In the post-Communist situation, the Orthodox manifest an ambivalence and incoherence when encountering the possibility of traditional Eastern European countries becoming liberal democracies. This ambivalence is evident even in Greece, an Orthodox country that has been a liberal democracy for decades. Such ambivalence seemingly lends credence to the assertion that a "clash of civilizations" exists between the traditional Orthodox countries and modern Western liberal democracies, that Orthodoxy simply cannot produce the culture conducive to liberal democratic forms of state. While appeals to the past are abundant, what is missing in sporadic Orthodox comments on liberal democracy is any assessment based on the axiom that no good Orthodox would deny—the principle of divine-human communion.

Chapter 2 will undertake the more constructive task of considering political theology in terms of divine-human communion. It will begin with ecclesiology because recent attempts at political theology, both Orthodox and non-Orthodox, have attempted to argue that Christian political theology must begin with the Christian conception of the church. This approach is advanced especially by those Christian theologians who are convinced that humans were created for *theosis*. Based on the latter, church becomes, in one form of the argument, the communal realization of divine-human communion, most manifest in the Eucharist. The Eucharist becomes the communal space of divine-human communion insofar as the faithful are constituted as the body of Christ by the Spirit. It is thus in the Eucharist that one locates the church as the communal realization of communion with the divine in Christ. As such, the church must exist in constant prophetic tension with any form of political community. More strongly, a eucharistic understanding of the church must judge modern liberal democracy as antithetical to the type of community realized as church, especially to the anthropology that grounds and is promoted by liberal democratic polity. In short, a eucharistic understanding of the church and modern liberal democratic forms of political community are mutually exclusive. I will argue against that claim, and through a form of immanent critique I will demonstrate that a eucharistic understanding of the church actually leads to a Christian endorsement of a liberal democratic form of polity. Insofar as the measure of the presence of God consists in the patterns of relationship enabled and realized within a community, the patterns of relationship enabled and realized within modern liberal democracies more iconically realize a eucharistic understanding of the church—as body of Christ and kingdom of God—than prevailing options. If the principle of divine-human communion leads to a eucharistic understanding of the church, which I think it does, it does not follow that such an understanding of the church results in the wholesale Christian rejection of modern liberal democracy; in fact, it implies something like a modern liberal form of democratic polity.

Chapter 3 will continue the immanent critique of the Christian assault on modern liberalism that targets the notion of human rights, which centers mostly on the understanding of the human being to which human rights language seems inherently tied. Through human rights language, modern liberalism advances an understanding of the human as autonomous, self-sufficient, with unlimited freedom of choice so long as such freedom does not result in the unwarranted infliction of harm on another. By unequivocally supporting human rights language, the critique goes, Christians are unwittingly promoting an understanding of the human antithetical to that which sees the human as created for communion with God. In order to refute this claim, I will draw on recent Christian theological understandings of personhood as relational that emerged within the Orthodox tradition and within the framework of a trinitarian theology that conceptualized the God-world relation in terms of communion. I will do so in conversation with Nicholas Wolterstorff's work on rights language. While it is irrefutable that human rights language cannot be so easily grafted onto Christian understandings of the self as created for communion with the divine, based on a Christian theological understanding of personhood as relational, I will demonstrate the logic of divine-human communion leads to a qualified Christian support of human rights language.

Chapter 4 will engage two of the more vociferous critics of modern liberal democracy—Stanley Hauerwas and John Milbank. Both Hauerwas and Milbank argue that a Christian understanding of the church cannot lead to support of modern liberal democratic principles without compromise; moreover, Milbank's understanding of church is explicitly informed by an ontology of participation. I will also engage recent work in political theology that is less deductive— that is, a certain idea of the church leads to this conclusion of modern liberal democracy—and focuses more on Christian practices in the world. I will amplify this turn to Christian practices for constructing a Christian political theology through the lens of the ascetical strug- gle to learn to love. The political space cannot be imagined as the space in which Christians perform de facto practices toward the ac- quisition of love but are challenged to engage in those practices. Put another way, the political space more than any other space may mag- nify to Christians how far they are from realizing the commandment to love. The Christian attempt to be Christian matters for the Chris- tian imagination of political space. Chapter 4 will also address the prediction issued by much recent Christian political theology, both those inimical to and sympathetic to liberal democracy, that liberal democracy itself will implode without some referent to the transcen- dent. While I agree with that prediction, I do not think that the tran- scendent referent need be the divine, but can take the form of the common good. What I try to propose is that there can be a non– natural law defense of the common good that is grounded in the real- ism of divine-human communion.

Chapter 5 will continue the focus on Christian practice by turn- ing to the theme of forgiveness in politics. Insofar as forgiveness in politics has been evoked primarily as a means to foster communities of difference, it will deal with the issue of democracy indirectly. Atten- tion primarily will be given to how the Christian understanding of confession can inform the idea of political forgiveness. To do so, how- ever, I will argue that Christian confession itself must be conceptual- ized less juridically and more in terms of a practice of truth-telling that can realize the presence of the divine. In my estimation, there is no clearer practice in and through which Christians learn how to love than truth-telling because love simply cannot exist without truth- telling. A phenomenology of truth-telling will thus inform a theology of confession, which, thus, informs a theological consideration of po- litical forgiveness. The chapter will end with a reflection on how the notion of truth-telling I am advancing could be suggestive for a theological understanding of democratic free speech.

Although I am concerned to fill a gap by providing what might be interpreted as an "Orthodox political theology," my concern is less to provide an "Orthodox perspective" and more to engage recent Christian political theologies that have erected a barrier between Christianity theology and modern liberal democracy. These Christian political theologies have unabashedly grounded their theopolitical imaginations in Christian principles, many of them in the Christian notion of *theosis*. It was once suggested to me by David Tracy that the Orthodox have a certain advantage—they did not go through the well-known chain of events within the West, meaning the Reformation, Counter-Reformation, Enlightenment, Romanticism, modernity, postmodernity. Because of this, those within the tradition have the advantage of knowing what it is like to think like a tradition. One could, indeed, argue that Orthodoxy is a tradition of thinking on the principle of divine-human communion and that the continuity of this tradition was facilitated by Orthodoxy not being forced to, or not being able to, confront the usual chain of historical events within Western Europe. The Orthodox cannot but think from the principle of divine-human communion, and what I am attempting to do is bring this tradition of thinking to bear on recent discussions of political theology. Such a tradition of thinking, in my view, does not lead to a mutually exclusive relation between an ontology of divine-human communion and modern liberal democracy.

—— As I have indicated, what also prompts this book is the confusion one discerns in recent Orthodox attempts to negotiate its new, somewhat unprecedented place in a post-Byzantine/Tsarist/Ottoman/Communist world—the Orthodox, for the first time in their history, are uniformly living without emperors or dictators. This confusion is, in part, understandable, since both the Ottoman and Communist occupations did not leave the Orthodox much leisure for reflection. Much of what emerges in contemporary Orthodox thought in general is a reflexive anti-Westernism, but the latter cannot be properly understood without taking into account Orthodoxy's long history of oppression. When one hears of colonial-discourse theory and post-colonial theory, one often thinks of the relation between colonizer and colonized. One aspect of postcolonial theory is analyzing the ongoing impact of colonization on the colonized, even "after" the end of colonization. The colonized always seems to face the colonizer, even when the colonizer has evacuated the colonized space of his oppressive structures. The colonized's postcolonial construction of identity seems haunted by the other of the colonizer.

In the Orthodox situation, the colonizers were non-Christians—Ottoman Muslims and secular atheists. In the case of the Ottoman Muslims, the Orthodox in those spaces never felt themselves to be inferior to the Ottomans. The Ottoman conquest was the result of simply a stronger army and not of any superiority in civilization. Though the Orthodox did need to develop strategies of survival, they were never not conscious of being inheritors of the great civilization of the Christian Roman Empire. If there was a relation of inferiority-superiority between the Orthodox and the Ottomans, it was restricted to military power, not to culture and civilization. The Communist oppression is more complicated insofar as the Communists, unlike the Ottomans, defined themselves over-and-against religion; they sought to eradicate religion from spaces that were traditionally deeply religious. Survival was more urgent for the Orthodox under Communism than under the Ottomans.

When both Ottoman and Communist oppression was lifted, in their inevitable search for a reconstructed identity, the "other" for the Orthodox was not their former colonizers but the "West," which encompassed not only Protestant and Roman Catholic Christianities, but also Western modernity. In contemporary Orthodox theology, narratives were constructed that described Western Christian thought as deviating from the Orthodox emphasis on divinization, with this deviation beginning with Augustine's rejection of the essence/energies distinction. Christos Yannaras, for example, would trace the nihilism of Nietzsche to Augustine's rejection of that distinction. What would emerge in contemporary Orthodox theology would be a discourse constructed in opposition to the West, one that focused on the Orthodox affirmation of divinization that was said to be rejected by the West and, moreover, one that saw the essence/energies distinction as central to the expression of divinization and that, again, was rejected by the West.[3] The narrative assumed hegemonic-like status insofar as an unspoken consensus would emerge around this narrative that is evident in most works of contemporary Orthodox theology. In the postcolonial attempt to define who the Orthodox are, the answer was a distorted apophaticism—what the West was not. Postcolonial understandings of Orthodoxy are invested in diametrical opposition to the West, in a way that is simply not evident in precolonial Orthodoxy.

This anti-Western framework would ultimately function as the horizon for the glimmers of contemporary Orthodox political theology evident either in the work of Vigen Guroian or Christos Yannaras, as discussed in chapter 3, or in statements made by representative persons or bodies of the Orthodox churches. Orthodox equivocation and, at times, rejection of Western democratic liberalism seems guided by this postcolonial understanding of Orthodoxy as on the other side of the West. The Orthodox have established a high wall of separation between West and East, and anything originating in the West, such as human rights language, cannot be so easily integrated in an Orthodox narrative that self-defines itself against the West. This Orthodox postcolonial situation does not so easily fit the present contours of postcolonial theory because the Orthodox almost ignore their previous colonizers, except where they are unable to do so, such as in Constantinople, northern Africa, and the Middle East. The despised other for the Orthodox became the West, whose theological and political thought was deemed opposed to Orthodox thought. This opposition, however, was more projected than real for the sake of a particular kind of construction of Orthodox thought.

This book, then, attempts to forge a (non-radical) Orthodox political theology that goes beyond a reflexive opposition to the West or a nostalgic return to a Byzantine-like, unified, political-religious culture. It attempts to force Christians to be more consistent with the core principle of divine-human communion. In the end, I argue that an Orthodox political theology, or a political theology grounded in the principle of divine-human communion, must be one that unequivocally endorses a political community that is democratic in a way that structures itself around the modern liberal principles of freedom of choice, religious freedom (implied in the former, but needs to be articulated), the protection of human rights (which I use interchangeably with natural rights), and church-state separation. I further argue that such an endorsement need not come with the anthropological or ontological commitments of modern liberalism. I do not engage the discussion on the various theories of democracy, but limit myself to the minimalist conception of liberal democracy that embodies modern liberal principles minus the philosophical architecture within which these principles were developed. I also fully recognize that such a liberal democratic political community may be realized under multiple state structures, so I am not arguing for a particular form of a democratic state; nor am I arguing necessarily for the nation-state, which was invented at the inception of what we are now calling the modern era. Again, I am not oblivious to the fact that what is known today as modern liberal thought often developed with ontological and anthropological commitments antithetical to those implied by the principle of divine-human communion, and often explicitly with an antireligious rhetoric. This reality, however, does not make democracy nor the basic principles of modern liberalism mentioned above antithetical to the Christian notion of divine-human communion. It would appear that Christian theology, and not just Orthodoxy, needs another Vatican II moment in order to end the current Christian equivocation on liberal democracy. And while I would never presume to equate myself to John Courtney Murray, I hope this book begins a conversation with John Courtney Murray–like results.

Chapter One

Orthodox Political Theology
through the Centuries

It is quite a remarkable fact that in the history of theology in the Christian East, there exists a core and guiding principle that is never challenged within the movement of the tradition: the principle of divine-human communion. This principle may sometimes be ignored, or often under-emphasized, but there are always trajectories within the tradition at any given moment in history that keeps its memory alive. Divine-human communion, or *theosis,* sparks the theological imagination of Orthodox Christians, and the influence of this principle is visible in writings related to questions of political theology. This chapter will trace the influence of this principle on Orthodox political theologies, and the effects of the forgetfulness of this principle in thinking about church-state relations. Although the principle of divine-human communion is discernible in the political theologies of Eusebius of Caesarea, John Chrysostom, Sergius Bulgakov, and Vigen Guroian, a consensus does not exist on the implications of this principle for political theologies. Implicit is a debate about what an Orthodox political theology should look like given the consensus on the realism of divine-human communion. I will end the chapter

13

with a description of the post-Communist ambivalence of the Orthodox Churches to modern liberal democracy, which indicates the urgency for a more exhaustive political theology grounded in the principle of divine-human communion, an outline for which is given in the remaining chapters.

Eusebius's Trinitarian Model

The earliest Christian documents give no clear or consistent statements of Christian theologies of state or culture. Christianity was an emerging religion within the Roman Empire, and although they would reject the various forms of pagan religion, Christians expressed a more ambiguous attitude toward the civic and political institutions of the Roman Empire. The Gospels present a Jesus who is not particularly clear on what is being called today a "political theology," but this vagueness does not mean that the portrait of Jesus that is given in the Gospels is not without its political implications, as various forms of liberation theology have rightly reminded us. One consistent thread in the earliest Christian texts is a nonidentification of the kingdom of God with any form of political community.

The political reality at the time of both Jesus and Paul was the kingdom of the Romans, or more commonly put, the Roman Empire, and the kingdom of God was often portrayed as diametrically opposed to the Roman Empire or to any kingdom of this world. The Gospel narration of Jesus's few comments on political matters, such as his proclamation to "render unto Caesar the things that are Caesar's and to God the things that are God's" (Mt 22:21), together with his stance before Pontius Pilate, could be interpreted in such a way as to justify a condemnation of all political institutions as falling short of the promised kingdom of God. Further support for such an interpretation might come from the fall of Babylon in the book of Revelation (Rv 17:1–18:24), the rejection of the "world" in the letters of John (1 Jn 2:15), and the metaphor of the "two ways" in the early Christian document *Didache*. A trajectory within Christian thought emerged in which, although Christians knew they had to live within the world until the promised kingdom of God, all other kingdoms were seen as the anti-kingdom, a form for arranging power and human relations structured according to all that is opposed to God's kingdom. The common description for this Christian positioning vis-à-vis political communities is in terms of the distinction between "this world" and "the other world," a dualism that often gets hardened into a Manichean mutual exclusivity. Although it was within the context of the Roman Empire that such a separation developed, it is still evident in contemporary Christian approaches to political theologies.

A less hardened opposition to the structures of political power is discernible both in the book of Acts and the writings of Paul, the latter appearing even to offer divine sanction of political institutions when he writes that "those authorities that exist have been instituted by God" (Rom 13:1). While appearing to offer a divine grounding to political power, what the book of Acts and Paul both have in common is the affirmation of the nonidentification of the kingdom of God with political kingdoms.[1] This nonidentification does not necessarily entail a complete absence of the divine from the political, but it has left open the ambiguity of whether political institutions are to be tolerated until the coming kingdom of God, or whether Christians are to actively work toward a good particular to political communities, a good not in competition with the kingdom of God but one that the latter perfects.

There is no evidence of a strong current of Christian anarchy: until the coming of the kingdom of God, political institutions were deemed necessary. The real question was whether to judge those political institutions, that is, the Roman imperial structures, as antithetical to the kingdom of God or as in some way divinely sanctioned by God. Since the fall of the Roman Empire was not imminent, focus was less on the form of political community, since there was no real chance to challenge the imperial structures, and more on the way Christians should relate to the already existing imperial structures, addressing such questions as serving in the army and holding political office. Christian writings on particular involvements in Roman society always reflected an awareness of a self-identity that was distinct from the prevailing political and civic structures in which they participated, even in those writings that suggested a noncombative relationship to those structures.

A third option would emerge, one that would closely align the Christianized Roman Empire with the kingdom of God without, again, strictly equating the two.[2] This option is coterminous with the ascendancy of Constantine I (324–37) to the throne. In 313 the emperors Constantine I and Licinius issued the Edict of Milan, which granted religious freedom within the empire but was also the first step toward Christianity becoming the established religion of the empire.[3] It became the first step because of Constantine's "conversion" to Christianity. Although scholarly debate continues on the question of the authenticity of Constantine's conversion, there is no disputing the popular belief in his conversion and the patronage Constantine bestowed on Christian institutions and churches, which seemed to support the perception of conversion. Christianity was not declared the official state religion until 380, under Theodosius I (379–95), but a particular understanding of the Christian state started to take shape under Constantine, especially in the writings of Eusebius of Caesarea.

Although it is common to name the empire after Constantine's conversion as Byzantine in order to indicate the change that occurred to the empire, specifically its Christianization, the word "Byzantine" can be misleading in relation to the attempt to understand the development of political theology after Constantine's conversion. Notwithstanding the invention of the term as a way of contrasting the empire after Constantine's conversion with the glorious, multicultural, tolerant "Roman" Empire, the Christians within this empire never thought of themselves as "Byzantine" but as "Roman"; not as creating something opposed to but as the genuine heirs and guardians of the Roman civilization. Such a self-perception is even evident today in the Ecumenical Patriarchate's understanding of itself as an institution that preserves *romiosyne,* which is argued to encompass "Hellenism" while surpassing it.[4] It is also used to distinguish the Ecumenical Patriarchate from the Greek state without necessarily renouncing "Hellenism." Christians only repudiated the empire's pagan past, not its civic and political modes of being. In the end, the persecutions notwithstanding, Christians were also proud Romans, and such a sentiment explains why there is a virtual absence of a developed political theology in the 1100-year existence of the Byzantine Empire.

The first signs of a distinctively "Orthodox" political theology, one that would wield considerable influence on what would become the Orthodox Church even beyond the definitive fall of the Byzantine Empire in 1453, are seen in the writings of Eusebius of Caesarea (260–340). Although Christianity was still in the minority during Eusebius's time, or perhaps because it was the minority, this did not stop him from describing the Emperor Constantine as the "Viceroy of God"[5] or the empire itself as an image of the heavenly kingdom.[6] Eusebius's *Ecclesiastical History* is an account of history that has divine providence as its guiding force toward the culminating point of the reunification of the Roman Empire under a Christian emperor. Although a history of Christianity, the *Ecclesiastical History* offers a political theology insofar as its pages express a certain understanding of God's power and sovereignty in relation to the course of events that took place over nearly three centuries. Maximin's defeat by Licinius and Constantine is attributed to his being "bereft of divine Providence," while his death was caused by an "invisible, divinely sent fire," a "stroke of God." After Maximin's death, the "other enemies of godliness" were also struck down, beginning with those closest to Maximin, so that "when the impious ones had been purged away, the kingdom that belonged to them was preserved steadfast and undisputed for Constantine and Licinius alone; who . . . made it their very first action to purge the world of enmity against God."[7] Throughout the *Ecclesiastical History,* any movement that led to the culmination point, the reunification of the Roman Empire under the Christian emperor, was attributed to divine providence. For Eusebius, God is clearly "leading . . . his servant Constantine" (10.8.19), who is described as "the friend of God" having "God the universal King and Son of God, the Saviour of all, as their [Constantine's and Crispus's] Guide and Ally" (10.9.4).

Eusebius further links God's providence in the Christianization of the empire with the history of salvation. Salvation, according to

Eusebius, is the restoration of the soul, which was created by the Son of God "in His own image," from its fall in love for what is earthly, sensual, and material (10.4.55–58). After the Word had "paid the just penalty of her sins, [and] once more again restored her . . . first, then, choosing unto Himself the souls of the supreme Emperors, by means of these men most dearly beloved of God He cleansed the whole world of all the wicked and baneful persons and of the cruel God-hating tyrants themselves" (10.4.55–60). This allowed the bishops to be "brought out openly and honoured worthily with the great gifts of His [the Word's] Father's bounty" (10.4.60). The bishops as pastors could then do their work in offering the instruction that would restore the image of the Word in individual souls. The implication here, of course, is that the extension of the salvation offered in Christ depends on the Christianization of the empire, because only then could the pastoral care of the bishops be extended as widely as possible.

The benefit of the Christianization of the Roman Empire was not limited to the spread of truth to individual souls: it also extended the peace that was offered through the pre-Christianized Roman Empire. Eusebius proclaims that "by the express appointment of the same God, two roots of blessing, the Roman Empire and the doctrine of Christian piety, sprang up together for the benefit of men."[8] The Roman Empire put an end to war among the nations and established a peace throughout the world. It was lacking, however, true religion. With the latter, it could facilitate the uniting of the whole world as "one well-ordered and united family," manifesting the sovereignty of the Word and, thus, imaging the Father's kingdom. While it may sound oxymoronic to theorists of empire today, Eusebius actually saw the unity of the Roman Empire and Christian doctrine as a vehicle for peace.

It is tempting to attribute Eusebius's providential view of history to a strict Christian monotheism: the one emperor and his empire are extensions of the one God and God's sovereignty.[9] There is some truth to this assessment, though it needs nuancing, since Eusebius espoused a radically trinitarian monotheism, albeit a subordinationist one.[10]

Eusebius does not present a picture of the one God standing over and against the not-God exercising God's power at will. His emphasis is somewhat consistent with the early Christian writings insofar as his focus is on the Father's kingdom. The kingdom of God (the Father) is mediated by the "divine Word, who administers his Father's kingdom on behalf of all who are after him and subject to his power."[11] The divine Word, "who pervades all things and is everywhere present, unfolding his Father's bounties to all with unsparing hand, has accorded a specimen of his sovereign power even to his rational creatures of this earth."[12] What Eusebius presents, then, is not a picture of God wielding divine power over the not-God, influencing the course of history simply by the divine will but, rather, of God the Father realizing the Father's kingdom through the divine Word, who is already present in the not-God, particularly in the souls of humans, which image the Word. As image of the Word, humans have the capacity to participate in the sovereignty of the Word, and do so by being lords and masters of the created and material world. Insofar as the Christianization of the empire for Eusebius means a form of sovereignty that is rooted in divine truth, he cannot but see it as reflecting the sovereignty and, thus, presence of the divine Word; as the soul is an image of the Word, so is the collective Christianized empire an image of the heavenly kingdom. Rather than presenting a nominalistic God with absolute power over creation, Eusebius presents what looks like a sacramental image of the empire insofar as the structures of the Christianized empire make present the sovereign presence of God and thus the heavenly kingdom. It is this sacramental imagination that would exercise a decisive influence over Orthodox understandings of politics and culture well into the twentieth century, as Orthodox thinkers would not limit this communion simply to the individual soul but extend it to all of the materiality of creation, including the constructions of society and culture. The whole of societal space was destined to be infused with God's presence in all its constitutive parts so as to realize a mode of being that reflects communion with God and, hence, the active presence of the Word.

It is not surprising then that, for Eusebius, the Christian emperor is an image of the sovereignty of the Word insofar as this sovereignty is directed toward the collective, while the bishops image the Word insofar as their own influence is directed to the individual soul. This dual imagining of the Word was expressed liturgically in the Church of Agia Sophia, with the emperor's throne given a prominent place in front and to the right of the altar. The emperor as image of the Word's sovereignty depends on his commitment to the Christian truth because only then can the emperor hope to form "his soul to royal virtues according to the standard of that celestial kingdom."[13] In what reads like a response to Plato's understanding of the philosopher king, Eusebius describes Constantine as a

> Victor in truth, who has gained the victory over those passions which overmaster the rest of men, whose character is formed after the divine original of the supreme sovereign and whose mind reflects as in a mirror the radiance of his virtues. Hence is our emperor perfect in discretion, in goodness, in justice, in courage, in piety, in devotion to God; he truly and only is a philosopher, since he knows himself, and is fully aware that supplies of every blessing are showered on him from a course quite external to himself, even from heaven itself.[14]

The fact that Constantine was not all that Eusebius made him out to be does not detract from Eusebius's sacramental vision of the role of the emperor—the true philosopher king—since he is devoted to the truth of the divine Word, and only through the knowledge of such truth can the emperor embody the royal virtues that allow him to mediate the sovereignty of the Word to the empire. This particular role of the emperor, a kind of sacerdotal role that facilitates the presence of the divine Word throughout the empire—further guaranteeing the unity and peace of the empire—could be the reason why Eusebius rejects democracy as "anarchy and disorder," and argues that "monarchy far transcends every other constitution and form of government."[15] Democracy reflects more the disorder of the pagan gods than the unity of truth of the Word of God.

Eusebius's political theology, then, is born of necessity to account for the changes occurring in the Roman Empire, which were favorable to Christians. He is not simply giving an account of the past, but self-consciously laying the groundwork for a future for Christians within the Roman Empire that is not yet guaranteed. Eusebius's understanding of God is monotheistic but not nominalistic; the divine Word, incarnate in Christ, is also the active mediator of the Father's kingdom in history. Eusebius could not help but see the Christianization of the Roman Empire as in some way the realization of the truth of the divine Word, and, as such, an iconic presence of this Word. For Eusebius, the soul is created in God's image, but a Roman Empire that is grounded in the truth of the Word, that is structured in a way that Eusebius imagines will allow for the guidance of a virtuous emperor who promotes a society of virtuous citizens, cannot but also iconically image the divine Word insofar as the latter administers the Father's kingdom within the earthly realm. The more the Christian truth penetrates the crevices of culture and society in the Roman Empire, the more is realized the truth of the divine Word. According to Eusebius's understanding of the iconic presence of the Word, a division of labor naturally follows in which the emperor functions as a sort of priest in relation to the manifestation of the Word in the wider society of the empire, while the bishops were charged with the cultivation of the image in individual souls. The two would have to work together insofar as their own spheres of responsibility were mutually conditioning. The cornerstone of Eusebius's political architecture is not, thus, a simple notion of monotheism but his affirmation of divine-human communion in the Word. The theological debates in which Eusebius would find himself embroiled were not about the principle of divine-human communion per se but about the degree to which creation communes with the divine. There is a logic to Eusebius's political vision, even if it is not the only logic possible, that takes as its basic axiom the principle of divine-human communion.

Although the specific details of Eusebius's vision may not have been endorsed, he provided the basic building blocks for a political theology that would go unchallenged, even by his theological adversaries. Christians never challenged the empire; they just tweaked it according to Christian values and norms. In the end, Eusebius provided the language for describing the Christian emperor and the Christian empire that would become common in later Byzantine political theory, especially after Christianity became the state-sponsored religion. The emperor as the Christian ruler of a Christian empire was eventually seen not as one option among diverse theologies of state but, rather, as the particular constitutional form "willed by God and sustained by Him."[16]

The Greek Fathers after Constantine

If Eusebius was writing in the midst of the transition of the Roman Empire to a Christian emperor (not yet a Christian empire), the context for Christian thinkers after Constantine was an increasingly Christianized empire that culminated in the declaration of Christianity as the official religion of the empire under Theodosius I. Even after Constantine, the inevitability of the Christian takeover of the empire was by no means certain. In the latter half of the fourth century, however, there was a palpable sense that Christianity was the privileged religion, with the exception of the period of the brief reign of Julian the Apostate (360–63). Although most of the Christian thinkers of this time were preoccupied with theological debates about the person of Jesus Christ, enough was written on matters of government to stitch together the semblance of a political theology. There are clear parallels in the thought of the late fourth- and early fifth-century Greek writers with that of Eusebius, but they are clearly not as concerned with legitimizing the Christian emperor, nor with constructing a providential account of history seeing the construction of the Roman Empire as a providential step in the Christianization of the *oikoumene*. Their writings betray a givenness to the Christianization of the empire, in spite of Julian's reign and in spite of the fact that they are still surrounded by a visible paganism. The focus is more on the role of the government in light of the eschatological future that awaits all of creation.

The one who writes the most on matters of government during this period is John Chrysostom (349–407). Chrysostom would touch on themes that would find echoes in other fourth-century writers, such as Athanasius of Alexandria (293–373), Basil the Great (330–79), Gregory of Nyssa (335–94) and Gregory of Nazianzus (329–90). Chrysostom first affirms the need for government. We must keep in mind that he is writing in the midst of the Christianization of the empire when he affirms that government is an institution ordained by God for the avoidance of chaos and anarchy. Dramatizing a conversation with Paul in which his audience is imagined to ask, "Is every ruler appointed by God?" Chrysostom imagines Paul answering: "That is not my meaning. . . . I am not talking about each ruler individually, but about the institution of government. That there should be structures of government, that some should govern and others be governed, that things should not drift haphazard and at random, with whole populations tossed like waves to and fro: this, I say, is the achievement of God's wisdom."[17] Such an institution must be hierarchical, since "equality of rank often breeds strife," and "[i]n every context anarchy is an evil, a source of disturbance."[18] Not only must there be hierarchy, but division of roles, especially between the two highest—priest and ruler: "The king, then, is entrusted with the care of our bodies, the priest with our souls."[19] Chrysostom even intimates that of the two roles, the "priest's office is higher."[20]

The most pervasive of all themes touched on by Chrysostom and the other fourth-century writers is that of government as an educator of virtue of the citizenry.[21] According to Chrysostom, the ruler "makes virtue easier for you by meting out punishment to the wicked, rewards and honor to the good, and cooperating with God's will; which is why Paul calls him God's 'minister.' . . . So he is a collaborator and assistant to us, sent by God for this purpose."[22] There are simply citizens who will not act morally if not for fear of punishment or promise of some sort of reward. As an institution that can mete out punishment for wrongdoing, government assists in putting the citizenry on the path to morality and virtue; thus, making "it more ready for the word of instruction." As a result of this role, it "is quite reasonably described as the servant of God."[23]

Lying behind this role of government as educator of the citizenry in virtue is what has recently been called an "ecclesial theory of politics."[24] Chrysostom reflects the views of Basil and both Gregory of Nyssa and Nazianzus in seeing the commonwealth as, ultimately, an icon of the church,[25] a little church,[26] or a church to a lesser degree. Church does not signify simply the visible, institutional church, but the eschatological unity of all-in-all, which finds its most visible iconic expression in the eucharistic celebration. The idea is that the church is the vision of an ideal society in which that which is true, good, and beautiful is realized in the communion of one with the other. All forms of society, then, are judged in light of this ideal. The political society will always fall short of the ideal insofar as its presence is made necessary by the fact that the kingdom of God itself is not realized. Being a society that is not the kingdom of God does not translate into being an anti-kingdom of God. In other words, Chrysostom envisions political society as contributing to the movement toward the realization of the kingdom of God. The commonwealth would contribute both to individuals in their own quest for salvation and to the church in its efforts to bring salvation to the world. As such a community, it serves and realizes a certain good, and by so doing, iconically reflects the church, which itself is an image of the kingdom of God.

In comparison to Eusebius, then, these Christian thinkers more explicitly reference the church, or ecclesiology, as the source for Christian thinking about political societies. Although Eusebius does mention the church in writings other than the *Ecclesiastical History* and the *Life of Constantine,* his is a more cosmic vision in which the distinction between state and church are often blurred.[27] One gets the impression from Eusebius's writings that the empire is the church, even if emperor and clergy have distinct roles; Eusebius also betrays a confidence that a Roman Empire fused with true religion will inevitably lead to the permeation of the truth of God's Logos throughout every corner of the material world.

Chrysostom makes a clear distinction between ecclesial and political societies, and although he affirms the fact that government must enforce the true religion, there is no hint of Eusebius's evolutionary unfolding of the Word in history. His emphasis is more on individual souls and the realization that, without fear of punishment, individuals will simply betray their relationship with God. For Chrysostom, the *telos* of creation is communion with God, that is, deification.[28] Although separated by more than two centuries, Chrysostom echoes Maximus the Confessor's understanding of the spiritual life: that it begins with fear of God as it struggles toward perfect love, in which fear of punishment is cast off. Chrysostom is a realist in the sense that he knows that humans need first to be motivated by fear of God. A community constituted by perfect love for God is the church; until then, government needs to play its role by regulating human conduct through fear of punishment. If the achievement of perfect love entails the casting away of fear of punishment, then the obvious conclusion is that government only plays a provisional role in the formation of the individual Christian. If perfect loves casts away fear of punishment, it also casts away the need for that which enforces fear of punishment—government. Political structures are positive for Chrysostom insofar as they contribute to the formation of virtue through fear, but they are necessitated only because humans need this kind of fear in the beginning stages of their spiritual lives.

Eusebius, Chrysostom, Basil, and the two Gregories thus share a singular focus on the kingdom of God, and, in so doing, on the realism of divine-human communion. The institutional manifestations of these distinct societies, church and government, must work together toward a goal that is the very source and justification of their existence—the eschatological unity of all-in-all. Since, however, creation is in process toward the realization of this communion, political societies are deemed necessary. Government thus must work together with the church in attempting to move all of creation toward the realization of this eschatological vision. Their difference notwithstanding, the result is the same for Eusebius and Chrysostom: the political society itself must be Christian, with a Christian ruler who embodies

Christian virtue, who governs in cooperation with the church and its leadership, for the sake of that for which we were created: union with God.

Symphonia

The understanding of the emperor as God's representative on earth would inevitably raise the question of the role of the bishop and the institutional church within the empire. There was little ecclesial opposition to the newly emerging understanding of the Christian emperor. Although they were distinctive institutions, the roles of the emperor and of the bishop were understood and justified within the same Christian framework. This Christian political vision called for the emperor and the bishop to cooperate for the sake of the unity of the Christian empire, the unity of the faith, and formation of virtue.

Justinian I (527–65) gave classical expression to this understanding of harmony, or *symphonia*, between the emperor and the bishop, having in view both the patriarch of Constantinople and the pope of Rome. Justinian continued the political theology of Eusebius, as seen by such phrases attributed to him: "By the will of God we govern an empire that has come to us from His Divine Majesty," or "God alone, and the Emperor who follows God, can rule the world with justice."[29] Justinian makes a distinction between the *imperium* and the *sacerdotium*: the former refers to the emperor and is responsible for "human affairs," whereas the latter refers to the priesthood, symbolized in the person of the bishop, and "serves divine things."[30] In his sixth *Novella*, Justinian declares that "for if the priesthood is in every way free from blame and possesses access to God, and if the emperors administer equitably and judiciously the state entrusted to their care, general harmony (*symphonia tes agathe*) will result and whatever is beneficial will be bestowed upon the human race."[31] Justinian, however, ultimately affirmed the emperor as responsible for the harmony between the *sacerdotium* and the *imperium*. As Meyendorff himself states, "The Church and the State . . . represent the internal cohesion of one single human society, for whose welfare on earth the emperor alone is responsible."[32]

The absolute authority of the emperor within the empire was never questioned. Such authority, however, did not stop the bishops, and in particular the patriarch of Constantinople, from functioning as the "keeper of the empire's conscience. On matters of morals the Emperor must listen to the priesthood."[33] Not only on matters of morals, but also on matters of faith the patriarch of Constantinople would often challenge the emperor. Within the empire, monastic communities would often resist both the patriarch and the emperor. There was a certain accountability of the emperor to the church, either in the form of the bishops or the monks. It is important to note, however, that there was little, if any, resistance to the notion of a Christian empire within the ecclesial community. Challenge to the emperor did not mean a challenge to the system. The patriarch and the monks wanted a Christian monarch and empire; they just wanted to assure that the emperor was orthodox in beliefs and a person of moral rectitude. Although tensions would often flare between the *imperium* and the *sacerdotium* throughout the history of the Byzantine Empire, and even though the authority and independence of the patriarch vis-à-vis the emperor increased as the empire declined,[34] the notion of a Christian empire was never questioned.[35]

With the conversion of the Roman emperors to Christianity came the slow but sure conversion of the Roman Empire from a pagan to a distinctively Christian empire, which Eusebius would have interpreted as confirmation of his own vision of the extension of the Word within creation. The principle of cultural unity within the empire was Orthodox Christianity, with its system of beliefs, institutions, practices, literature, and art. The emperors saw themselves as enforcers of both civil and religious laws. Canon law governing ecclesial life was also enforced as civil law. Throughout the history of the Byzantine Empire, the notion of an Orthodox Christian culture, in which the constitutive aspects of ecclesial life formed constitutive aspects of the culture of the empire, was as unquestioned as the idea of a Christian empire. The latter implied the notion of a particular "Christian"

culture. Although the Christian Roman Empire is often referred to as
a "multinational" empire, it is clear that other "cultures" embodying
either non-Christian beliefs or Christian beliefs distinct from the
reigning orthodoxy in the empire did not enjoy the same privileges as
the established Orthodox Churches within the empire. There is some
evidence that Lactantius, who in his *Divine Institutes* gives a theological justification for religious freedom, may have influenced Constantine.[36] This influence may extend to the Edict of Milan, which
one could argue stands in tension with the Eusebian understanding
of Constantine and the empire. It is clear, however, that the Eusebian
model, in which government was justified as the enforcer of true religion, did serve to justify various forms of religious coercion during
and well after Constantine's reign, as the Christian emperors were
attempting to forge a Christian society. During various periods within
the empire, Jews and the diverse forms of non-Chalcedonian Christianities were not only not tolerated, but were actively persecuted.[37]
It is probably the case that non-Chalcedonian Christianities were
considered more of a threat to the unity of the empire than were non-
Christians. Under the Eusebian model, the emperor was charged with
protecting the civic and cultural space of the empire from nontruth,
since the coexistence of competing truths would mean that empire
would no longer image the truth of the Word. Eusebius's original vision of the empire iconically imaging the heavenly kingdom insofar
as it was rooted in the truth of the divine Word could not tolerate the
free expression of deviations from what was endorsed as that truth. If
the Roman Empire and Christian truth were wedded for furthering
peace, it was a peace based on exclusion and purity of space.

The Non- and the New Christian Empires

After the fall of Constantinople in 1453, the only political theology
available to Orthodox Christians under the Ottomans for five centuries was strategies for survival. A political form was thrust onto the
Orthodox by the Ottomans in which the Ecumenical Patriarch was

appointed by the Ottoman sultans as the political leader, or ethnarch, of the Orthodox in an Ottoman imperial space. Ottomans forced the Ecumenical Patriarch to assume a position that is theologically unjustifiable within the grammar of the Orthodox tradition and that was not welcomed by Orthodox Christians not previously under the jurisdiction of the Ecumenical Patriarchate. A further consequence of the Ottoman occupation was the decimation of the Orthodox intellectual tradition. Not only was there really no opportunity or reason for Orthodox Christians under the Ottomans to engage the political thought emerging in Western Europe, there existed no vibrant intellectual resources or tradition that could engage the political sources of Western political thought with any real rigor.

What was constructed as the Russian Empire would emerge between the sixteenth and the early twentieth centuries as the only Orthodox space not under the oppression of the Ottomans. It is not surprising, then, that there existed a movement of thought that saw the Russian Empire as the natural successor of the Byzantine Empire, and the tsars of Russia as the successors of the Byzantine emperors. There is little evidence, however, that the Russian Empire inherited the civic, political, and legal infrastructure of the Christian Roman Empire; nor is there any real sign that a tradition of thought on "political theology" was ever transmitted within what would emerge as the Russian Empire, in the same way as were the dogmatic, liturgical, canonical, monastic, and iconographic traditions. The absence of the transmission of any substantive political thought is indicative of how questions related to political theology were never central within the Byzantine Empire. The point of continuity between the Russian and the Byzantine Empires was the recognition of ecclesial and political spheres of authority united by an allegiance to a common Christian perspective and the ongoing negotiation of the proper roles of these spheres of authority within the empire. Justinian's notion of *symphonia* was a guiding principle within the Russian Empire, but there was not a clear transmission of a tradition of thinking on the shape of *symphonia* in the long history of the Byzantine Empire.[38] The Russians were left to apply the principle of *symphonia* in its own history without any recourse to a body of work from the Byzantine Empire that could help guide them.

The basic frame of the Russian Empire did resemble the Byzantine Empire: an Orthodox Christian emperor and an Orthodox patriarch attempting to work in harmony for the good of the Orthodox Christian society. How the church and state were to relate to each other in the course of the history of the Russian Empire was not self-evident and always in flux. There are various landmarks in the history of the Russian Empire that are considered decisive for the shape of church-state relations.[39] The first of such landmarks is the presence of a decentralized form of theocratic republicanism in Novgorod from the middle of the twelfth century until 1478, when Novgorod, Pskov, and the Novgorodian colony of Vyatka were annexed by Moscow in 1478.[40] It would be a mistake to see Novgorodian republicanism as a form of modern democracy, but it is appropriate to contrast it with the autocracy that developed with the centralization of power in Moscow. Although Novgorodian republicanism died with the annexation of Novgorod to Moscow, it remained alive in Russian memory and served as inspiration to eighteenth- and nineteenth-century revolutionaries.[41]

The second of such landmarks is the sixteenth-century debate between the nonpossessors and the possessors. The nonpossessors favored a strict separation of church and state, together with a divestment of church property that was acquired as a result of the privileges given to the clergy by the Mongol Khans.[42] The possessors were not in favor of such a divestment and also supported a mutual cooperation between the church and the state for the advancement of Christian truth. One of the possessors, Joseph of Volokolamsk (1440–1515), was "an extravagant apologist of royal absolutism," who introduced into Russia the notion of the divinization of the tsars.[43] In the sixteenth century, Philotheus of Pskov (d. 1542) would present what would be the most developed form of the theory of Moscow as the Third Rome, an idea that would circulate within Russia without gaining much traction.[44] The rhetoric of the possessors was instrumental in consolidating the Russian Empire and the power of the tsars, the first of which would be Ivan IV(1533–84); it would also contribute to a more autocratic and absolutist understanding of imperial power than was witnessed within the Byzantine Empire.

The third landmark in the history of church-state relations within the Russian Empire is the ecclesial reforms of Patriach Nikon in the mid-seventeenth century.[45] These reforms led to the split from the institutional Russian church by those who would be called the Old Believers, a schism that still reverberates in post-Communist Russia. Although Nikon's intent with the reforms was to strengthen the clergy in relation to the imperial state, and even if Nikon himself argued for the primacy of the patriarch over the tsar, since the Old Believers were the more faithful participants within the Russian Orthodox Church, their departure weakened the position of the church vis-à-vis the state.

The schism left the church vulnerable in such a way that it could not mount a defense against the abolition of the patriarchate by Tsar Peter I (1682–1725), the fourth landmark in the history of church-state relations in Russia.[46] Instead of the patriarchate, Peter created the Holy Synod as a branch of the state bureaucracy, engineered by Feofan Prokopovich, "the chief mastermind and the head of Peter's Holy Synod."[47] The head of the synod was the overprocurator, an appointed government official, one of whom was a self-proclaimed atheist, while another was openly hostile to Orthodoxy.[48] Peter's configuration of church-state relations was unprecedented in the history of the Orthodox Church and weakened substantially any possibility of ecclesial resistance, either hierarchical or monastic, to imperial power. This particular Russian structure highlights the fact that *symphonia* within the Byzantine Empire entailed some form of independence and distance between the ecclesial and political spheres of authority, which allowed for a dynamic of constant negotiation between these spheres.[49] The common presupposition of these spheres of authority was an Orthodox Christian society, but the bishops, monks, and emperors could not always agree on the details of such a society. In addition to the abolition of the patriarchate, the establishment of a Holy Synod as an institution of the bureaucratic state, together with the newly created position of the overprocurator who ran the Synod, Peter's reforms entailed the requirement of priests to pledge "to defend unsparingly all the power, rights, and prerogatives belonging to the High Autocracy of His Majesty," to report any incriminating information obtained in confession, to denounce political dissent, and to cooperate with police in defending state authority. Moreover, Peter seized the last of the church-owned lands, made priests into civil servants on the government payroll, and outlawed the construction of private family churches.[50] After Peter I, the balance of power was decisively on the side of the tsars. One could rightly ask whether anything of the Byzantine notion of *symphonia* remained after Peter's reforms.

In the nineteenth century, after the American and French Revolutions, challenge to imperial authority would extend into Russia. Some scholars argue that Peter's reforms effectively discredited the moral authority of the clergy and the monks, leaving no other option than secular ideologies for resistance to imperial authority.[51] Although ecclesial resistance to imperial authority was evident in the Byzantine Empire, such resistance was in response to what was considered threats to Orthodoxy and never to the imperial structure itself. In nineteenth- and early twentieth-century Russia, a variety of Christian political responses emerged, including the preservation of the monarchy either through the maintenance of the status quo or a revival of *symphonia* that would grant greater independence to the church from the secular state in the form of the reinstitution of the Patriarchate. The reaction of the bishops and priests to the political turmoil that was brewing around this time was far from uniform.[52] Bishops were mostly against the autocracy of the Russian tsars, and called for a greater independence of the church from the imperial state. Among the priests, there were many who sympathized with the more radical elements within Russian political life. It was a Russian Orthodox priest, Grigorii Petrov, who initiated an Orthodox version of the social gospel that called for a rejection of the institutional church and a Christian form of social action that would establish the kingdom of God on earth.[53] By the eve of the revolution, some estimate that as many as 90 percent of the church's top officials welcomed the revolution when it came.[54]

In addition to the Christian responses, there existed the atheistic humanist call for either the liberal strict separation of church
and state or the more radical Marxist abolition of religion altogether.
Nineteenth-century Russia was the place where, for the first time in
its history, the basic framework of the Orthodox Christian political
theology—Orthodox Christian emperor and Orthodox Christian
church working in relation toward the maintenance of an Orthodox Christian society—would come under question. What was considered a given of Orthodox political theology, even if its form was
under constant negotiation, would now come under attack. It was
not simply that alternative Christian political theologies were being
proposed, but the very legitimacy of religion was being questioned
by atheistic ideologies. One could argue that for the first time in its
history, questions related to Orthodox political theology received an
urgency and centrality that had not been evident since Eusebius. Orthodox thinkers were forced to respond to challenges and questions
that could simply be ignored prior to the nineteenth century. As a result, nineteenth-century Russia was one of the most productive periods for Orthodox political theology.

The first systematic attempt at a political theology emerges in
mid-nineteenth-century Russia in the person of Vladimir Solov'ev.[55]
Solov'ev has been dismissed as not being a theologian but a Russian
religious philosopher who is outside the mainstream of the tradition.[56]
Based on this identification, some might argue that his political theology is symptomatic of the "Western" character of his thought.
Again, this labeling of Solov'ev as Western is more of a strategy of dis-
missal rather than a theological argument. Both Solov'ev and his
greatest disciple, Sergius Bulgakov, based their thought on the Christological principle of the unity of the divine and the human in Christ.[57]
No good Orthodox theologian today can ignore Solov'ev's attempt to
address questions of political theology on the basis of divine-human
communion.

Besides being the first to offer a coherent systematic response to
questions of political theology, the other notable element of Solov'ev's

political theology is that he connects the conclusions of the theological controversies of the fourth century to questions related to political theology in such a way that the adequacy of a particular political
form is judged by whether it reflects the expansion of the divine presence within material structures. Like Eusebius, he offers a political
theology that is based on a cosmic vision of the principle of divine-
human communion, but without Eusebius's subordinationist lean-
ings, and with an understanding of divine-human communion that
Eusebius may have considered pantheistic. For both Solov'ev and Eusebius, if created reality was destined for union with the divine—or
something like the divine, in the case of Eusebius—then this union
included the political order. Also relevant is that although Eusebius
was crystallizing his political theology in the midst of debates about
the divinity of the Word and in the midst of the Christianization of
the empire, Solov'ev was constructing his political theology when
both the dogmatic tradition of the Orthodox Church and the notion
of a Christian empire were being questioned.

Based on this principle of divine-human communion, Solov'ev
rejected both atheistic humanism and the Slavophile glorification of
the Russian Empire. He very much believed that creation was destined for deification, and based on this principle of divine-human
communion he advocated for a system that he called a "free theocracy."[58] Solov'ev endorsed a Christian liberalism: he argued that the
Christian principle of divine-human communion leads to a vision of
society in which the church and state are separated, and that the state
is structured to protect human rights, which would even include religious pluralism. In the end, divine-human communion cannot be
enforced or imposed but must be freely realized, which means protection of freedom to reject particular beliefs, even belief in God. In
Solov'ev's political theology, one can detect a fusion of Eusebian and
Chrysostomian elements: like Eusebius, there is a blurring of the ecclesial and political orders in Solov'ev's vision, such that a particular
form of political society enables the realization of the Word, or, for
Solov'ev, *Sophia,* in material reality; unlike Eusebius, and more like
Chrysostom, the realization of the divine within the created reality

relies on the free, ascetical struggle of the human person.[59] Where Solov'ev departs from both Eusebius and Chrysostom is the use of the power of the state for the realization of divine-human communion. For Eusebius, the power of the state is necessary to expand true religion and to eliminate false religion; for Chrysostom, it is needed for education in virtue of the individual Christian through fear of punishment in order to facilitate their communion with God; for Solov'ev, the political order must be such so as to maximize the conditions for the possibility of a free response to and, hence, realization of the divine in creation. There can be no forced imposition of religion if, in fact, creation is destined for communion with God.

The "theocracy" part of his vision, however, entails arguing that modern political liberalism is mistaken in thinking that freedom and equality can be secured without being grounded or connected to the love of God. Solov'ev even argued for a kind of secularism that grants independence to various spheres of society, such as government, law, commerce, science, and the arts. He absolutely rejected a version of theocracy that placed these spheres under the authority of the church. He did, however, think that freedom is an illusion if not grounded in something transcendent; specifically, the love of God.

Suggestive in Solov'ev is his attempt to integrate modern Western liberal notions of the secular, human rights, freedom, and church-state separation into an Orthodox vision of divine-human communion. If *symphonia* served as a guiding principle for church-state relations from Eusebius through the history of the Russian Empire, one could argue that it progressively became disconnected from Eusebius's grounding of such a model in divine-human communion, which allowed for the never-ending negotiation of the relationship between the realms of church and state. Peter's reforms reflect more the overpowering sovereignty of the nominalist God that is often, misleadingly, associated with Eusebius. Solov'ev can be credited with returning Orthodox political theology back to its core principle of divine-human communion. Such a logic, however, leads to a political form that is different from that of Eusebius—to a form of political liberalism that is grounded in the love of God. This option, perhaps, was not conceivable for Eusebius; he did, however, know of and reject democracy, though the democracy he was thinking of may have looked different from that motivated by Western political liberalism. Solov'ev and Eusebius both have in common the affirmation that God must somehow be in the horizon of a political community. What is remarkable is that for Solov'ev the principle of divine-human communion, which, as with Eusebius, is the realization of the truth of the Word, leads to a political form that endorses religious pluralism and liberal understandings of church-state separation. In other words, Solov'ev does not see the Christian empire as the image of the heavenly kingdom. Solov'ev opens for Orthodox political theology the possibility that the principle of divine-human communion could lead to a vision of the political form that is not imperial, and it is likely that Solov'ev's own context allows him to think that very possibility.

Solov'ev exercised an enormous influence on the intellectual life of Russia, especially in the late nineteenth and early twentieth centuries when there was a backlash against the positivism that dominated Russian intellectual life in the nineteenth century. The most sophisticated theological elaboration of Solov'ev was accomplished by Sergius Bulgakov, at the time arguably the most profound Orthodox theologian since Maximus the Confessor, especially in terms of a cosmic theological vision based on the unity of the divine and the human in the person of Christ. Like Solov'ev, Bulgakov also thought that the principle of divine-human communion must translate into a Christian political and economic vision.

What is slightly different from Solov'ev's and Bulgakov's contexts is that the latter was writing during a period in which the political situation in Russia was reaching a boiling point. The clash of political ideas was no longer theoretical, but was realizing itself in on-the-ground confrontations. There was a palpable sense of revolutionary change; it was simply a question of who would have the greatest chance of winning the hearts and minds of the general population. Bulgakov sensed the real dangers of the popularization of Marxist socialism, to which he proposed his own Christian socialism.[60] He knew, however, that the credibility of Christianity had been so badly damaged by the institutional church's collaboration with the imperial state that to persuade the general population that Christian socialism was a more attractive option than atheistic, Marxist socialism would be a challenge.

Having converted from a quasi-Marxist position, Bulgakov's Christian socialism first started to find shape in 1905 in his own efforts to form the Union of Christian Politics. Toward this end, and in the wake of the 1905 revolution, he published "An Urgent Task," which he defined as the formation of a new "Christian politics."[61] Bulgakov argued that Christians can find common ground with socialist movements insofar as they are concerned with the social liberation of the poor and laboring classes. He decries the fact that these socialist movements have a "monopoly on the sincere defense of the laboring classes and on the defense of social truth," which he attributes to the obscurantism, misanthropy, and despotism that have been identified with Christianity as a result of its perceived conservatism and institutional collaboration. He harshly criticizes the official church for having "disgraced the Christian religion" and "poisoned the national soul" by allying itself with prevailing state and social systems.[62] Bulgakov was not anti-church, as other Russian religious thinkers were during his time, even if he agreed that the institutional church betrayed the spirit of Christianity. His version of Christian politics sought not only to liberate the poor and laboring classes but the institutional church as well. Although Bulgakov's own sense of politics would continue to evolve and mature theologically over the course of his career, one thread was consistent throughout: he denounced all forms of ideology and political philosophy that presupposed atheism. In this group, he included liberal, "enlightened" forms of democratic theories that are inherently atheistic insofar as they are grounded in an immanentist and hence materialist conception of the human person, and called for the marginalization of religion from the public sphere.

As early as 1905, however, Bulgakov's sympathies with the American style of democracy are discernible, though he consistently refused to identify Orthodoxy with any specific political philosophy. He endorsed Solov'ev's idea of "free theocracy," arguing that Christian politics must be guided above all by belief in the freedom and dignity of the human person, and it must concern itself with spreading the love of one's neighbor beyond inner moral feeling and into concrete political economic relations. The ideal of Christianity is free theocracy understood as a kind of religious anarchism in which humanity is united by love free of all compulsion. But the corruption of human nature that makes this ideal presently impossible leaves Christians with only one course of action, and that is "to subject the Leviathan of the state to Christian tasks, to strive for its inner enlightenment, forcing it to serve Christian ideals in approaching the absolute ideal of the freedom of the person, of universal love."[63] Christianity can do this only when it liberates the oppressed from their enslavement and when it gradually destroys "force, despotism, and bureaucratic tutelage" through "the development of self-government and social self-determination, under which government, authority, and society gradually emerge."[64] Bulgakov states that "at one end of this path stands centralists, autocratic despotism, which turns those who have the misfortune of being its subjects into slaves; at the other is the free union of self-governing communes, a federative union of democratic republics, a worldwide United States. I repeat, none of these forms in themselves has any absolute significance; they all are merely *historical means*. However, if their approximation of the ideal were measured, then the Christian form of government is in no way the Tatar-Turkish type of despotic autocracy, which has been elevated to its rank by Byzantium and the cringing official Church, but rather the federative democratic republic, as the English dissidents who emigrated to America understood so well in their time."[65] In, then, a somewhat ironic twist, Bulgakov agrees with Eusebius and Chrysostom that, in principle, government must perform "Christian tasks," but such tasks involve the non-imposition of any particular form of religious truth, including Orthodoxy. By signaling to American forms of democracy, Bulgakov is arguing that a cosmic vision that entails a union of materiality with the divine is realized freely only through a political form in which church and state are separated.

Bulgakov also anticipated many of the themes that circulate in contemporary liberation theology. He argues that Christian clergy must also learn to judge which groups in Russia's social struggles are the truly oppressed ones, so that they may work on the side of true justice. In general, Bulgakov argues, Christians should stand on the side of labor, supporting the masses against exploitation by the capitalists. Bulgakov gives credit to the democratic and socialist parties for having already discovered this truth, and it is Christianity's job to immediately adopt it and integrate it into Christian politics.[66] Christians should support the formation of labor unions, the education of the working classes, the shifting of the tax burden off of the poor and onto the rich, and the gradual transference of the land from the aristocracy to the laborers who work it. He further argues that the social sciences will reveal the means by which Christian ideals are to be realized, and for that reason Christianity must abandon its suspicious attitude toward them. Bulgakov decries the "shocking" ignorance of clergy who attempt to speak on matters of law and political economy and complains that knowledge of such disciplines has been surrendered almost entirely to the secularists and atheists, who in turn have almost sole power to determine the course of their development. Pastors therefore have an obligation to be trained in the social sciences so that they can adequately respond to current events.[67] The church could then offer its own political and economic science, which would draw on Marxist analysis while resisting the positivism that undermined the role of human personality in historical development.[68]

Bulgakov also emphasized how Christian politics is distinct from clericalism. While clericalism seeks to use politics to serve the private interests of the church and the clergy, Christian politics seeks "the emancipation of all humanity, universal freedom, for which there can be no distinction among nationalities, religions, or denominations."[69] For this reason, believers of all different denominational backgrounds can unite around the cause of Christian politics, since they can see in its program the fulfillment of Christ's love commandment. Christian politics is an ecumenical task, and it may even help to heal the historic rifts between the churches.[70]

While Christianity can and must accept what is true and good in the democratic and socialist parties, it must reject the parties' atheistic commitment to the religion of the mangodhood and its attempt to build "heaven on earth" without reference to the heaven above. Atheistic socialism is a totalistic worldview, whereas for the Christian, socialism and democracy are only external means to an end and derive their meaning from religion. Thus, there is an irreconcilable difference between the socialism and democracy of radical atheists and of Christians; yet Bulgakov cautions that these theoretical differences should in no way divide by mutual animosity human beings who subscribe to these worldviews nor prevent them from working together toward common goals, since the public goals can be separated from the private motivations that drive them.[71]

In the present, Christians must strive to establish the foundations of authentic Christian "community" (*obshchestvennost'*—a complex and untranslatable term used by the radical intelligentsia and the Soviets to denote both social engagement and the group of people who participated in it), so that the atheists no longer have a monopoly on community and in order to break the misconception that religion is identical to political indifference or reaction. The "church" of atheistic humanism has been able to attract the best people of Russia because of "the valor of its followers, who sacrifice their lives for the sake of fulfilling the biddings of their religion" and reveal its holiness in deed, while official state Orthodoxy, "blasphemously passing itself off as a church, is being eaten away by the mold of indifference, by the mildew of malice, by the rot of impotence and decrepitude."[72] In order to change the present situation, socially minded Christians must organize into a Union of Christian Politics, which should organize congresses, collect funds, publish and disseminate its ideas among the people, and establish new societies to be active among the people and work alongside them. The Union must be willing to enter into alliance with the democratic parties when shared goals justify doing so. The Union is to understand itself as a "center of ideological propaganda, not a political party."[73]

To conclude, Bulgakov summarizes five parts of his "urgent task": the formulation of a Union of Christian Politics that sees "political activity as a religious action, the fulfillment of God's precepts"; the cooperation of all denominations; dedication to the political and economic liberation of the human person with the principles of early Christian anarchic Communism as the ideal; the unequivocal denunciation of and struggle against the Black Hundreds and a pragmatic alliance with democratic parties; and the dissemination of Christian socialist ideas to the people.[74]

Later in his life, Bulgakov would develop the most systematic theological development of Solov'ev's sophiology,[75] and his first major work after his sophiological turn was his *Philosophy of Economy*, which he published in 1911.[76] For Solov'ev, *Sophia* is the divine principle in the material reality moving all of creation toward an original unity with the divine; his "sophiology" was a Christologically grounded cosmic vision fused with German idealism that attempted to account for a God-world relation in which the world is a repetition of the divine in what is other than God. Bulgakov would attempt to channel Solov'ev's sophiology toward a more traditional dogmatic idiom. After this sophiological turn, even toward the end of his career and after he was exiled from Russia, Bulgakov did not change his view much on Christian politics. The sophiological turn entailed an understanding of the world as already participating in the life of God and moving toward a realization of created *Sophia* in the world, which is an image of or a repetition of the eternal life of God-as-Trinity-as-Sophia.[77]

Christian work in the world is to transform the material so as to fulfill its created capacity to presence the divine, which is created *Sophia*. There is necessarily, then, for Bulgakov a Christian politics and a Christian economics, insofar as Christians are called to transform all relations so as to realize created *Sophia* that is already latently present in the material creation. Toward this end, Christianity cannot be identified with any particular political philosophy or any particular economic theory. What Bulgakov is looking for is the form of government that allows for the realization of principles most consistent with his sophiology, the realization of which *is* created *Sophia*.

From this sophiological vantage point, which is one of divine-human communion, Bulgakov does not stray much from the conclusions he drew in "An Urgent Task." In 1935, he published *The Orthodox*

Church, which although not overtly sophiological, is written at a time when his mature sophiological theology had moved toward its final form. In a lengthy passage, worth citing in full, he writes on Christian understandings of the church-state relations:

> Separation of Church and state, under different forms, has replaced the ancient alliance. This separation, at first imposed by force, has been accepted by the Orthodox Church also, for it corresponds with its dignity and its vocation. . . . The liberty we find in the United States is now the regime most favorable to the Church, most normal for it; it frees the Church from the temptations of clericalism and assures it development without hindrance. Doubtless this system is valid only provisionally, depending upon its historic usefulness. . . . New dangers, new difficulties arise in this way, analogous to those which existed at the time of the alliance between Church and state. The Church may be led to interfere in party politics: the latter, in its turn, may divert the Church from its true path. But an essential advantage remains: the Church exercises its influence on souls by the way of liberty, which alone corresponds to Christian dignity, not by that of constraint. Constraint leads more quickly to certain results, but it carries with it its own punishment. Contemporary history in both East and West proves this. We cannot close our eyes to the less desirable results of the separation of Church and state; in our time when personal liberty is more and more disregarded, the separation often becomes direct or indirect violation of the rights of the Church, extending even to persecution. But we must have faith that, in spite of these trials, Providence is leading the Church to free itself from heterogeneous, parasitic formations which have invaded its body during the centuries. The ultimate influence of the Church on life, and especially on the state, will be only increased by separation of Church and state.[78]

For Bulgakov, the church is a politics and an economics that hope to realize "its spiritual domination" in a "struggle towards victory *from within.*"[79] The political form most conducive to the church's work is liberal democracy. By endorsing liberal democracy, Bulgakov is not accepting what some argue to be the atheistic presuppositions of modern liberalism; he is simply recognizing that the principle of divine-human communion requires a political form in which this communion is realized freely and without coercion. He is also affirming that something like a liberal democratic polity more than other political forms actualizes sophianic principles without identifying liberal democracy with the kingdom of God, or Solov'ev's idealized "free theocracy," which Bulgakov endorsed even in his mature sophiological phase of his career.[80]

Ethnotheology

The Russian Revolution would put an end to the productive thinking on questions related to political theology in Orthodox Russia. While Russian Orthodoxy would begin its own period of oppression, more brutal than the Ottomans, other Orthodox spaces were starting to emerge from the grip of the Ottomans and reassert their identity. After nearly five centuries of Ottoman oppression, the Orthodox countries would begin the long road of rebuilding their intellectual tradition, which was interrupted by Communist occupation of most of the Orthodox world, with the exception of Greece. As an indication of what Ottoman occupation had effected on the Orthodox mind, Nichifor Crainic, one of the leading Romanian intellectuals between 1922 and 1944, inferred only after studying German medieval mystics in Vienna that Orthodoxy must also have a tradition of mystical theology![81] He then "studied the great patristic sources of mystical theology and practice not much consulted by theologians in Romania at that time."[82]

The situation in the Orthodox spaces in Europe after independence from the Ottomans was not necessarily ripe for thinking through questions related to political theology. In the effort to solidify both a national identity and national borders, religion played a constitutive role in these Orthodox spaces. Something like the Christian Roman idea of *symphonia* was uncritically grafted onto the Western European conception of the nation-state. Orthodox nation-states would be carved out in Europe—Greece, Romania, Serbia, Bulgaria—and religion would become part of the homogeneous national identity within particular national borders. It is not by accident that the autocephaly granted or claimed—depending on one's interpretation of history—by particular national churches occurred in the nineteenth century in the midst of the efforts by these countries to forge national identities and borders and while the Ottoman Empire was collapsing. The institutional churches of these newly emerging Orthodox nations would play a prominent role modeled uncritically after the Byzantine notion of *symphonia*—the political and ecclesial authorities working in harmony for the good of the one Orthodox Christian nation. Such a nation would now have to contend with atheistic ideologies, particularly Communist, which favored the marginalization of religion from public life, or, in its more extreme versions, the eradication of religion.

Such antireligious movements within Europe prompted some Orthodox intellectuals to construct a defense for the homogeneity of the Orthodox nation and culture, forming a genre that is now being called "ethnotheology."[83] Examples of such "ethnotheology" occur particularly during the interwar years in Romania in discussions on ways of organizing the new Romanian state. Nichifor Crainic, as one of the leading Romanian intellectuals of the time, was involved in such debates.[84] Crainic was distrustful of Western democratic ideals, seeing them as a threat to the unity of a Romanian Orthodox culture. Crainic proposed an ethnocratic state that would secure the primacy of Orthodoxy as a cultural and civic force. Although accused of fascism, Crainic's ideas are probably best understood in relation to his own epiphany about the presence of mystical theology in the Orthodox tradition. This epiphany led Crainic to discover the centrality of the principle of divine-human communion in the Orthodox patristic tradition. His notion of the ethnocratic state is rooted in the deduction that if, in fact, creation is already called to more fully participate in the life of God, then such a participation must be reflected in the life of the national group.[85] Without necessarily referring to Eusebius, Crainic transplants his political theology in the context of nation-states. Crainic, like Eusebius, but in contrast to Bulgakov, thought the logic of divine-human communion leads to the Orthodox rejection of democracy.

After the War

After World War II, most of the Orthodox world was under another brutal occupation, this time by the Communists. Once again the Orthodox within the Communist space were forced into a political theology of strategies for survival. Millions of Orthodox Christians were murdered under Communist governments; thousands of churches and monasteries were destroyed. Government spies infiltrated institutional church structures, a fact that influenced the institutional ecclesial response to Communist oppression. Greece was the only Orthodox nation-state that managed to escape Communism, though there was an active and influential Communist party in Greece in the postwar years.

After both the Russian Revolution and World War II, many Orthodox Christians flooded into both Western Europe and the United States. The Orthodox Diaspora was formed, and although a vibrant intellectual tradition would emerge, beginning in Paris and then migrating primarily to the United States, this intellectual productivity entailed very little reflection on political theology.[86] At a time when "political theology" was being launched within the contemporary theological scene, Orthodoxy theology was being identified with mystical theology, in no small part due to the English translation of Vladimir Lossky's *The Mystical Theology of the Eastern Church*. It is not exactly clear why the movement in theology identified with a "neopatristic synthesis" ignored questions related to political theology. Even though hundreds of thousands of Orthodox poured into the United States, a necessity for reconciling Orthodoxy and American democracy was never felt to be urgent as it was for Roman Catholicism;

the Orthodox produced no John Courtney Murray as none was felt to be needed. The Orthodox seemed to have no problem theologically with their new democratic surroundings, both in the diaspora and in Greece.

Prior to the fall of Communism, the most notable and substantive political theologies come from the Greek theologian Christos Yannaras and the Armenian-American theologian Vigen Guroian.[87] Both Yannaras's and Guroian's reflections take aim at modern Western liberalism as inherently anti-Orthodox. In this attack, they are joined by other Orthodox voices, especially within Eastern Europe, as well as other notable non-Orthodox theologians, such as John Milbank and Stanley Hauerwas. The thrust of Guroian's and Yannaras's critique is that modern political liberalism is a political philosophy that was constructed as part of the modern critique against religion. Consequently, modern political liberalism is based on a worldview that is mutually exclusive with an Orthodox worldview. Both Yannaras and Guroian criticize modern Western notions of human rights as inherently individualistic, and, thus, in contradiction with the Orthodox notion of the relationality of persons. They also reject the modern Western notion of the exclusion of religion in public life, which sometimes takes the form of the principle of church-state separation. This critique of Western liberalism would be echoed in the post-Communist Orthodox world, in which for the first time in nearly six hundred years, most Orthodox spaces would not be in a situation of oppression and would have to (re)negotiate the relation between the political and the ecclesial.

The Current Situation

After the fall of Communism in the early part of the 1990s, most of the Orthodox world was thrust into a situation of political upheaval for which it was not theologically prepared. Communism was to be repudiated—that much was clear.[88] But the role of the Orthodox Churches within the changing cultural and political landscape of Russia, Romania, Yugoslavia, Bulgaria, Georgia, and Armenia was not clearly envisioned. At first, it appeared that the Orthodox Churches in these formerly Communist countries would embrace democratic re- forms as the antithesis to Communism. When faced with concrete situations, however, their attitude to democracy was more ambiva- lent. Such was the case when Russia was bombarded with evangelical Christians attempting to re-evangelize what they thought was a god- less country, no doubt inspired by proclamations similar to the one given by Pat Robertson, who on his Christian Broadcast Network showed a map of Russia and declared that Russia had never known of Christianity. In addition to the issue of religious pluralism, these newly emerging democracies would be faced with issues such as the role of religion in public schools, religion on identification cards, chaplaincy in militaries, and state financial support of the institu- tional church.

As Communism was falling, the European Union was consolidat- ing its financial and political influence within Europe, which would affect both Orthodox countries within and outside of the European Union. The relation of Orthodox countries to the European Union either as member states or aspiring member states would inevitably raise issues of the role of religion in public life within these Orthodox countries. In relation to the European Union, these Orthodox coun- tries would also be invested in the debate about the mention of the Christian roots of Europe in the constitution of the European Union. In the post-Communist Orthodox countries, the Orthodox churches would fear the influence of the secularized European countries as they attempted to reassert the cultural influence of Orthodoxy within their respective countries, which they tied to the national identity and history that had been purported to be lost and decimated by the Communists. Finally, the negative portrayal of the Serbian people by the media during the Bosnian and Kosovo wars would contribute to an Orthodox sensibility that became mistrustful of all that was West- ern, including the basic principles of democratic liberalism. The post- Orthodox Communist countries were confronting this new situation virtually without any grounding. What emerged in the decade of the

1990s was an Orthodox world that was not really sure how it felt about Western democratic liberalism.

The first major event that would highlight Orthodox ambivalence is the by now infamous "Russian Law on the Freedom of Conscience and Religious Association."[89] After a period of embracing religious pluralism, the Russian Orthodox Church (ROC) soon realized that Russia was being flooded with evangelical money proselytizing Russians toward evangelical Christianity and, thus, away from the Russian Orthodox Church. At that time, the ROC did not have the financial resources to compete with American evangelicals, so it supported the law that restricted religious freedom.[90] In response to the criticism that such a law is a violation of a basic human and democratic right, the argument was made that the restriction of such a right is warranted for the sake of the unity of Russian culture. In other words, since Orthodoxy has been integral to the history and formation of Russian culture, it has the right to privilege within Russia and the legal protection of that privilege.

Not long after the Russian law was enacted, an ROC Bishops' Council released in August 2000 a comprehensive social document, *The Orthodox Church and Society: The Basis of the Social Concept of the Russian Orthodox Church,* together with *Basic Principles of Attitude to the Non-Orthodox.*[91] The *Social Concept* reaffirms a 1994 Bishops' Council declaration that "the Church does not give preference to any social system or any of the existing political doctrines" (3.7). The ROC does not advocate democracy, nor does it reject it; implicit is an acceptance that democracy would be the de facto *modus operandi* for Russian society for the foreseeable future. Given the new democratic situation in Russia, however, the *Social Concept* clearly affirms that it would not be one in which there existed a strict wall of separation between church and state. Even if the ROC rejects any formalization as a state church, it is indicating that it expects a *symphonia* between the church and state, in which the state would guarantee Orthodoxy a privileged placed within Russian society, and the church would do its part to promote the construction of civil society within Russia. The *Social Concept* rejects a democracy that is based on the marginalization of religion in the public realm, the latter being defined as morally neutral. It sees its role as promoting a civil society that is under a moral canopy approved by the ROC. Furthermore, although it does not repudiate religious pluralism, it is clearly a managed pluralism that does not threaten the primacy of Orthodoxy within Russian culture. It also promotes the teaching of the place of Orthodoxy within Russian history and culture, the teaching of the faith to Russian Orthodox students, and moral education to non-Orthodox students. The form of government is, thus, irrelevant to the ROC, so long as it helps the ROC reconstruct and maintain an Orthodox culture, which, theoretically would value the inviolable dignity and equality of all participants within the culture. As a result of Russian history, and because of a theological perspective that does not accept the privatization of religion, the ROC expects Orthodoxy to be privileged in Russian culture, and for such privilege to be facilitated in the various spheres of society.

In addition to this law and these documents, at the Joint Russian-Iranian Commission on the "Islam-Orthodoxy" Dialogue held in Moscow in June 1999, then Metropolitan Kirill of Smolensk and Kaliningrad, Chairman of the Department of External Relations of the Moscow Patriarchate and presently Patriarch of Moscow, and Aya Mohammed Ali Taskhiri, president of Iran's Culture and Islamic Relations Organization, expressed their unified stance in protecting their traditions against what they perceived as an attack from Western liberal values.[92] All the documents released by the ROC, together with statements made by high-ranking ROC hierarchs, are consistent in their attack on what they describe as an inherently antireligious, liberal, atheistic humanist agenda that is individualistic, narcissistic, and mutually exclusive with Orthodox understandings of the person. This atheistic humanism is the reigning ideology of the United States of America and Western Europe, and the ROC does not want Russia to follow that path.

A similar post-Communist ambivalence to democracy is evident in Romania and even in Greece, which escaped Communist oppression. The situation in Romania parallels that of Russia, in which the

Romanian Orthodox Church is attempting to maintain a critical distance from the state while advocating for the formation of an Orthodox culture.[93] The church in Romania is attempting to effect a model of managed pluralism, where the teaching of Orthodoxy is privileged in public education, and in which Orthodox moral principles shape public morality on issues such as abortion, homosexuality, and legalized prostitution. In Greece, the relations between the Church of Greece and the state are always in flux, even if Orthodoxy is the constitutionally established religion of Greece. There are few who doubt the compatibility of an established church and democratic government, but certain issues and events manifest the church's own ambivalence toward democratic structures.[94] In the past decade the issue of removing religious identification from the national identification cards betrayed the church's own perpetual fear of the secular erosion of Orthodoxy's influence on Greek culture.[95] It should be made clear that the synod of the Church of Greece did not object to the removal per se, but argued that it should be made optional. They also objected to the fact that the state did not discuss the issue with the church before deciding on the removal. Many Orthodox hierarchs, both within Greece and outside Greece, did not agree with the official position of the synod, claiming that the church should have nothing to do with a matter for which the state alone is responsible. The ambivalence to democracy is also evident in the Church of Greece's support of a ban of a controversial book that made suggestions of sexual encounters experienced by Christ.[96]

For antidemocratic tendencies, some might also point to the response by the hierarchs and clergy of the Serbian Orthodox Church during the wars in Bosnia and Kosovo. During the Bosnian War, the responses by members of the hierarchy and clergy of the Orthodox Churches in Bosnia and Serbia were confused and contradictory.[97] Such responses lead some to identify the Orthodox Church as inherently antidemocratic. Miladin Zivotic, former philosophy professor at Belgrade University, argued that "the church's ideology is common to that of all authoritarian ideologies. . . . It was because of the Orthodox Church that this society was easily convinced that it had to become obedient followers of the Communist Party"; while Mirko Djordjevic, retired literature professor, assessed that "the Roman Catholic Church announced in the Second Vatican Council that it was the duty of believers to support democracy and human rights. . . . But the church in the east has never addressed these issues and found itself unprepared with the fall of Communism."[98] As the war progressed, the Serbian Orthodox Church more consistently declared publicly its opposition to Yugoslav President Slobodan Milošević and its support for the implementation of democratic reforms and structures in Serbia itself and throughout Bosnia and Kosovo.[99] The church's position culminated in its immediate acceptance of Vojislav Kostunica as the legitimate president of Yugoslavia.[100] While it turned toward supporting democratic forms, it attempted, some might argue contradictorily, to make the teaching of religion compulsory in public schools.[101] Although there exist extreme nationalist and fanatical elements within the Serbian Orthodox Church, the conflict in the Balkans during the past three decades is a manifestation of an Orthodox Church being unprepared to deal with the consequences of the fall of Communism, and of a church in search for an understanding of its proper role in relation to a state and culture whose identity it has played a constitutive role in forming.

Their different histories notwithstanding, a consistent pattern starts to emerge in the Orthodox attitude to modern democracy. First, there is never unequivocal support for democratic forms of government over other options, even if there is not repudiation of democracy. The Orthodox churches always promote what looks like democratic values, especially the inviolable dignity and equality of the human person. Second, there is a clear concern for maintaining (as in Greece) and reestablishing a cultural hegemony. Finally, there is a unanimous condemnation of a form of liberal democracy that calls for a strict wall of separation between church and state, an ideology that is seen as inherently antireligious and atheistic, and that only leads to a degraded form of individualism. In short, there is an ambivalence on the part of the Orthodox to modern Western forms of democracy, which is ironically best summed up by an American

Orthodox theologian, and former Dean of Saint Vladimir's Orthodox Theological Seminary: "As the grandson of Carpatho-Russian immigrants to the United States, I cannot imagine my life in any other society, and I feel extremely grateful for my personal destiny. But as an Orthodox Christian . . . I cannot imagine a way of life more insidious to Christian Orthodoxy and more potentially dangerous to human being and life."[102] What is absent from all these post-Communist responses is any rigorous theological reflection on the implications of the central principle of Orthodoxy—divine-human communion—for thinking about a coherent Orthodox political theology.

Conclusion

Contrary to the normal caricatures of Christendom, political theology in the newly emerging Christianized Roman Empire was attempting to negotiate Christianity's new position within the empire through the theological lens of divine-human communion. Although Eusebius was Christologically a subordinationist, he shared the conviction that created reality was destined for communion with the Logos of God, even if the Logos was not all that God is. The Christianization of the empire seemed a natural, evolutionary expansion of God's Logos in creation, for which the *pax romana* paved the way. The fusion of the truth of the Logos with the *pax romana* seemed liked the mirror image of the kingdom of God. Both Eusebius and Chrysostom did not shy away from asserting that government was to enforce the true religion of Christianity: for Eusebius it was the true religion that was missing from an otherwise praiseworthy Roman civilization; for Chrysostom, the empire simply served the function of inculcating virtue through fear of punishment, for the sake of individual salvation. For Eusebius, empire merged with church, while for Chrysostom empire was functional toward realizing the fullness of the church. Although both would see government playing a certain role in relation to God's salvific plan, and even if Eusebius blurs empire and church, both affirmed the distinction between governmental and ecclesial authority, a relationship that would be constantly negotiated during the long life of the Byzantine Empire.

The Caesaro-Papist caricature often attributed to the Byzantine Empire would actually take hold in the emerging Russian Empire. The unilateral authority of the imperial government over all matters ecclesial makes nineteenth-century reemergence of a political theology based on a vision of divine-human communion all the more remarkable. Even more surprising is the move toward endorsing aspects of liberal democracy on the basis of this principle. Eusebius and Chrysostom hated democracy; Solov'ev and Bulgakov saw it as the necessary precondition for realizing divine-human communion.

This newly emerging political theology would come to an abrupt halt with the shadow of Communism lurking over much of the Orthodox world. For the first time in nearly six hundred years, the Orthodox Church has no shadow, and yet it remains somewhat in the dark on how to respond to the political realities it confronts. A somewhat half-hearted endorsement of democracy with a push toward assuring a cultural hegemony seems to have emerged as the norm. The result is a lack of sustained reflection on what the Orthodox affirmation that creation was created for communion with God would mean for an Orthodox response to the given political and cultural situation. In the end, the logic of divine-human communion shaped the Orthodox political imagination in predominantly two ways: (1) an openness to a variety of forms of government so long as it prioritizes the Orthodox Christian faith toward a predominantly Orthodox Christian culture, seeing such permeation of Orthodoxy in the space of culture and politics as entailed in the logic of divine-human communion; and (2) an affirmation of a liberal democratic form of government, in which church-state separation is seen as a liberation for the church that allows for the free realization of the divine presence in the materiality of creation. There is a consensus that no aspect of creation can be isolated from the divine presence, that is, that divine-human communion is not limited strictly to the human person, even if it relies on the response of the human person. Debate remains, however, on whether such a divine presence requires the established presence of the Orthodox Church, or, ironically, a politics free from politically and culturally established religion.

Throughout the centuries, one thing has remained consistent: the ecclesial is distinct from the political. And because for the Orthodox the ecclesial is the space of divine-human communion, one must begin with ecclesiology in order to carve out a consistent contemporary political theology grounded in the realism of divine-human communion.

Chapter Two

Eucharist or Democracy?

When Roman Catholics immigrated to the United States, it was not at all clear whether they could accept American democracy, together with its separation of church and state, without compromise. Among others, John Courtney Murray emerged to convince Catholics and non-Catholics alike that Western democracy is not antithetical to Catholic teachings. When Orthodox Christians started coming to the United States prior to World War I and then again after World War II, no visible tension existed between their adaptation to American democracy and their ecclesial commitments. One of the reasons why such a tension was not necessarily visible was the fact that the Orthodox Church lacked a visible transnational institutionalized authority that could function as a focal point for framing the difference between its visible ecclesial structures and the political structures of American democracy.

Its lack of visibility notwithstanding, the tension was latent and became manifest in a theological dispute between two of the more well-known American-Orthodox ethicists of the last few decades: Stanley Harakas and Vigen Guroian. Harakas attempted to justify Orthodox acceptance of American democracy through the prism of the

Byzantine legacy of *symphonia*. Guroian challenged this appeal to the Byzantine past, naming it a form of accommodationism. Instead, Guroian argued that a Christian political theology must begin with an account of the church—an ecclesiology. His understanding of the church is based on what has become known as eucharistic ecclesiology in contemporary Orthodox and Roman Catholic theologies. According to eucharistic ecclesiology, "the eucharist makes the church,"[1] which means that the church *is* church in the eucharistic assembly, where those congregated are constituted as the body of Christ. As the body of Christ, the community exists as a communion with the divine. Thus, the Eucharist is not simply a practice reenacting the meritorious sacrifice of Christ, and contributing to fulfilling one of many obligations needed for salvation; it is, rather, the space of divine-human communion.

On the basis of this eucharistic understanding of the church, Guroian, together with the Roman Catholic theologian William Cavanaugh, have joined a host of other Christian thinkers who have targeted liberal democracy. If the church as Eucharist is the space of divine-human communion, and if the mission of the church is to "eucharistize" the world in the sense of transfiguring all created reality with the presence of God, then such an understanding of the church is diametrically opposed to all for which liberal democracy stands, especially its nihilistic anthropology and its violence against religion.

I will analyze the contours of this current Christian attack on liberal democracy, and while I side with an ecclesial approach to political theology grounded in the principle of divine-human communion, I do not agree with the conclusions put forth by Guroian and Cavanaugh. Contrary to their positions, I argue that a eucharistic understanding of the church needs to be tempered by the ascetical tradition within Christianity. I will further argue that a eucharistic ecclesiology that integrates the ascetical tradition leads to an endorsement of the principles of modern liberal democracy, and that such an endorsement is not a betrayal of the ecclesial vision of the world being created for communion with God.

The American-Orthodox Debate

The legacy of the theory of *symphonia* in the Byzantine Empire and its influence as a frame of reference for contemporary Orthodox discussions on democracy are evident in the debate between two contemporary Orthodox ethicists, Stanley Harakas and Vigen Guroian, on Orthodox understandings of church-state relations.[2] Although the first evidence of sustained reflection on modern democratic notions of church-state separation by Orthodox theologians was given by the Russian thinkers of the late nineteenth and early twentieth centuries, the Harakas-Guroian debate is the first sign of substantive Orthodox reflection on democracy in the American context. Harakas's own position is detailed in a 1976 article entitled "Orthodox Church-State Theory and American Democracy."[3] Though the bicentennial that year probably played no small part in inspiring him to write the piece, the reflections themselves are the natural result of the later generations of an immigrant church forced to give some understanding to a church-state relation that has no precedent in its own history. Although the Byzantine Empire was not democratic, the past for Harakas still holds the key for understanding the present situation of the Orthodox Church within the American democratic society, particularly on the issue of the separation of church and state.

For Harakas, the *symphonia* that existed between the church and the monarchical state during the period of the Byzantine Empire constitutes the paradigm for Orthodox understandings of church-state relations, whatever form the state may assume. In relations of *symphonia*, "the Church and State cooperate as parts of an organic whole in the fulfillment of their purposes, each supporting and strengthening the other without this causing subordination of the one to the other."[4] Harakas adds that "the harmonious relationship of State and Church is a result of the belief that both Church and State are creatures of one Lord."[5] The one God assigns to each institution, church and state, its own sphere of influence: church is responsible for spiritual matters, while the state is responsible for worldly needs.

Harakas identifies more precisely what he terms the "elements" that constituted the symphonic relationship for the church and the state during the Byzantine period. These elements are (1) the affirmation of God as the source of both church and state; (2) the independence and sufficiency of both church and state; (3) the identity of the constituency, that is, that the people of the church and the state are of one faith; (4) a religious and political authority—a patriarch and an emperor; and (5) what Harakas terms "methods of relationship," by which he means the fulfillment of the respective functions of the church and the state, whereby the church influences the state toward a more just society and the state defends and protects the church.[6] For Harakas, these elements are normative for an Orthodox understanding of church-state relations.

The central question that Harakas wishes to address is whether the Orthodox in America, who have traditionally understood church-state relations on the model of *symphonia*, can accept the separation of church and state within this country. Harakas provides an ironic response to this question by suggesting that a reinterpreted understanding of the elements of the *symphonia* model allows for an acceptance of the U.S. situation of church-state separation. Put another way, what one sees in church-state relations in America is *symphonia*, albeit in a different form from that which existed in Byzantium.

Regarding the first element, Harakas argues that God is mentioned in the founding documents as the source of the state and the foundation for human rights. The second principle, the independence and self-sufficiency of church and state, is one on which the country itself was founded. One might expect Harakas to confront insurmountable hurdles with the next two elements, the unity of the faith of the people and the coexistence of a patriarch and emperor. Harakas reinterprets the notion of the one faith in terms of the one common good. In other words, the Orthodox Church exists in a society in which it shares not a specific religious faith but rather a common good that is included in—though not exhaustive of—the Orthodox understanding of *the* good. As Harakas puts it, "Orthodoxy can make the adjustment if its own identity with the nation becomes sufficiently broad and deep so that the concerns of the Church transcend its own membership and seek the welfare of the whole people. Admittedly this is not the same as the identity of constituency as presupposed by the 'symphonia' theory. Yet, if Orthodox Christianity can learn to speak to the nation as a whole, to concern itself with the common problems of the people of this country, if it can seek to become in some measure the 'soul' of the nation, it will have made great strides in overcoming that inapplicability."[7] The notion of the common good is contained in the Orthodox faith, and as the one faith did during the Christian Roman Empire, it serves as a focal point of unity in the country.

Regarding the fourth element, there is neither emperor not patriarch in the U.S. Instead of the latter, there is the church, which for Harakas means both the laity and the various degrees of clergy; instead of the former, there is not the president as much as the people, "who rule through their elected representatives. . . . The Church can now speak to the political authority by and through the people."[8] In the people of the church, church and state converge because the people of the church are the people of the state. Finally, in terms of what Harakas calls the "methods of relationship," although the patriarch is no longer whispering in the emperor's ear for social and legal reforms, the church exercises its influence on legislation and public policy. The state offers protection to the voice and integrity of the church, while the church, "through its example, its teaching and its preaching . . . points to a goal for the State and its society."[9] Reinterpreted, each of the five elements constituting the Byzantine model of *symphonia* can thus be located in the American context of church-state separation. For Harakas, this allows Orthodox Christians to view the present arrangement not as strange but as consistent with their tradition. More importantly, it avoids sectarianism and encourages Orthodox participation in public life.

Vigen Guroian, an Armenian[10] Orthodox ethicist, takes a position diametrically opposed to Harakas's. He has no love lost for the Constantinian era, as the title of one of his books, *Ethics after Christendom*, might suggest. Guroian confronts Harakas's positions head-on:

here "is a sense in which Harakas has merely picked up where the Constantinian and Justinian synthesis of church and state left off."[11] For Guroian, the Byzantine model of *symphonia* is an inherently accommodationist approach to church-state relations in which the true nature of the church is sacrificed to the interests of the state. Guroian accuses Harakas of the same accommodationist attitude, claiming that Harakas is in "the same pit of cultural accommodation into which the mainline Protestant churches in America thrust themselves earlier in this century."[12] He further criticizes Harakas for reducing the church's role in relation to the American democratic state to the functionalist one of raising social consciousness and promoting the common good. In this sense, for Guroian, the church becomes simply another interest group. Moreover, with Harakas's model of *symphonia,* the church loses its critical and prophetic edge vis-à-vis the state. As Guroian puts it, Harakas "would have the Orthodox Church assume its place beside the other mainline churches in America as contributor to and custodian of a common American faith and identity."[13]

For his understanding of the church, Guroian is drawing off what became the most influential form of ecclesiology in twentieth-century Orthodox thought—eucharistic ecclesiology. Although Orthodox thinkers will claim that its roots are patristic, the articulation of the general outlines of such an ecclesiology first emerges with the Russian émigré theologian and historian Nicholas Afanasiev. Its influence, however, is evident in such Orthodox thinkers as John Romanides, Georges Florovsky, Alexander Schmemann, and John Meyendorff. The most developed systematic expression of eucharistic ecclesiology comes from John Zizioulas.[14] A brief review of the logic of Zizioulas's eucharistic ecclesiology provides a broader context for understanding Guroian's identification of the church with the Eucharist and why such an identification implies, for Guroian, a particular positioning of the church in relation to society.

For Zizioulas, if the church is the body of Christ, then it is only in the Eucharist that the body of Christ is realized; thus, the church is to be identified with the eucharistic assembly.[15] This identification of Eucharist/church/body of Christ is, for Zizioulas, evident in early

Christian spirituality. It is by now well known that much of Zizioulas's early work consists in historically grounding this claim both in New Testament texts and early Christian writings.

Zizioulas, however, also grounds this claim theologically with what he calls a pneumatological Christology. According to Zizioulas, the Holy Spirit has two fundamental roles following the resurrection of Christ: to constitute a communion of persons, and to constitute this communion as an eschatological reality. These two aspects of pneumatology are ultimately implied in the central Christian claim of the resurrection of Christ, which is itself accomplished by the power of the Holy Spirit. If the Son is the one who "becomes history," then the Holy Spirit is the one who breaks through history and makes present the eschaton; this eschaton is nothing else but the resurrected body of Christ in whom all of creation is united without being absorbed. Zizioulas's logic is that, insofar as the resurrection of Christ is the realization of a divine-human communion, the Holy Spirit's presence cannot be restricted to the individual ascetical ascent; the presence of the Spirit is simultaneously the re-presencing of the resurrected body of Christ, which is a communion of all of creation with the divine. The Eucharist is, thus, the space for the communal realization of divine-human communion.

This understanding of the church as an eschatological community in and through the Eucharist is what defines the church's mission in the "world." For Guroian, the state is part of the "world" or unredeemed reality; how the church relates to the "world" is the basis for how it relates to all forms of "state." Because of this understanding of church, it would be a betrayal of the Orthodox Church's true nature if it were reduced to a functionalist role vis-à-vis the state or another denomination alongside others. As Guroian puts it, "The field of the Church's mission is nothing less than the whole fabric of human life, not just individuals, but the social, economic, and political relations, the institutions and values of human community."[16] Moreover, because of its eschatological identity, the church must exist in a permanent state of tension with the world. As Guroian argues, there is a necessary antinomy between the church and world that *symphonia* inevitably blurs.[17] This antinomy must be maintained if the church is not to lose its prophetic distance from the state. For Guroian, this distinction or antinomy between church and world/state does not mean separation or sectarianism. "Sectarianism," according to Guroian, "is impermissible on Christological grounds."[18] The logic is that the church is distinct from the world, and is not to withdraw but to engage the world in order to transform it. The missionary goal of the church, because of its nature, is the transfiguration of the world to realize its divine destiny. For Guroian, "It is not the business of the Church to impose a new, presumably more just ethic of power on the world. Rather it is the calling of the people of God to demonstrate his love for the world through their obedient service to his Kingdom."[19]

It is on the basis of this understanding of the church that Guroian rejects, contrary to Harakas, the separation of church and state, and even religious pluralism inherent in democratic forms of polity. For Guroian, "It is impossible to treat the arrangement [the separation of church and state] as normative, since it is not consistent with the truth of its ecclesiology and soteriology."[20] In such an arrangement, a juridical understanding of the church replaces an eschatological vision.[21] It "perpetrates the secular notion that the world really does not need the Church or God."[22] It defines the church in privatistic and functionalist terms, contrary to its own understanding of embodying a message of salvation for the whole world.[23] The religious pluralism that is secured and promoted under the separation clause is also problematic for Guroian: "Furthermore, an expanding religious pluralism within, somewhat paradoxically, an also increasingly secular society does not correspond with past Orthodox experience of the world, the Orthodox Church's historic definition of its relationship to the world, or its experience for the world."[24] The bottom line for Guroian is that the separation of church and state forces the Orthodox Church into an understanding of itself that is contrary to its nature. By accepting this definition, the church allows itself and its mission to be defined by the state. The church accommodates itself to the interests of the state, and, for Guroian, "there is something inherently contradictory about Orthodox Christians coming together in worship to declare that they have experienced such a thing and promising that they will behave consistently with that truth and then going out into the world to take their directives from a legal arrangement which declares that none of this is really so."[25]

The Harakas-Guroian debate indicates in part how the Orthodox Church's Byzantine legacy is ultimately shaping the debate over church-state relations within Orthodox thought. It is also interesting to note that the debate I have presented is between a Greek Orthodox and an Armenian Orthodox, members of two traditions that have different experiences and assessments of the Byzantine past. In more practical terms, it is this legacy that the Orthodox churches, especially those in Eastern Europe, must grapple with as many of these countries attempt to move toward more democratic structures.

Eucharist as Politics

Orthodox theologians are not the only ones arguing that a Christian positioning in relation to politics, culture, and society should ultimately be grounded in an ecclesiology—a theology of the church. Each in their own way, such notable theologians as John Milbank, Stanley Hauerwas, Graham Ward, and Catherine Pickstock claim that the Christian church is its own politics, culture, and society. The Roman Catholic theologian William Cavanaugh has developed an understanding of a Christian politics that has affinities with that of Vigen Guroian's insofar as Cavanaugh also understands the church in terms of the Eucharist, even if Cavanaugh's primary inspirations are Henri de Lubac and Jean-Luc Marion, rather than Afanasiev, Schmemann, and Zizioulas.[26] Much like Guroian, the place of the church for Cavanaugh is the Eucharist, and it is in the eucharistic event that the church finds itself positioned in relation to culture.

The Eucharist, for Cavanaugh as well as Guroian, is an event of the eschatological body of Christ, and it is the Eucharist that makes the church.[27] Christians do not participate in the Eucharist in order to merit entry into the kingdom of God; rather, the eucharistic act is a proleptic presence of the unity of all in Christ. The logic of the Eucharist dictates an understanding of time different from the secularized notion of disconnected moments between past, present, and future. In the Eucharist, past, present, and future collapse in God's eternal now. The remembering that occurs in the Eucharist is of a future fulfillment of the past event; a re-presencing of the past event of Christ's resurrection and of the future expectation: "The present, then, is not a self-sufficient reality defined over against the nonpresence of an extinct past and a not-yet-existent future; in the Eucharist the future fulfillment of the past governs the present."[28]

Cavanaugh stresses that the Eucharist is a doing, a performance, and a practice that forms the body of Christ, and, in so doing, forms those Christians who constitute the body of Christ. The doing of the Eucharist by those participating in the Eucharist is simultaneously a doing, performance, and practice of the body of Christ. It is a happening that is a making present of Christ in the world; time and space are not so much ruptured or interrupted as fulfilled—formed into what they were created to be. This eschatological presence of Christ's body is, however, a disruption of "the secular historical imagination," which is essentially nihilistic as it endlessly marches toward an undefined future. Although Cavanaugh affirms that in the Eucharist "the heavens are momentarily opened," he cautions against any strict identification in history of the "earthly church" with the whole Christ. Given that he already identified "the church" with the Eucharist, the notion of the earthly church must also include the institutionalized form of the church. While the Eucharist is the visibility of the fulfillment of the church as the body of Christ, which as a performance has both spatial and temporal dimensions, there is also the non-eucharistic institutionalized form of the church, the earthly body, in process toward the kingdom.

This understanding of the Eucharist means that the church's politics is the Eucharist; put another way, the Eucharist is simultaneously a politics. Cavanaugh rejects any understanding of the Eucharist that restricts it to an act of grace operative on the individual soul. The Eucharist has both a temporal trajectory, insofar as it is a present presencing of the future fulfillment of a past event, and a spatial dimension, insofar as it is a work of the people on the material conditions that they both embody and inhabit. The Eucharist is an act of creatively working on creation so as to shape materiality into a form that reveals the eschatological presence of God. In the eucharistic act, the individual is not guaranteed a future reward in heaven, but all of creation created is affected by this act insofar as creation becomes that which it was intended to be—a manifestation of communion with the loving Creator in the body of Christ. In the space of the Eucharist, creation cannot but be affected by the eucharistic act; if the Eucharist is an event with temporal and spatial dimensions, then it is its own politics, culture, and society.

If the Eucharist is an event in which the material creation's capacity to presence God is actualized, then it realizes a relation of church to society different from the one envisioned by Jacques Maritain's notion of a "New Christendom." According to Cavanaugh, Maritain's New Christendom model emerged as the most influential within the Catholic world and exercised a decisive influence in the understanding of church-society relations in both Europe and Latin America. Maritain makes a distinction between a temporal and spiritual plane that is grounded in the Catholic natural law tradition. Each of these planes has its own autonomy and integrity, though it is the spiritual plane that is superior. The distinction of planes allows Maritain to claim that society, together with its constitutive elements of government, law, culture, and so on, possesses a common good, which is an end in itself that is distinct though not separated from the good of the supernatural plane. Since the church is moving toward a supernatural end, it exists as a community distinct from a political community. Though it exists within particular societies and cultures, the church is called to spiritually penetrate and transform culture.[29] Given that a political community has its own distinctive natural end, the church must resist the temptation to embody itself as a temporal authority within society. Maritain was attempting both to extricate the Catholic Church from specific political alliances and to provide Christians a way in which to accept a pluralistic society, that is, one that is not homogeneously Catholic.

Maritain's New Christendom model is, for Cavanaugh, simply bad ecclesiology, as it does not cohere with the logic of the church as a eucharistic community. If, in fact, the "place" of the church is the Eucharist, then the distinction of planes does not make any sense. Even though Maritain attempted to avoid a separation between the natural and the supernatural, his distinction of planes allows for a conception of the natural that entails its own distinct integrity and end. The Eucharist reveals, according to Cavanaugh, that there cannot exist a natural plane whose end is not the supernatural. The natural does not have its own distinctive end; echoing Henri de Lubac, Cavanaugh asserts that the supernatural is nature's true end. In fact, the Eucharist as an event of communion with God is one in which nature's true end is fulfilled. Maritain's mistake was to attempt to ground the church's relation to society on the basis of a particular understanding of the Catholic natural law tradition rather than on the logic of the Eucharist.

Despite its best intentions, Cavanaugh argues, Maritain's New Christendom resulted in catastrophic effects, made especially visible in Chile. Insofar as the New Christendom justified the autonomy of the temporal plane, it resulted in a tentative, weak, and ultimately ineffectual response to the reign of terror and torture initiated by the Pinochet regime. Although the church did issue condemnations against the torture, the New Christendom model caused it to initially be tentative in response to the Pinochet dictatorship and shaped a policy whereby the church thought it could be more effective in changing the regime if it maintained good relations. The notion of the distinction of planes also provided a basis for the state to criticize the church for interfering in temporal affairs, which are not under the church's designated sphere of influence. In short, even though New Christendom extricated the church from the ambiguities of party politics, it also functioned to play into the hands of the ruthless dictatorship of the Pinochet regime.

Cavanaugh's critique of New Christendom goes one step further: the latter also acquiesces to modern liberalism's notions of the nation-state, church-state separation, and human rights. Maritain's distinction of planes allowed Catholic Christians to accept a model of political community in which the church was not the established religion and in which the state did not function to defend the prerogatives of the church. New Christendom provided justification for Catholic endorsement of democratic pluralism, church-state separation, and the protection of the freedom and equal dignity of all humans through the concept of equal rights. This endorsement of modern liberalism is according to Cavanaugh ultimately self-defeating as it supports principles that are mutually exclusive with a eucharistic understanding of the church. A Christian support of modern liberalism pays little attention to the latter's origins. Although the familiar narrative of the birth of modern liberalism describes the so-called religious conflicts as the impetus for a political philosophy that could contain the potentially explosive violence of religious division, a genealogy of modern liberalism reveals a different story. The so-called religious conflicts have nothing to do with religion; in fact, Cavanaugh argues, Protestants and Catholics often fought on the same side, and Catholics often fought against Catholics. The theological divisions between Catholics and Protestants merely provided the pretext for a political conflict, which resulted in the centralization of power in the modern state.[30]

A constitutive element of this centralized sovereignty of the modern nation-state was an ideology that religion needed to be controlled by the state, and eventually marginalized through privatization or, in some cases, elimination. This exclusion of religion is reinforced through modern liberal notions of church-state separation and human rights. Although human rights, on the surface, appears to be a concept that coheres with Christian notions of the uniqueness of each individual person, it is problematic for at least three reasons: it is used to justify exclusion of religion from the public sphere; it is rooted in a faulty anthropology that conceptualizes the human as an autonomous, self-defined, non-relational entity; and it has proven ineffective in preventing violence on a mass scale.[31] In fact, according to Cavanaugh, although the modern liberal state is built on the myth that it contains violence, it is in fact created and sustained through violence.

One obvious form of violence is the exclusion of religion from the public sphere; but, as Cavanaugh argues, the history of the modern liberal state is a rhetoric of human rights that masks various forms of exclusion and violence. Cavanaugh takes this argument one step further: there is no discernible difference between the violence of the modern nation-state and the torture of the Pinochet regime. The logic of the nation-state is, Cavanaugh argues, torture; put another way, torture is the necessary mechanism of its survival. Cavanaugh, then, is not juxtaposing the church as Eucharist against the Pinochet regime because of this particular regime's use of torture; all modern nation-states are implicated in torture, since the latter is the necessary mechanism for the centralization of power inherent to the modern nation-state. As Cavanaugh himself declares, "For this reason I refer to torture not as the state's imagination, but as the imagination of the state."[32]

To promote modern liberalism is a self-subversive and self-destructive act insofar as the discourse of modern liberalism is incompatible with Christian discourse. Violence in the form of torture is the tool of the modern nation-state that "aims . . . at the destruction of social bodies and the construction of walls around the individual."[33] Under the guise of freedom and human rights, the modern nation-state creates a situation in which the individual depends on the state for protection, rather than local social groups, thus consolidating the power of the nation-state. The Eucharist exists as a social body that is a counter-politics to that of the state, one that exists through practices of peacemaking rather than violence and that actualizes the irreducible uniqueness of the person through particular relations rather than through the negation of relations.

In relation to Pinochet's reign of terror, Cavanaugh argues that an ecclesiology centered on the Eucharist would have prioritized the eucharistic community as a spatial and temporal moment that counters the regime's indiscriminate use of torture. Such a community would form persons who would resist Pinochet, even in the face of death; it would exist as an indestructible social body against the attempts to atomize society toward the centralization of power; it would excommunicate all those who cooperate with Pinochet in order to mark clear borders between the eucharistic community and those who enable Pinochet's abuse of power, thus functioning to make the body of Christ visible in the world; it would not demand human rights but manifest a way of being in the world that actualizes the irreducible uniqueness of each human. As Cavanaugh states, "true resistance to torture depends on the reappearance of social bodies capable of countering the atomizing performance of the state."[34]

Eucharist and Democracy

The affinities between Guroian and Cavanaugh are, perhaps, best summed up in Cavanaugh's declaration that the "point is not to politicize the Eucharist, but to 'Eucharistize' the world."[35] For both Guroian and Cavanaugh, the logic that leads to the identification of the church with the Eucharist is one that cannot accept a church that is marginalized or privatized in relation to the state. The very mission of the church is to eucharistize, to expand its visibility to all aspects of the material creation, which is simultaneously to actualize God's presence as the body of Christ in the material. In spite of the criticisms, the Guroian/Cavanaugh position is not intentionally sectarian, insofar as it self-consciously avoids seeing the eucharistic community as being over-and-against the world. It may appear to be sectarian, but only to those who are unable to discern that their position is ultimately grounded in a logic of divine-human communion, which affirms that all of creation is destined to participate in the life of God. Divine-human communion is normally associated with individual spirituality and mystical experience. What is both innovative and challenging in Guroian's and Cavanaugh's thought is their attempt to extend the implications of the principle of divine-human communion toward a political theology. For both, this extension occurs in, through, and *as* the Eucharist; put another way, the Eucharist is an event of deification, having both spatial and temporal dimensions, but not limited to a particular space and time. To build on Cavanaugh's "eucharistize," the logic of deification affirms that all of creation is eucharistizable, not just the human being. For the two theologians, if in fact the world was created to be deified, then it is absolutely inconceivable for the church as the eucharistic body of Christ to accept a functional, privatized, or marginalized position in society. Guroian and Cavanaugh are to be credited with reviving the political implications of the Christian conception of divine-human communion, which one also witnesses in nineteenth- and twentieth-century Russian thought, though there it is grounded in the patristic development of the cosmic dimensions of deification. The Christian thinkers of the Byzantine Empire never exhaustively developed the political implications of this principle, but such implications are implied in their understanding of the cosmic dimensions of the Christian affirmation of deification. The simple logic is that if divine-human communion is not limited to the individual mystical experience but has cosmic dimensions, then it must also inform Christian thinking of politics, culture, economics, and society. What was once thought to be simply a private concern is now shown to have public ramifications: the mystical is the political.

Any Orthodox assessment of the church's relation to a political community must agree on inner theological grounds with Guroian's claim that the model of *symphonia* can only make sense in an imperial context and not in a democratic one. The fundamental flaw with Harakas's method is that it seems to imply that because *symphonia* was the model in the Orthodox past it should exist as the norm for Orthodox understandings of church-state relations in any present situation. He gives insufficient attention to the fact that *symphonia* emerged more as a practical necessity that resulted from the increasing ascendency of Christianity within the Roman Empire. Since *symphonia* was forged within an imperial structure that was more and more dominated by a particular form of Christianity, to try and apply it to what could be argued is a political structure that is self-consciously anti-imperialist ignores the contextuality of *symphonia*. Put another way, the rise of Christianity within the Roman Empire was the impetus to *symphonia;* the question now is whether *symphonia* is adequate to the modern postimperialist context.[36] In confronting modern political thought, the Orthodox confront specific questions and challenges that were unimaginable during the transition of the Roman Empire's official embrace of Christianity. Harakas sees *symphonia* as a response to modern political thought without considering whether the new situation may give rise to a political theology that is different from *symphonia*. It is not necessarily the case that the new situation would lead to a disavowal of *symphonia*, but it is also not self-evident that *symphonia* is adequate to the new questions and challenges of the present situation.

Harakas also fails to analyze *symphonia* as a political *theology*, providing no attempt to justify *symphonia* as being theologically normative. *Symphonia* is a form of political theology, and Guroian is right to question whether its inner coherence does not emerge from the principle of divine-human communion. It is tempting, and fashionable, to dismiss *symphonia*, otherwise known as "Christendom," as simply antithetical to the gospel message. A closer reading, however, would reveal that, prior to its distilled, theologically weak form in Justinian's *Novella*, Eusebius argued that something like *symphonia* is the result of the progressive realization of the Logos in history. Even after Eusebius, Chrysostom, among others, saw the state as an instrument of coercion, motivating out of fear, for the sake of promoting virtue. For Chrysostom and other Christian thinkers of his time, virtue was not for virtue's sake but for the sake of communion with God. In other words, Chrysostom saw the role of the state in light of the ultimate destiny of humanity, which was divine-human communion. Insofar as such a communion is a progressive ascetical realization, the state is necessitated by virtue of the fact that all are working toward this communion. Until one can move toward the love of God for God's sake, like a child, he must be motivated through fear. The church, then, must work with the state to exercise the coercion necessary so as to make the civil society a training ground in virtue. The point here is that *symphonia* within the Byzantine Empire did emerge against the background of a Christian understanding of God's relation to the world in terms of divine-human communion. But Harakas nowhere makes that connection. Even if Guroian were to recognize this aspect of *symphonia*, he would still be correct in questioning whether in fact the church-state incarnation one sees in the Byzantine Empire is most consistent with the principle of divine-human communion.

Harakas also seems to base his application of *symphonia* on an understanding of the role of religion in public life that has since become highly contested within American political discourse. The fact that "God" is mentioned in the founding documents is hardly any grounds for affirming that America is a religious nation or that all Americans self-evidently accept that God is the source of authority for American democracy. While there are some who argue that America is a Christian nation, this version of American history is highly contested. Even if America were a "Christian" nation demographically, it is not necessarily the case that it need remain so. Second, the common good that Harakas recognizes as the new "unity of faith" is a concept not accepted by all theorists of democracy; there are those who would argue that the very notion of a common good is not inherent to democratic structures. Even if one were to accept the idea of a "common good" within American democracy, it is not the case that all would agree that religious institutions should have a voice in the formation of this common good. In short, for Harakas to make the application of *symphonia* work in relation to the Orthodox Church's positioning within American democracy, he must present an understanding of American democracy that is both highly contested and not necessarily reflective of what actually is the case within American democracy.

Cavanaugh and Guroian are, thus, correct in asserting that a proper understanding of church-state relations requires first and foremost an understanding of the nature of the church, that is, an ecclesiology. Both argue for an identification of the church with the Eucharist, what is called by the Orthodox "eucharistic ecclesiology" and by Catholics "communion ecclesiology." Such an understanding of the church, however, does not lead to their conclusions regarding church-state relations and liberal notions of democracy.

The first criticism of Cavanaugh and Guroian's position is that it is untenable. They reject sectarianism as indefensible on the basis of the principle of divine-human communion; but their rejection of accommodationism is fairly clear, either in the form of a Christian state or in the form of a Christian affirmation of the discourse of democracy, which might include such concepts as human rights, church-state separation, the public good, and religious pluralism. Included in this rejection of accommodationism is the status of the church as a denomination. By denominationalism is meant the existence of a plurality of religious expressions within a public space in which religious association is voluntary and based on religious freedom.

Guroian, in particular, anticipates that his positions might be labeled as sectarian, but he resists such an identification because it implies a withdrawal of the church from the world. Guroian's eucharistic understanding of the church defines the mission of the church as one of engagement with the world. The church itself is a presence of salvation for the sake of the world. His attempt to weave a social ethic between the extremes of accommodationism and sectarianism is also evident in his reflections on the Armenian community in the U.S.[37] The fact that he criticizes the Armenian community in America, on the one hand, for prioritizing its ethnic identity over its religious identity and, on the other hand, for becoming more American "uncritically and at great cost to the Orthodox faith" suggests that his "ecclesial" ethics tends toward sectarianism.[38] He does not intend sectarianism, but he leaves unclear what it means to become "critically" more American and be true to one's religious identity. The impression left by Guroian is a mutual exclusivity between being American and being Orthodox.

Cavanaugh also resists the tag of sectarianism, arguing that a eucharistic community is a practice and performance in the world and, as such, is its own politics. The eucharistic community is not an enclave withdrawn from the rest of the world but an active presence transforming all who participate in its sphere. As such, it is a counter-politics to regimes of torture. Cavanaugh, however, does not limit the identification to particular regimes but to the very existence of the nation-state. All nation-states are constituted in and through violence, implying there is no difference in kind between the nation-state of Chile under Pinochet and that of American democracy. The church as eucharistic community exists as a counter-politics to all nation-states, insofar as the eucharistic community is constituted through practices of peace and not violence. If the nation-state is antithetical to the eucharistic community, especially if the concept of the nation-state is grounded in the attempt to marginalize religion from the public sphere, Cavanaugh does not suggest an alternative form of political community. In fact, by identifying the Eucharist as a politics, he has cornered himself into the position that all other forms of political community are contra the Eucharist, inevitably leading to a sectarian position. The only position for Christians is one over and against the political community within which they stand, since it embodies a form of politics that is not eucharistic. Christian participation in the mechanisms of the nation-state or any other imaginable form of political community would ultimately be a tacit affirmation of a form of politics that is not eucharistic. The only option left for the Christian is, then, to prophetically position herself in opposition to a politics that is non-eucharistic, as she simultaneously attempts to expand the visible spatial borders of the eucharistic community. Although the eucharistic community is active in the world, in relation to all other political forms of community, it is de facto sectarian.

Guroian and Cavanaugh could argue that the church is already excluded from having any impact on public life and is thus compelled into sectarianism against its very nature by virtue of the church-state separation; Cavanaugh amplifies this statement by claiming that the nation-state is constituted through violence against religion. This leads to a second problem in their argument, which is a too monolithic understanding of the notion of church-state separation that entails de facto marginalization or privatization of religious voices from the public realm. The strict "wall of separation" in the democratic notion of church-state separation is by no means self-evident or inherent to the idea of democratic pluralism; in fact, it has become the minority opinion. Jeffrey Stout has argued that such exclusion of religion from public life is counterproductive, insofar as it only incites a reactionary form of religious expression in public life; is fundamentally undemocratic in silencing a particular voice within the democratic process; and precludes possible alliances between religious and nonreligious affiliations toward social causes that may actually advance the democratic goals of freedom and equality.[39] Both Charles Taylor and José Casanova argue that although something like secularization has occurred in terms of the functional differentiation of the nonreligious spheres of society, such as the state, economy, and education, from an all-encompassing common theological perspective this differentiation need not necessarily result in privatization or marginalization of religion.[40] Casanova then illustrates the variety of forms public religion takes in the modern world through case studies on religion in Brazil and Poland, and on Evangelical Protestantism and Catholicism in the United States. Rather than theorizing the impending or naturalized privatization of religion in the modern world, sociologists should be theorizing the variety of forms public religion can take in the modern world. As Casanova states, "It is the major purpose and thrust of this study to show both theoretically and empirically that privatization is not a modern structural trend. In other words, this study has tried to show that there can be and that there are public religions in the modern world which do not need to endanger either modern individual freedoms or modern differentiated structures."[41] Finally, Ronald Thiemann has argued, "Particular moral and religious beliefs can be developed with sufficient generality to provide an overarching framework within which an overlapping consensus can be developed. If that is the case, then it surely follows that religious beliefs should not be prohibited from providing public justifications within a democratic polity, as long as those beliefs genuinely contribute to the building of an overlapping consensus."[42] Both Guroian and Cavanaugh presume that democratic structures exclude the religious voice from public life, but this perception is both empirically false and no longer the majority opinion among political philosophers and sociologists. Religion in public life is not necessarily the Rortyan "conversation stopper."[43] Although it remains a matter of debate in what way the religious voice can participate in public discussion without threatening democratic principles of freedom and equality, it is safer to predict that it will always be a part of the public scene, rather than to predict or await the completion of the modern privatization of religion. The debate is also rightly focused not on whether but on how religion can be a part of public life.

Even if church-state separation need not entail exclusion of religion from public life, Guroian and Cavanaugh would argue that the very notions of public life, common good, and a public morality based on democratic principles involves the church in a compromise of its nature and its mission. The central question is whether the affirmation of a public space that promotes diversity, religious pluralism, and a public morality that is not exhaustive of the church's morality is a betrayal of the church's nature and its mission. Can the church preach a message of salvation for the whole world and accept a religiously, culturally, ethnically, and morally diverse political community? Presupposing the understanding of church as an eschatological community in the eucharistic worship, I would argue that the acceptance of such a political community is not a betrayal. More than this, it is called for by the very nature of the church as an eschatological community.

First, the church is church, that is, it is an eschatological community in the eucharistic worship through faith or persuasion and not coercion, a principle with which Guroian and Cavanaugh would agree. The church's mission is to call the world to the salvation offered in Jesus Christ not by christianizing the state but through persuading others to freely join its eucharistic communion, that is, its communal praise, worship, and offering to God; by its very definition, a eucharistic community is one of noncoercion. Such persuasion is the only legitimate way to expand the boundaries of the church throughout the world. Until the world is included in the church through persuasion, then the church must confront a political community that is distinct from itself but to which it is necessarily related, together with the institution of the state that administers, symbolizes, and expresses the nature of such a political community. The question becomes whether the Christian church that understands its *telos* as one of communion with the divine could support a democratic form for the political community and the state, and not be in contradiction with its own self-understanding as church.

If the church relates to the world through persuasion, then in order to be consistent with itself, the church must accept a community distinct from its own that consists of religious, political, and cultural diversity, and a state that affirms and protects such diversity. The forms of political community and state that best express and affirm such diversity are liberal democratic, for such diversity is what it means, in part, to be a democracy. The logic of the eucharistic ecclesiology demands the existence of a liberal democratic state that is by definition an institution that is distinct from the church, in which a community of religious and political diversity is symbolized and that is made necessary by the fact that all the people of the world are not members of the church's worshipping community. The important point here is that the existence of a politically diverse community in which the church is one voice among others is not a betrayal of the church's nature but, rather, the necessary result of the church as an eschatological community. Insofar as the church has not fulfilled its mission to persuade others to become part of its eucharistic worship of God, then it must accept the existence of political and religious diversity. The state as a politically diverse community is not contrary to but, rather, inherent in the very notion of the church as an eschatological community.

Second, the support of democratic forms of public morality and a common good is not a compromise of the church's mission. The terms "public morality" and "common good" refer to the consensus or unity of a society around shared moral values. My own position agrees with those who argue that democracy itself implies a particular notion of the common good including freedom, equality, justice, fairness, inclusivity, participation, diversity, and otherness. More concretely, it includes those institutions and structures designed to preserve and protect such goods and that provide the space for the conversation over further concrete determinations of democratic goods. Certain forms of diversity, such as religious, political, and cultural, are concrete expressions and embodiments of the common good of the democratic community.[44] Guroian and Cavanaugh cannot envision a Christian at one and the same time assuming a missionary attitude vis-à-vis the world and accepting the limits placed on the church's voice in the notion of a public morality. But insofar as the notion of a politically and religiously diverse community is the necessary result of the church as an eschatological community in the world, it is not a contradiction for the church to attempt to missionize the world and simultaneously recognize the need for a common good around which diverse groups unite to form a community. As Harakas suggests, the common good is included in, though not exhaustive of, Orthodox moral principles. As a necessary part of the political community, the church should have a voice in the construction of the common good. As an example, in its attempt to missionize the world the church may attempt to persuade others not to commit murder and to engage in fasting practices. In relation to a democratic form of the common good, the church must accept its own limits and recognize that the goal is not the formation of a eucharistic community through persuasion but, rather, the construction of a community in which diversity and cultural difference are affirmed and protected and in which the recognition of such diversity must be enforced if they are not voluntarily accepted. In light of this particular end, the church can affirm that laws against murder must form a necessary part of the common good but not laws regulating fasting, for rules of fasting presuppose a Christian community formed through persuasion and whose end is distinct from that of the political community. As Ronald Thiemann notes, "Even if liberal societies cannot agree on the ultimate *telos* for all human beings, it does not follow that they are unable to generate a limited but still real consensus which concerns the common good such societies should praise."[45]

Guroian might object that there can be no ends or good within the "world" other than that of union with God, which is the ultimate *telos* for God's creation. Although it may be true that a eucharistic ecclesiology implies that the sole *telos* for the whole world is union with God, the existence of a politically diverse community is made necessary by virtue of the fact that such a *telos* is as yet unfulfilled. Until such a fulfillment, the existence of a politically and religiously diverse community has a *telos* distinct though not separate from that of the church, which is, according to the logic of eucharistic ecclesiology, to form a community of diversity in which the integrity of life is affirmed and protected until such time that all are one with God. Even though the principle of divine-human communion precludes a strict separation of nature and grace, and thus the understanding of the church as eucharistic participation in the life of God leads to the natural law–like conclusion for a political community as a space with a *telos* distinct though not separate from that of divine-human communion.

My position, then, stands somewhere in between that of Chrysostom's and Eusebius's. Like both Christian thinkers, it affirms that a Christian can only think politics within the horizon of the eschatological, though potentially immanent, goal of divine-human communion. Like Chrysostom, the state is clearly distinct from the church and functions only in relation to the realization of church—a community of communion with the divine. Unlike Chrysostom, the state is not to function so as to form citizens of virtue through fear with an eye toward their union with God. The function of the state, rather, is to maximize the conditions for the possibility of free realization of this communion. This is not to say that only in a liberal democracy is divine-human communion possible, but simply to assert that if God is calling for a free response to God's initiating love, then the state must maximize the conditions for such a free response, even if such a response is "no." More like Eusebius, the state is not simply functional, but iconic. While it is necessary to reject Eusebius's blurring of the distinction between state and church, the structures of a political community are by no means symbolically neutral. Although no Christian could ever equate state with church, this does not mean that political communities cannot be understood as allowing for the presence of the divine to some degree. If Christians maintain that all of creation is meant to be saturated with the divine without losing its created otherness, then this principle serves as a criterion of judgment of various forms of political community—there are simply some that iconically presence the divine more than others. A political community that fosters a common good that promotes the treatment of all human beings as irreducibly unique iconically presences the divine more than Hitler's Third Reich or Pinochet's regime, even if that community takes the form of a nation-state. Like Eusebius, then, Christians need to attempt to discern forms of political community that embody the Logos of God, even while asserting that the fullness of the Logos of God is the church.

Furthermore, as I will show more extensively below, Christians who shape their lives toward the realization of communion with the divine will ultimately act in such a way as to work toward a political community that affirms, in a broad sense, the basic axioms of liberal democracy. The Christian striving for communion with the divine, while maintaining a prophetic distance to any and all forms of political community, would never demand a culturally and politically privileged Christianity, even if it meant being the last to be convinced of the Christian truth of divine-human communion. As Christians progress to realize the divine in their lives, then the inevitable result would be a liberal democratic form of political community. Otherwise put, the church is meant to perfect the political community not abolish it, which means that the political community exists in an analogical relationship to the church, not one of diametrical opposition. Theoretically, once all have become part of the eucharistic community, the community of praise, worship, and offering to God, the existence of the state is no longer necessary. One could argue that this is consistent with Pauline theology, wherein the necessity of the state is affirmed in Romans 13, though in 1 Corinthians (6:1–11), Christians, regarded as the body of Christ, are chastised for resorting to non-ecclesial institutions for resolving disputes.

It is, then, not a contradiction for the church to simultaneously be engaged in missionizing the world and be committed to supporting public discussions of the common good. In the end, the understanding of "church" in the Orthodox tradition as an eschatological community through the eucharistic worship demands engagement in both types of activities. More explicitly, it lends support to democratic forms of government as most consistent with its own theological principles.

Issues with Eucharistic Ecclesiology

My argument up to this point has engaged in a form of immanent critique, which takes for granted the assumptions of both Guroian and Cavanaugh that the church *is* Eucharist, is constituted in the eucharistic event, but questions whether, in fact, such a claim leads to their conclusions, namely, the mutual exclusivity between the church as eucharistic community and a political community structured around the principles of modern democratic liberalism. I have argued that a eucharistic ecclesiology does not lead to such a mutual exclusivity, a church-world dichotomy, but actually leads to the affirmation of the necessity of a political community with a *telos* that is internal to such a community, and distinct though not separate from the *telos* of an ecclesial community. Guroian and Cavanaugh simply offer no other alternative, nor can they, since to do so would be to legitimize a form of political community other than the church; but, this would be, according to their logic, to diminish all that the church is as a politics. In the end, they are caught in a contradiction of affirming that the church's mission is to eucharistize the world, but, until that is fully accomplished, can only exist as an enclave or sect in relation to the world. Their understanding of the church as Eucharist is grounded in the realism of divine-human communion, but such a communion is parochialized in small communities throughout the world and, thus, absent everywhere else. I would argue that to understand the church in this way follows, ironically, a Gnostic either/or logic that is incompatible with the realism of divine-human communion.

The other problem with a eucharistic political theology, or, more generally, a eucharistic ecclesiology, is that the claim that the Eucharist is the experience of the kingdom of God simply does not resonate with human experience.[46] Such a lack of resonation does not necessarily make the identification of the church as a eucharistic event incorrect; in fact, according to the logic of divine-human communion, the church as the body of the faithful is the event of communion with God and, as such, is the kingdom of God understood as the unity of all creation in the body of Christ. It makes sense also to say that in such an event humans are constituted as persons, understood as unique and *ecstatic*. The image of the kingdom of God as an event of eucharistic exchange, in which persons are constituted as unique in relations of freedom of love, and that such an event *is* the realization of divine-human communion, is persuasive, powerful, and, simply, beautiful.

As beautiful as it is, it simply does not appear to be realized in all its fullness in the eucharistic gatherings of local parishes. Such a gap between the eschatological vision and the local reality does not necessarily mean that the eschatological vision should not continue to inform institutional ecclesial structures; nor does it mean that the eschatological is absent from such communities. It simply means that the claim that the Eucharist is an event of the kingdom of God must intersect with the ascetical struggle to more fully realize the presence of the divine in one's mode of being. Put another way, the event language of eucharistic ecclesiology needs to be tempered with the insights of asceticism that although the material is created to embody the divine, such an embodiment is a never-ending movement realized in and through particular practices. One could say that the ascetical struggle is to exist as eucharistic, that is, to *be* in such as a way so as to relate to the other in and by giftedness. It is in relating to the other eucharistically that one has the power to render the other irreducibly unique and free. The ascetical struggle recognizes that humans do not exist in that way, and the movement toward that mode of existence is through practices that allow for the divine presence to be more fully manifested. If through ascetical struggle one realizes that one is more loving and, thus, more eucharistic, then all one has done is allowed the love of God that is already there to manifest itself in the human person more fully. To understand the ascetical life as individualistic and nonrelational is incorrect; the purpose of the ascetical is a relational mode of being that is eucharistic. Moreover, eucharistic ecclesiology's understanding of the Eucharist can be interpreted as unfree insofar as it is focused on the inbreaking of the Spirit in history without any dependence on the human struggle to realize the Spirit that is already present in one's life.[47] The Eucharist is the gathering of all those attempting ascetically to struggle to realize the presence of the divine in their lives and, by extension, as community.

If eucharistic ecclesiology presents a vision of the Eucharist as a communion of persons, who are constituted as unique and free in relations of love, then the Christian ascetical tradition reminds eucharistic ecclesiology that humans need to learn how to love. As Maximus the Confessor puts it, "Blessed is the man who has learnt to love all men equally."[48] If the eucharistic vision is the fulfillment of the greatest commandment to love God with all of one's heart, soul, and mind, and to love the neighbor as one's self, then obedience to this commandment is neither willed nor imposed by the Holy Spirit but realized as a growing presence of the Holy Spirit in the face of all that pulls one away from following this commandment. The Eucharist is a practice that both contributes to embodying this presence and, momentarily, constitutes the faithful as the body of Christ. The eucharistic participants, then, must scatter into the world where they confront the stranger, who more than blood or ecclesial kin provokes a challenge to the ascetical struggle to love; above all, one rarely finds oneself loving the stranger. Notwithstanding its strangeness, politics is an arena of community of strangers and, for the Christian who cares about communion with God, the space for ascetical struggle. If we broaden the political beyond simply what legislators do to include the forms of practices in and through which strangers relate to one another, then the political is not insignificant to the Christian ascetical struggle to learn how to love. The political is one of the deserts where the Christian confronts images of demons that provoke demonization of the stranger.

One such demon that provokes demonization in politics is anger. Maximus the Confessor claims that "Christ does not want you to have hate for anyone, or grief, or anger, or resentment in any way at all or for any temporal reason whatsoever."[49] He then advises, "When you are insulted by someone or offended in any matter, then beware of angry thoughts, lest by distress they sever you from charity and place you in the region of hatred."[50] So much of what passes as Christian politics in the United States and in traditional Orthodox countries is a form of righteous anger. Christians often engage in political issues with an anger that they justify in the name of truth. This anger then justifies a demonization and destruction of the other who appears to be the enemy of God's truth. If the principle of divine-human communion interprets God's truth as an embodiment of the greatest commandment that must be learned through ascetical practices, then the notion of Christian righteous anger is an oxymoron. In this view, anger is corrosive. One does not need anger to struggle for social, economic, and racial justice, nor to argue for a particular concrete realization of the common democratic goods of equality and freedom. If one's political struggle is motivated by anger, then that is a sign, at least for the Christian, that more ascetical work needs to be done in learning to love, since this learning includes even the other we are tempted to demonize: the stranger who most hurts or threatens us. In the end, there is no space in which this ascetical struggle to learn to love does not take place, including family, church community, and political community. In confronting the stranger, however, we are more likely to come face-to-face with the magnification of how much learning to love we have ahead of us, since it is much easier to justify anger, hatred, resentment, and demonization of those who threaten our identities. The temptation is to justify the violence that emerges from these vices in the name of truth. So-called Christian politics often masks an idolatrous self-interest. True Christian politics would work toward the realization of Christian principles specific to a political community without demonizing the "godless" other, even if that other persuades more people of his position. One thing is for sure: Christian politics stands against all forms of violence, both physical and rhetorical.

To interject the ascetical into the eucharistic gathering does not challenge the fundamental logic of eucharistic ecclesiology. The eucharistic gathering is the church par excellence, and it is an event of the inbreaking of the Holy Spirit and, as such, a realization of the body of Christ. It is also clear, however, that the community is in movement to participate and, hence, realize the body of Christ more fully. Understanding the ascetical dimension of the eucharistic community also does not mitigate the fact that the eucharistic community is a distinct community from the political community, as well as the various subpolitical communities, such as voluntary associations. It does not allow for the hard and fast borders between the political community and the idealized form of the eucharistic community put forth by Guroian and Cavanaugh. There is no question that the Eucharist is a practice internal to the ecclesial community whose distinctive *telos* is divine-human communion. The fact, however, that such a community is in process makes its borders much more porous to all that surrounds it. As a eucharistic community it witnesses to an alternate politics while realizing it does not fully manifest this alternate politics. Moreover, there are some (not all) who move from this eucharistic community and bring a eucharistic engagement to those that are not part of this eucharistic community, and to all that exists and to which they relate in some way. This engagement is one of treating the other as a creation of God, no matter who they are or what they do. Insofar as such an engagement is a hope for a noncoercive, eucharistic transformation of the material as the icon of the divine presence, then, quite ironically, Christian eucharistic work is to maximize the conditions for the possibility of rejecting God, since eucharistizing the world is only possible through an ascetical struggle in which the presence of God is freely embodied.

What the eucharistic and communion ecclesiologies do not fully nuance is how Christians do not live up to being Christians. Again, this does not negate the validity of these ecclesiological visions, but it does mitigate the claim of identification of the Eucharist with the kingdom of God. The entire Christian ascetical architecture is built on the premise that to be all that one was meant to be requires ascetical struggle. The Christian community itself has to organize itself so as to guard against Christians not being all that they can be; and what is paradoxical (and a little sad) is that Christians have to think about political communities that guard against Christians not being Christian. Cavanaugh and Guroian do not give sufficient attention to that reality. What is the form of political community that would guard against Christian support of slavery? That would guard against Christian denigration of women as unequal to men? That would guard against Christian persecution of those who express sexuality different from heterosexuality? History confirms that such a political community is not likely to be one in which chuch-state separation does not exist. The biggest problem with Cavanaugh and Guroian's account of a eucharistic politics is that one cannot rely on Christians being Christian. Given that, the church as Eucharist is an already–not yet reality, and Christian thinking on political community must take that into account. It must recognize the need for a political community with a good internal to itself that is in continuity with the good being realized in the eucharistic community, but with neither being collapsed into the other. Such a community is one that looks like a liberal democracy, minus the anthropological baggage of modern liberalism.

Immanent
(of GOD) permanently
pervading + sustaining
the universe –
(pervasive, pervading
permeating)

Chapter Three

Personhood and Human Rights

This chapter will continue the immanent critique of the Christian theological assault on modern liberal democracy. The focus will be on the modern liberal notion of human rights, and the theological ground will shift from ecclesiology to theological anthropology, even if the two are theological mutually constitutive. Christian thinkers of late, quite surprisingly, have argued for a mutual exclusivity between modern liberal notions of human rights and a theological anthropology based on the principle of divine-human communion. This ambivalence to the notion of human rights seems to exist for several reasons, among them: (1) its seemingly inherent link to atheistic humanism; (2) a secular, human rights rhetoric implies a marginalization of religion from public life that is especially problematic for traditional Orthodox countries; (3) human rights language is grounded in an anthropology that is individualistic, a-relational, and solipsistic and, as such, incompatible with a Christian theological anthropology. The first section of this chapter will survey the various contemporary Orthodox voices on human rights discourse.

My own angle will be to explore whether the notion of human rights is compatible with recent Orthodox understandings of personhood, which itself is an attempt to give anthropological flesh to the

—*Inter*—

realism of divine-human communion. In the second section, I will outline the main aspects of this theology of personhood, which has been developed in relation to trinitarian theology and eucharistic ecclesiology. According to contemporary Orthodox theology, personhood is an event of freedom and uniqueness realized in relations of love in union with Christ by the power of the Holy Spirit.

I will end the chapter in conversation with Nicholas Wolterstorff's recent attempt to theistically ground the notion of human rights. There are affinities between Wolterstorff's dignity-based approach to human rights and the relational notion of personhood put forth by recent Orthodox theologians. I will argue that, based on the principle of divine-human communion, the Orthodox (and Christians, more generally) must unequivocally support the language of human rights, though fully realizing that such language falls short of expressing all that the human is created to be.

Recent Debates about Human Rights in Orthodoxy

One of the features of modern liberal democracy to which the Orthodox have shown an ambivalence is the modern liberal notion of human rights. The debate within Orthodoxy about modern liberal human rights language mirrors that occurring in Islam.[1] These debates about human rights are not restricted to the religious sphere, as some nonreligious political philosophers think that the modern liberal architecture of human rights has been an utter failure.[2] Most Orthodox resistance to human rights language comes from the insistence that such language is incompatible with Orthodox theological anthropology. The Orthodox detractors of human rights argue that it is inherently linked with a nonrelational, autonomous, individualistic understanding of the human person that does not resonate with experience. Some more strongly connect human rights language with an atheistic humanism, which thus promotes either implicitly or explicitly an atheistic, antireligious agenda. Although he is in the "radical" Orthodox camp, John Milbank encapsulates this Christian resistance to human rights language:

[Giorgio] Agamben rightly warns us not to be sanguine about the end of totalitarianism, because the line between totalitarianism and liberal democracy is not after all so distinct. The liberal notion of natural rights guaranteed by a sovereign state itself plays directly into a first constitutive *aporia* of sovereignty. If these rights are "natural" (and follow from certain given facts regarded as prior to valuation) as if they belonged to an animal, yet are only operative and recognized—and therefore existent—within the State, then the State assumes to itself a power over nature, a right even to define nature, and indeed defines itself by this power, and therefore secretly reserves to itself alone a supreme *de facto* right of pure nature prior to contract, by which in exceptional circumstances it may withdraw any right whatsoever. If you accord people "human rights" by nature, it means (as Alain Badiou argues in his *Ethics*), that you already envisage people *primarily* as passive if freely wandering animals, who *might* be victimized: the ban actually creates the space for its own violation, just as St. Paul saw was the case with all law outside the counter-law of charity. Agamben cites instances of reduction to half-life by liberal democracies and especially the United States: dangerous experiments upon prisoners condemned to death; drug testing in the third world; the dubious treatment upon fetuses and late abortion which is but disguised infanticide. Recently we have had instances of American politicians declaring that Taliban prisoners or suspected terrorists enjoy *neither* the rights of criminals *nor* the rights of prisoners of war. They have therefore become *homo sacer,* denied contradictorily *as* humans (since we would not really treat animals like this) any humanity whatsoever, and any mark of the *imago dei*.[3]

One of the first Orthodox theologians to challenge an uncritical acceptance by Orthodox of the modern notion of human rights is Christos Yannaras.[4] Yannaras, throughout his work, operates with a view of history in which "Western" thought, which begins with Augustine, is diametrically opposed to the Christian thought that developed in the Byzantine Empire. Although there exist common sources in Latin and Greek Christendoms, such as the so-called Cappadocian fathers, from Augustine forward, Western thought carved an intellectual path that would culminate in the narcissism of Nietzsche.[5] The problem with Western thought, according to Yannaras, is that it rejected the Greek patristic notion of *theosis*—the deification of the material creation. This rejection of the incarnational principle of divine-human communion began with Augustine's rejection of the essence/energies distinction, which was crucial to the Greek patristic expression of divine-human communion. In the end, this rejection led to the gulf-like split between Creator and created, which led to other forms of hardened dualisms such as reason/faith, body/soul, and sacred/secular.

The Enlightenment privatization of religion, enshrined in the principle of the church-state separation, is not a rejection of Western Christianity, but the logical outcome of a mode of thinking that separates the material from the divine. It is not a surprise then that political thought degenerated, according to Yannaras, into an understanding of the political based on individuals over-and-against other individuals. The usual Enlightenment narrative is that abuses of power on the part of religions and the interminable religious wars made it necessary to assert the inviolable rights of each individual against other individuals and against the state without any reference to God: "The idea was that normative principles and rules of justice should not be deduced from the hypothetical 'law of God' which was arbitrarily handled by religious institutions, but by the logic of the laws of nature which was objective and controllable."[6] In the end, "The 'paradigm' of modernity was grounded on the egocentrism of 'human rights,'" both in terms of bracketing the transcendent and in terms of injecting the individual with ultimate value.

Yannaras argues that, although there was no concept of "human rights" in ancient Greek and Roman jurisprudence, there was a realization of the inviolable dignity and honor of the human person that was an event of community rather than either an attribution of individualized human nature or a legally protected claim on the other individual. According to Yannaras, "Ancient Greece's radical innovation in human history was that it transformed simple cohabitation into the achievement of a city, that it transformed necessary (for utilitarian reasons) collectiveness into an 'exercise of truth.' The city is the state of social relations which results when the aim and axis of collectiveness is metaphysical and not utilitarian."[7] The ancient Greek city is, at least philosophically, grounded in ontology—in a particular conception of "being." As such, as an event, the city mirrors "the way of existence 'according to the truth,' the way of incorruptibility and immortality."[8] It is simply by the city being such an event, by being as it is, that the human person is unique and irreducible. In other words, only a certain conception of being can realize what human rights language hopes to achieve.

This conception of being, however, must be relational, and it is only with Christianity and the realization of the church that this relational mode of being is actualized. According to Yannaras, "It is no accident that the first apostolic Christian communities borrowed from the ancient Greek political event the term *ecclesia* in order to express and reveal their identity and their specific difference from any other 'religion.'"[9] What Christians did was transform this "ancient Greek political event into the eucharistic body of the Christian Church," which is "an event and a way of communion between Church persons, a way of love: that is, freedom from the existence of nature, freedom from the physical limitation of time, attrition and death." Such an event is contrasted with what Yannaras calls "religion," which is "an individual event, subject to the natural need of every person to worship and to appease the unknown and transcendent—it is an individual effort towards individual faith, individual virtues, individual justification, individual salvation."[10] "Religion" is that into which Roman Catholics and Protestants transformed Christianity, thereby laying the groundwork for the modern Western liberal emphasis on the individual. It was this individualized relation to the transcendent that set the stage for modern conceptions of individual rights: "the opinion that, in European history, religious individualism preceded the egocentrism of a religionized (from Charlemagne and after) Christianity and set the pattern for the absolute importance of individual rights in modernity, is not arbitrary. When the tyranny of metaphysics was rejected, the aim of individual metaphysical salvation was replaced by the aim of a secularized (legal) protection. And thus was born the political system of so-called 'representative democracy,' which lies at the antipodes of ancient Greek democracy (in the same way that religionized individualized Christianity lies at the antipodes of the Orthodox Church)."[11] Yannaras thus echoes a growing number of Christian thinkers in claiming that the modern notion of human rights is based on anti-Christian presuppositions. Further, he amplifies Milbank in implying that the modern language of human rights is simply a result of bad theology, and that only the church as eucharistic event realizes what the language of human rights aspires to accomplish. Yannaras's grand narrative of the demise of the West, however, extends further back to Augustine.[12]

Vigen Guroian has also written against any Orthodox affirmation of the language of human rights, and for similar reasons as Yannaras, based on the Orthodox affirmation of the human person's destiny for communion with God. According to Guroian, "human autonomy and rights in Western thought . . . contradict Orthodoxy's insistence upon the theonomous nature of humanity revealed by the divine Word's incarnate existence."[13] Like Yannaras (though without referencing him), Guroian attributes the language of rights to a theological divide between nature and grace: "from the perspective of Orthodoxy, and especially from an Armenian standpoint, the doctrine [of human rights] in all its varieties expresses a flawed understanding of the relation of nature and grace and of God and persons in Jesus Christ."[14] He amplifies that "[h]uman beings are not autonomous but theonomous."[15] Guroian sounds a warning that without attention to the propensity of sin in humans, the language of human rights will do little good toward safeguarding the inviolable human dignity it proclaims. Guroian, like Yannaras, proclaims that humans were created for more than human rights, and that human rights language has the potential to obfuscate this human destiny for communion with God and with others.

On the institutional level, the loudest resistance to human rights language has come from the Russian Orthodox Church. In 2008, the ROC published "The Russian Orthodox Church's Basic Teaching on Human Dignity, Freedom and Rights."[16] In this document the ROC unequivocally states its support for the notion of human dignity, which it argues is the essence of human rights language, but asserts that the Christian notion of human dignity is grounded on a different basis than modern liberalism, the latter being essentially atheistic. Human dignity, according to the ROC, is a result of the creature being created by the Creator; it is a gift given at creation. In this sense, the "dignity and worth of every human person are derived from the image of God" (1.2). The ROC explains that dignity is not inherent in the creature but is linked to moral principles. The human being realizes the dignity of the image of God if he acts according to God's moral law, that is, realizes the likeness for which he was created: "Thus there is a direct link between human dignity and morality" (1.5). What the ROC rejects is any understanding of dignity, and hence human rights, that translates into unlimited negative freedom, with the only restriction being no harm to others. Such an understanding of human dignity would allow for a relativistic notion of morality, which is unacceptable. Freedom according to Orthodox theology is not unlimited freedom of choice, but freedom of choice that is enabled to follow God's law. Thus, while freedom of choice should be defended, it must be regulated in order to freely choose what is good and moral (2.2).

In the realm of society, then, human rights must always be understood in light of the human being's relation and obligation to God's moral law. Such a principle would mean that rights are not unlimited and that such rights as freedom of expression cannot extend to "the public defilement of objects, symbols or notions cherished by believers" (3.2). Human rights cannot be extended to immoral actions that "cancel both the Gospel and natural morality. The church sees a great danger in the legislative and public support given to various vices, such as sexual lechery and perversions, the worship of profit and violence. It is equally inadmissible to elevate to a norm such immoral and inhumane actions towards the human being as abortion,

euthanasia, use of human embryos in medicine, experiments changing a person's nature and the like" (3.3). Human rights also cannot be
supported at the expense of the "religious and cultural traditions of
countries: One's human rights cannot be set against the values and interests of one's homeland, community and family" (3.5). The ROC extends the rights language to nations and ethnic groups, who have the
right to "their own religion, language and culture" and from protection from "the actions of destructive cults" (5.3).

The ROC, then, is not against affirming the inherent dignity of all
human beings, but sees this dignity tied to morality, which as an institution it has a duty to promote within Russian society in cooperation
with the state, but without being under the hand of the state.[17] Russian
history and culture justifies the rights of privilege for the ROC within
Russian society, which it translates into the rights of the Russian
people and nation over and against influence of other nations or destructive cults. Furthermore, such a conception of rights justifies legislation against defamation of sacred symbols or any movement that
might mitigate the influences of Orthodoxy within Russian culture.
The subtext of this particular document is a rejection of any notion of
human rights that relativizes morality and, by so doing, promotes an
atheistic humanist agenda or, somewhat less ominously, reduces the
ROC to one among many voices in a pluralistic public space.

Such a subtext is made more explicit in statements by individual
hierarchs, such as Metropolitan Hilarion (Alfeyev) of Volokolamsk.[18]
Echoing the ROC's emphasis on the divine origin of human dignity,
he argues that "the idea of responsibility is also present in humanism,
but with the absence of absolute moral norms this principle simply
denotes the limitation of one person's freedom by the freedom of
other people. From the standpoint of atheistic humanism, the realization of the potential of freedom is nothing other than the person's
unhindered realization of all his desires and aspirations, except for
those which hinder the realization of similar desires of other people,
as well as the realization of those rights of his that do not violate the
rights of others. This gives rise to the relativistic interpretation of all
moral norms and spiritual values."[19] Echoing Milbank, Alfeyev sees a
link between this atheistic humanist understanding of human rights

and the tragedies of the twentieth century: "Humanism of the second half of the 20th century, expressed in the Universal Declaration of Human Rights, arose as a reaction to the barbaric acts which fill the conscience of mankind with indignation, i.e. in reaction to the crimes of Nazism. However, humanists refuse to see the connection between these crimes and the anthropological theories born in the atheistic minds of the French enlighteners of the 18th century and developed by 19th century materialists. Humanists refuse to admit that the 'humanization' of morality through the rejection of religious norms was the main cause of the monstrosities of the French revolutionaries and later of the Communists and Nazis."[20] In short, an atheistic humanist conception of human rights is self-contradictory and implodes on itself.[21]

Not all Orthodox scholars and theologians take this hard line against the human rights language of modern liberal thought.[22] John McGuckin argues against Yannaras's notion that the language of "human rights" never appeared in the Christian Roman Empire.[23] While McGuckin agrees with the chorus of Christian thinkers that human rights language needs a grounding in the transcendent, the language of "rights" itself is replete both in the canons of the Ecumenical Councils, which attempt to regulate relations among the various churches, and in the Justinianic Code, which would later influence Western legal theory and lay the foundation for the Western conception of universal human rights: "Commencing with the notion of the Justinianic Code as a great historical enterprise, its influence extended out from the merely historical so as to enter western Renaissance mentality as the potential *idée maitresse* of European political cohesion. The rule of law, based upon notions of equity and systematic reason, entered the early modern European consciousness along this track bringing with it political concepts of a wider western legal civilization: and with that the seminal notion of the rights of Mankind."[24]

The most substantive defense of the compatibility of human rights language and Orthodoxy comes from Anastasios Yannoulatos, Archbishop of Albania, a country in which Orthodox Christianity is a vibrant minority. Before assuming the see of the autocephalous Church of Albania, Yannoulatos served as acting Archbishop of East

Africa. According to Yannoulatos, "Any coherent consideration of the 'Rights of Man' or 'human rights' necessarily involves a broader notion of what man is."[25] Yannoulatos recognizes that the presuppositions of the various declarations about human rights over the past century are different from those of the Orthodox for understanding the human being. He explains that "human rights declarations and the perspective of religion start out from different premises. The declarations under discussion seek to regulate human life based on the view that people are political beings and are therefore subject to the power that belongs to Caesar; human rights declarations are concerned with the relationship that exists between the individual and the state. . . . Christian faith starts and ends with God."[26] Further differences include the fact that "[d]eclarations seek to impose their views through legal and political forms of coercion, whereas the Christian message addresses itself to people's way of thinking and to their conscience, using persuasion and faith. Declarations basically stress outward compliance, while the gospel insists on inner acceptance, on spiritual rebirth, and on transformation."[27] He admits that behind the rhetoric of human rights language is a deification of humanity without God, which, in its extreme, can lead to an excessive individualism that abuses rights language.

Yannoulatos, however, does not issue an outright condemnation of human rights language, nor does he diametrically oppose such language to an Orthodox anthropology. Rights language is a "starting point" that must be coupled with an attempt to counter the real threats to human dignity, which are an excessive "egotism" and "the complex factors that operate in our modern technological society's multiform and impersonal structures."[28] Rights must ultimately serve a common good, must enable participation in and responsibility to a community, and not allow for an enclave-like isolation from society. A Christian cannot prescind from seeing rights from the angle of a thick, metaphysical description of human destiny; a human ultimately has a right "to become that for which we were created,"[29] which, in the end, is to love and to be loved.[30]

Yannoulatos, thus, although he is critical of human rights documents, is not rejecting them outright. He is attempting to deepen them with an Orthodox Christian understanding of the human being.[31] Rights language, then, is useful for shaping societal structures and institutions, but a Christian, for Yannoulatos, cannot but see the purpose of such rights in relation to society as enabling the human person to be all that she was created to be. In the end, for Yannoulatos, "Orthodoxy nurtures a willingness to accept people as they are, with deep respect for their freedom and without requiring them to adopt Christian views. . . . It also instills a deep respect for human rights and an eagerness to work with others to attain universal acceptance for human rights and to defend them."[32] What Yannoulatos appears to underline as a fundamental right consistent with Orthodox anthropology is the right to noncoercion with respect to religious beliefs. Yannoulatos believes that religion can offer "something radically different in quality and significance from anything promised by secular forces in our society." This something different is contributing to "an organic social whole made up of people who are complete personalities and whose relationships are based on love—not merely a form of coexistence shared by isolated individuals."[33] True Christian work is measured by "a spontaneous and sincere openness without expecting anything whatsoever in return."[34] There is not a hint in Yannoulatos of privileging Orthodoxy in a particular society, even if he advocates for a public role of religion within a sphere of democratic pluralism. In a tone that is distinct from the ROC documents, Yannoulatos states:

As to the Christian churches, if they want to make their own distinctive contribution to the cause of human rights, they should not limit themselves to fine analysis and admonitions, but should become in reality what they were meant to be: centers of moral and spiritual inspiration, where personalities can be molded; laboratories of selfless love; a place where the kingdom of God reveals itself on earth; a place where the level of human life is elevated from a collection of individuals, who merely coexist biologically, to a "communion of persons," which takes as its model the supreme reality: the Holy Trinity, whose praises the churches ceaselessly extol.[35]

Conspicuous by its silence is the sense that the church can and should do such work in society without having to either count on the state for certain forms of support or lay claim to a cultural privilege within a particular society.

There is thus a consistent thread in contemporary Orthodox discussions of human rights language: a critique of an understanding of human rights that presupposes an understanding of the human being that is nontheistic. The only way the Orthodox can make sense of the language of human rights is through the prism of divine-human communion,—that the human was created for communion with God. This consensus, however, as we have seen, has not led to similar conclusions. The ROC affirms human dignity language, but only when coupled with morality; based on the relation between these two concepts, it then, somewhat ironically, asserts the right to the privileging of Orthodoxy in Russian culture in light of Russia's history. Yannoulatos shares the Orthodox suspicion of advancing an atheistic agenda via human rights language and concern about the potential for human rights language for excessive individualism; but he affirms rights language only to challenge religions to broaden and deepen the concept in their work in the world. Yannaras completely rejects human rights language as antithetical to a relational ontology of personhood. Although Yannoulatos hints at it, Yannaras is the only Orthodox voice to base his rejection on contemporary Orthodox understandings of personhood, to which he contributed and which is present throughout his *oeuvre*. In light of this aspect of his thought, a more thorough treatment of the development of a contemporary Orthodox theology of personhood will follow. It is based on this understanding of personhood that I will offer my own assessment of Orthodoxy and human rights language—one that fundamentally disagrees both with Yannaras and the ROC.

Orthodox Understandings of Personhood

After centuries of neglect, Christian theologians renewed their attention to the doctrine of the Trinity in the latter half of the twentieth century.[36] This revival of interest in the Trinity was not restricted simply to an understanding of God: perhaps for the first time in the history of Christian thought, Christian theologians were claiming that the affirmation that God is Trinity has radical implications for theological anthropology, in other words, for thinking about what it means to be human. Christian thinkers, of course, had always linked the understanding of being human to the being of God, but only in the twentieth century was the more explicit claim made that since God's being *is* persons in communion, then human "personhood" must be defined in terms of relationality and communion. In other words, humans are truly persons when they image the loving, perichoretic communion of the persons of the Trinity.

Orthodox theology in the twentieth century was very much a part of this revival, and its influence is noticeable both in the theologies of the Trinity and in the attempt to relate the doctrine of the Trinity to theological anthropology. The Russian sophiologists of the late nineteenth and early twentieth centuries were the first to forge the link between Trinity and personhood. Beginning with Vladimir Solov'ev, the father of Russian sophiology, Russian sophiological understandings of person can be interpreted as applying a trinitarian corrective to the German idealist philosophy of the transcendental ego. The Russian sophiologists, especially Pavel Florensky and Bulgakov, identified the "person" with the absolute freedom and irreducibility of the transcendental ego that philosophy discovers through an analysis of self-consciousness. They argued, however, that such an understanding of person is incomplete without the trinitarian notions of love and relationality. This theological understanding of person reaches its most developed form in the work of Sergius Bulgakov, who, according to Michael Meerson, established "the Trinitarian structure of both the created and the divine personality, by moving from Fichte's *Ich*-philosophy through the Feuerbachian 'I-Thou' thesis to the methodological 'We' in the Russian notion of *sobornost*."[37]

These themes of freedom, irreducibility, love, relationality and their identification with the concept of person, minus, however, the reliance on German idealist notions of the transcendental ego, are all evident in contemporary Orthodox theology. Such an affinity is especially evident in the theology of Vladimir Lossky, the Russian émigré theologian who was better known than the other Russian émigré theologians to both Eastern and Western Christians. Lossky, however, was largely unsympathetic to Russian sophiology; it is thus likely that Lossky critically filtered Russian sophiological understandings of personhood into his own apophatic framework. It was Lossky's theology of personhood that influenced the Greek theologians Christos Yannaras and John Zizioulas, whose own writings evince no sign of Russian sophiological influence.[38]

Their differences notwithstanding, I will show that the theologians share a consensus on two points: (1) the doctrine of the Trinity implies an understanding of human personhood in terms of *ecstasis* (freedom) and *hypostasis* (uniqueness) that is constituted in particular relations of loving communion; and (2) such an understanding of personhood emerges from what constitutes the core of the Orthodox tradition—the affirmation of divine-human communion.[39] Unlike contemporary Protestant and Roman Catholic theologies, there is a remarkable consensus among Orthodox theologians that the very starting point of theology is the affirmation of divine-human communion. There is no disagreement on this point, but rather on the implications of this central axiom for thinking about God, Christ, theological anthropology, ecclesiology, and epistemology. Lossky, Yannaras, and Zizioulas share the consensus that divine-human communion could not be otherwise expressed than through the concept of personhood. I will also attempt to show that this particular understanding of personhood is not inimical to the notion of natural human rights.

Vladimir Lossky

The beginning of theology, according to Vladimir Lossky, is the Incarnation understood as the event of the union of the divine and the human natures in the person of Christ.[40] It is this event that reveals the antinomic God, that is, the God who is simultaneously transcendent to and immanent in creation. Given this revelation of God, theology must be apophatic. Lossky, however, means much more by apophatic than simply the assertion that one "knows" God through the affirmations of what God is not. Apophaticism does not mean that one can never make positive statements about God. Drawing primarily on Dionysius the Areopagite, Lossky explains that insofar as God reveals himself, cataphatic or positive names can be attributed to God, such as "God is good." God, however, is simultaneously the *transcendent* and immanent God; hence, language used to express what God is cannot be construed as literal. God's revelation is always excessive, which means that there is always a gap between our language about God and what God is. In an apophatic approach, theology attempts to stretch language in order to express the central antinomy revealed in the Incarnation—God's transcendence and immanence. As Lossky states, "The existence of an apophatic attitude—of a going beyond everything that has a connection with created finitude—is implied in the paradox of the Christian revelation: the transcendent God becomes immanent in the world, but in the very immanence of His economy, which leads to the incarnation and to death on the cross, He reveals Himself as transcendent, as ontologically independent of all created beings."[41]

The purpose of theology is not to resolve the antinomy, but to express it in order to lead one to union with the God who in his transcendence is radically immanent in Christ.[42] Dogmas are essentially, for Lossky, antinomic expressions of the mystery of the Incarnation whose purpose is to guide the believer toward an experience of divine-human communion. In the end, true knowledge of God is not propositional or conceptual; it is mystical knowledge that goes beyond reason without denying it, and is given in the experience of God—in *theosis*.[43]

The Incarnation reveals not only the antinomy of the transcendent and immanent God, but also the "primordial fact" that God is Trinity.[44] Apophaticism is a necessary condition for expressing God as Trinity insofar as the Trinity is the antinomic affirmation that each of the three is simultaneously the same yet irreducible to the other.[45] The challenge to theology is to choose the proper language for expressing the Trinity. The distinction that is widely accepted in the Christian tradition is that between "nature" and "person."[46] The language of the Trinity is the product of the Christian controversies over the person of Christ, often referred to as the "trinitarian controversies." On Lossky's reading, the nature/person distinction is the product of the genius of the Cappadocian fathers. Nature (*ousia*) referred to what was the same among the Father, Son, and the Holy Spirit; person (*hypostasis*) referred to what is irreducible either to the nature or the other persons. For Lossky, *hypostasis* was an especially suitable term since it was also used synonymously with *ousia,* and as such when used for the Trinity, indicates that the three are the same *ousia.* The Cappadocians did, however, have to "deconceptualize" *hypostasis* of its traditional philosophical content so that it can refer to the irreducibility of the three either to the *ousia* or to the other persons. In a deconceptualized form, *ousia* and *hypostasis* express the antinomy of God as Trinity, that is, the simultaneity of sameness and irreducible particularity.[47] In characteristically apophatic fashion, Lossky asserts that this is all that the distinction is meant to convey—the antinomic truth of God's being as Trinity. Lossky, however, has difficulty remaining faithful to his own apophatic restrictions, and in his interpretation of the antinomic use of the person/nature distinction for expressing the doctrine of the Trinity, he gives one of the constitutive aspects of his theology of personhood—uniqueness as irreducibility to nature. To be a person is to be more than simply the nature common to persons.

To be irreducible to nature, however, also implies another constitutive feature of personhood—freedom from nature. This latter aspect of personhood is developed by Lossky in relation to his understanding of the *monarchia* of the Father. In, again, characteristically apophatic fashion, Lossky affirms the monarchy of the Father—the Father is the principle of unity in the Trinity. If either the nature or the communion between the persons of the Trinity were the principle of unity, this would give priority either to what is the same or to what is particular in the Trinity. For Lossky, responding to Théodore de Régnon's axiom that theologies of the Trinity have either started with the one or the three, it is necessary that both what is common and what is particular in the Trinity be thought simultaneously.[48] The monarchy of the Father accomplishes this antinomic condition of theology of the Trinity. He argues that "[t]hus the monarchy of the Father maintains the perfect equilibrium between the nature and the persons, without coming down too heavily on one side. . . . The one nature and the three hypostases are presented simultaneously to our understanding, with neither prior to the other."[49]

Although he affirms the monarchy of the Father on the basis of his apophatic understanding of theology as expressing an antinomy, Lossky cannot help but go beyond this apophatic restriction. It is clear, especially in Lossky's later writings, that the monarchy of the Father does more than simply serve an antinomic function; it implies something for the meaning of personhood. If the Father is the principle of unity of the Trinity, then, for Lossky, the "cause" of the Son and Spirit is a personal principle. It is only, however, as a personal principle that the Father can be "cause" of the other persons of the Trinity, since it is only as person that the Father is not reducible to the divine nature, and, thus, free from nature in such a way as to give the divine nature to the Son and the Spirit.[50] This free movement beyond nature in order to give it to the other persons of the Trinity Lossky cautiously identifies as *ecstasis*, while wary of "introducing an expression too reminiscent of 'the ecstatic character' of the *Dasein* of Heidegger."[51] The Father as personal principle also implies that the movement toward the Son and Spirit is one of love.[52] To *be* a person of the Trinity is to be irreducible to nature, unique, in a movement of freedom from nature that is defined as love. Uniqueness is given when freedom exists as love.

Christos Yannaras

The general contours of Lossky's theology of personhood, together with his attack against neo-scholasticism, are all prominent in the thought of Christos Yannaras. Yannaras affirms all that Lossky does about personhood in terms of irreducibility, freedom (*ecstasis*), and love. He adds, however, three distinctive elements: (1) an engagement with Heidegger, who, he argues, provides the justification for a reappropriation of Dionysian apophaticism; (2) an identification of *ecstasis* with *eros;* and (3) a much more explicit rather than implicit, as it is in Lossky, identification of person as a relational reality.

Heidegger's singular contribution to the history of philosophy, according to Yannaras, was to discern how philosophical discourse on the question of God is essentially "ontotheological." God was reduced to the first cause of creation, but, as such, was reduced to the highest "thing" within creation, thus leading to conceptual idolatry. Heidegger's critique thus opens the door for a revival of Dionysian apophaticism that emphasizes knowledge of God as an experiential event. Apophaticism regarding the knowledge of God is really an apophaticism of the person insofar as the event of communion between God and humans is one between persons. In such an event, humans are encountered as uniquely irreducible to nature, and hence to conceptual knowledge; they are constituted as unique and free beings in relations of freedom and love with the trinitarian persons who eternally exist as a communion of persons.[53] Yannaras much more explicitly crosses the apophatic boundary between human and divine personhood in drawing an analogy between the persons of the Trinity and human personhood. This allows him to emphasize the element of relationality in personhood: *imago dei* becomes *imago trinitatis* for Yannaras, which means that personhood is not a quality of human nature but a relational event analogous to the communion that exists between the persons of the Trinity. Humans can image the life of the Trinity only in community, specifically, the ecclesial community, that is, the Eucharist.

The knowledge in the experience of union with God is, according to Yannaras, an "*erotic* affair" and the "gift of an erotic relationship."[54] Person is an event of freedom, or *ecstasis,* from the limitations of nature in a movement of love, which Yannaras identifies with eros. This movement is simultaneously a self-transcendence from the limitations of nature, a self-offering to the other, and a desire to be united with the other for the sake of the other.[55] Eros is a divisive and acquisitive force only in fallen humanity; when redeemed, it is a unifying force that does not annihilate but constitutes true otherness. Creation itself is a manifestation of God's eros, a desire for loving union with what is other than God and which inflames the human desire for return to God.

John Zizioulas

Zizioulas and Yannaras are contemporaries, but Yannaras was the first of the two theologians to form a developed theology of personhood, in his small book *On the Absence and Unknowability of God: Heidegger and the Areopagite* (1967 in Greek) and then more fully in his *Person and Eros* (1970 in Greek). Zizioulas's first attempt at a developed theological account of personhood appeared in 1975 in the article "Human Capacity and Human Incapacity," though one can detect traces of his theology of personhood in his dissertation, *Eucharist, Bishop, Church* (1965 in Greek). In his early writings, he continued to develop his theology of personhood primarily in relation to his ecclesiology. Zizioulas credits Yannaras and Martin Buber with influencing his own understanding of personhood.[56] There is thus a continuity of thought on personhood that can be traced from Lossky through Yannaras to Zizioulas. The early work on the Eucharist and ecclesiology is, however, key for understanding Zizioulas's own approach to personhood. The experience of God in the Eucharist is both the ground and the realization of human personhood. Zizioulas here is linking personhood to the eucharistic ecclesiology of twentieth-century Orthodox theology most evident in the work of Nicholas Afanasiev and his own mentor, Georges Florovsky. Zizioulas also links his theology of personhood to a theology of the Trinity in a way that is more developed than in Yannaras and less apophatic than in Lossky. Prior to this theological account of personhood, Zizioulas offers a phenomenological account of human existence that amplifies the human longing for personhood, that can only be fulfilled through a theological affirmation of the transcendent—not simply any notion of the transcendent, but one that would allow for the human longing for uniqueness and irreducibility to be realized. For Zizioulas, this understanding of the transcendent is fulfilled in the Christian doctrine of the Trinity.

Zizioulas himself is adamant that "person" as *ecstasis* and *hypostasis* is a strictly theological concept: "The Orthodox understanding of the Holy Trinity is the only way to arrive at this notion of personhood."[57] His writings, however, betray a philosophical argument for person as the only means to fulfill a fundamental drive in human existence. This drive is one away from death toward life realized in communion with others. According to Zizioulas, if such a drive is left unfulfilled, then non-existence defines the meaning of existence.

This philosophical argument for the centrality of the concept of "person" for human existence appears for the first time in his seminal article, "Human Capacity and Human Incapacity: A Theological Exploration of Personhood." In arguing "for an approach other than the 'substantial' one to the human being,"[58] which, of course, is the personal approach, Zizioulas outlines the constitutive elements of his theology of personhood, which he develops throughout his career. Early in the article, after discussing the difference between substantial and personal understandings of the human being, Zizioulas illustrates "the greatness and tragedy of man's personhood" through what he terms the "presence-in-absence paradox" inherent in all creaturely existence.[59] The human being's personhood and the tragedy of the presence-in-absence paradox are most evident, for Zizioulas, in the human capacity to create. For Zizioulas, to create as an individual is different from creating as a person. The former is a process of "*seizing, controlling and dominating* reality." Beings are turned into things, and insofar as such manufacturing is more often than not "a collective effort," the human being turns him- or herself into a thing, "an instrument and a means to an end."[60] To create as a person is to imbue the created object with the uniqueness and irreducibility of the person. Zizioulas uses art as an example of such personal creativity, in which the artist "becomes 'present' as a unique and unrepeatable *hypostasis* of being and not as an impersonal number in a combined structure." Reminiscent of Lossky's reference to artists to illustrate the uniqueness of person,[61] Zizioulas argues that "when we look at a painting or listen to music we have in front of us . . . a 'presence' in which 'things' and substances (cloth, oil, etc.) or qualities (shape, colour, etc.) or sounds become part of a personal presence."[62] Thus, a personal presence, which is one of uniqueness, irreducibility, freedom, is inherent in a work of art.

If art is a manifestation of personal existence, it is also a revelation of the "tragedy" inherent in creaturely existence. Tragedy is an important concept for Zizioulas's understanding of personhood, especially with regard to its philosophical justification. Concerning our present discussion, the tragedy of all works of art consists in the fact that art itself manifests the absence of the artist as much as his presence. "If we take again our example from the world of art, the fundamental thing that we must observe with regard to the 'presence' it creates, is that the artist himself is absent."[63] Art is just an example of the "paradoxical fact" that plagues all creaturely existence, namely, "that the presence of being in and through the human person is ultimately revealed as an *absence*."[64] It must be remembered that Zizioulas is speaking here of a presence that is personal. When a person is present, she is present as a unique, irreducible, free, relational being. "Pure presence" is a personal existence without absence, in other words, an existence in which the marks of personal existence are immediate and permanent. This pure presence is not possible so long as it is mediated or limited by the boundaries of the body.[65]

What ultimately constitutes this presence-in-absence paradox as tragic, for Zizioulas, is the fact that it indicates a fundamental *drive* for personal presence in created existence that is thwarted by the coexistence of absence. "All this means that the ecstatic movement towards communion which is part of personhood, remains for man an unfulfilled longing for a presence-without-absence of being as long as there is no way of overcoming the space-time limitations of creaturehood."[66] This "unfulfilled longing" is one for personal presence or personhood, and it is on this "longing" that Zizioulas bases his philosophical argumentation for the validity of an ontology of personhood. The longing for pure presence is, in effect, a desire to eradicate absence, and the definitive form of absence is death. Inherent in all creaturely existence is death and, consequently, all creaturely attempts for a personal presence without absence will always be reduced to the absence that is death. The important point here, however, is that Zizioulas isolates in human existence a fundamental longing for personhood, for an existence that is free, unique, and unrepeatable. Such a longing is, in the end, a longing to escape death: "All this means that the overcoming of death represents a longing rooted in the *personhood* of man."[67] Since death is inherent in all creaturely existence, "personal presence *qua presence* is something that *cannot be extrapolated from created existence*."[68] What Zizioulas means here is that the longing for personal existence can only be affirmed by uncreated existence. Personal existence, one that is both *ecstatic* and *hypostatic*, that attempts to transcend the boundaries and limitations of creaturely existence, namely death, through personal relations, becomes a reality only in an *ecstatic* and *hypostatic* movement and communion with the uncreated, with that which does not die. It is only in communion with that which is not-created that created being can fulfill its longing for personal existence. Implicit here is a proof for God's existence: "Personhood, understood in its terrifying ontological ultimacy to which I have tried to point in this chapter, leads to God—or to non-existence."[69] Either there is God who fulfills this longing for personhood and gives meaning to life; or there is death that envelopes all existence, and the only way to affirm one's personhood, one's freedom from the given, is to commit suicide, which, however, negates the very freedom one seeks in committing the act. For Zizioulas such meaninglessness is not an option, which leads him to conclude that this fundamental longing "reveals that there is a future, an *eschaton* or a *telos,* a final goal in creation, which must resolve the problem created by personhood."[70]

Zizioulas never speaks to this presence-in-absence paradox in his later work, though the basic thrust of this philosophical argument for personhood as the fundamental longing of all human existence remains intact. In the first chapter of *Being as Communion,*[71] Zizioulas describes what he terms "the *hypostasis of biological existence.*" This existence "suffers radically from two 'passions' that destroy precisely that towards which the human *hypostasis* is thrusting, namely the person."[72] The first passion Zizioulas calls "ontological necessity," and consists of the inevitable link between the *hypostasis* and natural instinct. The second passion is that of "*individualism, of the separation of the hypostases*."[73] Both passions as well as the drive to personhood are intertwined in erotic love, which conceals "in the deepest act of communion a tendency towards an ecstatic transcendence of individuality through creation."[74] This new creation, a human being, bears both the marks of personhood and of individuality: "He is born as a result of an *ecstatic* fact—erotic love—but this fact is interwoven with a natural necessity and therefore lacks ontological freedom. He is born as a *hypostatic* fact, as a body, but this fact is interwoven with individuality and with death."[75] Zizioulas's focus has shifted from the creation of an artist to that of an erotic couple. There is no mention of the presence-in-absence paradox, but the drive toward personhood manifested in the creative act of erotic communion indicates both the capacity for personhood and the inability to fulfill such a longing. "All this means that man as a biological *hypostasis* is intrinsically a tragic figure."[76]

More recently, in his "On Being a Person: Towards an Ontology of Personhood,"[77] Zizioulas explores how the personal and the particular can have ontological import. He analyzes the question "Who am I?" from an ontological perspective, indicating that "'Who' is a call for *definition* or 'description' of some kind. . . . The ingredient 'am' or *to be* . . . is a cry for security, for ground to be based on, for fixity. . . . The ingredient 'I' or 'Your' or 'He/She' . . . is a cry for *particularity*, for *otherness*."[78] In this basic question is the cry, for Zizioulas, for particularity and otherness to be permanent or to be grounded ontologically. In characteristic fashion, Zizioulas then argues how an ontology based on substantial categories is inadequate to secure the permanence of otherness. Zizioulas explains that "the inability of Greek thought to create a personal ontology is not due to a weakness or incapacity of Greek philosophy as *philosophy*. . . . Otherness cannot acquire ontological primacy as long as one begins with the world as it is, as did the ancient Greeks and all philosophy does, if it wishes to be pure philosophy. The observation of the world cannot lead to an ontology of the person, because the person as an ontological category cannot be extrapolated from experience."[79] Elsewhere Zizioulas explains that "the *ekstasis* of beings towards humanity or towards creation alone leads to 'being-into-death.'"[80] Zizioulas reiterates here what we saw in his earlier work, namely, that an ontology of personhood and the particular needs a beyond, an uncreated realm, since creation itself is inherently ridden with death. The particular is not ontologically absolute if it dies.

For Zizioulas, only a theological account of personhood can make sense of the human drive for particularity and uniqueness, which Zizioulas identifies with freedom. Specifically, only the Christian conceptualization of God as Trinity can ground a notion of personhood as unique and *ecstatic*. He is insistent, however, that the Christian doctrine of the Trinity is not simply a logical conundrum to be solved, but an expression of the Christian community's experience of God in Christ, by the Holy Spirit, in the Eucharist, which is the starting point of all theological discourse. From the time of the early Christians, church was identified with the eucharistic assembly. If the church is the body of Christ, then the church *is* the Eucharist since it is there that the community of the faithful is constituted as the body of Christ. The Pauline expression of body of Christ is not metaphorical for Zizioulas; the Eucharist is quite literally the event of the resurrected body of Christ.[81] It is such an event because of the presence of the Holy Spirit, who constitutes the faithful as the body of Christ. The Holy Spirit does not simply inspire or empower individual Christians, but completes the work of Christ by making present the divine-human communion accomplished in the person of the resurrected Christ. The Holy Spirit's role is thus primarily communal and eschatological, in that it constitutes the Eucharist as the eschatological unity of all in Christ. This understanding of the interrelation of ecclesiology and Christology is what Zizioulas refers to as a *pneumatologically conditioned Christology*.[82]

It is this experience of God in the Eucharist that forms the basis for the early Christian affirmation of the divinity of Christ and the Spirit. The challenge during the early Christian controversies was to find the proper language to express the eucharistic experience of God in Christ and, hence, of the Trinity itself. Like Lossky and Yannaras, Zizioulas credits the Cappadocian fathers with the *ousia/hypostasis* distinction that expresses what is the same and what is particular in the Trinity. For Zizioulas, however, the language of the Trinity must express more than what is the same and what is particular; it must signify the event of divine-human communion in Christ as experienced in the Eucharist, which is simultaneously an event of communion among the Father, Son, and the Holy Spirit. This event of divine-human communion is inherently a relational event which occurs in the *hypostasis* of Christ. *Hypostasis* cannot simply mean, according to Zizioulas, that which signifies particularity; it is a relational category insofar as it is *in* the *hypostasis* of Christ that the eschatological unity of all creation occurs. This unity is not an absorption of human personhood in the person of Christ, but the constitution of human personhood in its eternal uniqueness by being brought into relation to the Father through the Son by the Holy Spirit. Christ is, by the Holy Spirit, the one and the many in whom the many are constituted as children of God and, as such, eternally unique. It is only in Christ that humans are true persons, that is, unique and irreducible beings.[83] This personhood, however, is also a relational and an *ecstatic* event in which the human person transcends the limitations of finite nature toward an eternal communion with the Father in Christ by the Holy Spirit.

According to Zizioulas, *hypostasis* by itself cannot convey all that is accomplished in Christ and all that is revealed about God in Christ, primarily because *hypostasis* is not a relational category. *Prosopon* (person), however, is a relational category, but in both the ancient Greek and Roman context it lacked ontological content. The singular genius of the Cappadocian fathers, according to Zizioulas, was to identify *hypostasis* and *prosopon* so that the relationality and freedom signified in *prosopon* was now given ontological content.[84] In doing this, the Cappadocians were not initiating an "ontological revolution" so much as giving expression to the revolution in ontology implied by the divine-human communion in Christ. Such an ontology is mutually exclusive with the Greek philosophical ontology of substance in that the priority shifts to relationality, freedom, otherness, and communion. The latter are no longer accidents but what being *is;* human personhood *is* a relational event in which the person is constituted as eternally unique, other, and free. Thus *hypostasis,* both human and divine, is not simply that which is particular, but is a relational event of otherness and communion: "*The Person is otherness in communion and communion in otherness.*"[85]

Identifying being with relationality, freedom, otherness, and communion is not restricted to created being, but to divine being as well. For Zizioulas, this is the implication of the Cappadocian insistence on the monarchy of the Father, which itself logically follows, according to Zizioulas, the eucharistic experience of God in Christ. In what is probably his most controversial theological move, Zizioulas argues that the being of God as Trinity is "caused" by the person of the Father. Being, thus, is the result of the freedom of the person of the Father: "God, as Father and not as substance, perpetually confirms through 'being' His *free* will to exist. And it is precisely His trinitarian existence that constitutes this confirmation: the Father out of love—that is, freely—begets the Son and brings forth the Spirit."[86] The Father as person, as a being who is *hypostatic,* who is unique and irreducible to nature, and *ecstatic,* free from the necessity of nature, is the *aitia,* the "cause," of the persons of the Trinity, who are themselves *hypostatic* and *ecstatic* beings in and through an eternal communion of each with the others. For Zizioulas, only by asserting the monarchy of the Father can one ground the possibility of freedom from necessity, which is itself the condition for the possibility for uniqueness and irreducibility. Thinking of God in terms of a primordial concept of an eternal communion would subject the being of God to a given and, hence, to necessity. If God gives what God *is,* and if the experience of salvation in the eucharistic experience of God is a personal uniqueness constituted as freedom from the given, namely, the necessity of finite humanity, then God's very being must *be* as freedom from necessity.[87]

It is in Zizioulas's reflections on the monarchy of the Father that one sees clearly how his relating a theology of the Trinity to a theology of personhood cannot be labeled as a simple social trinitarianism, nor as a top-down approach. The constitutive aspects of Zizioulas's theology of the Trinity are grounded in the eucharistic experience of God in Christ by the Holy Spirit. This bottom-up approach is even more evident in Zizioulas's discussion of the tragic state of created existence. In the end, the longing for irreducibility is thwarted by death—the great leveler of uniqueness and otherness in rendering all the same. Salvation in Christ, experienced in the moment of the Eucharist, is the overcoming of this tragic longing insofar as it fulfils it. But the fulfillment of this longing, in the form of freedom from the necessity of finite nature, reveals that God's very being is freedom from necessity. It is not so much that because of human salvation God *must* be conceived as freedom from necessity; rather, for Zizioulas, the eucharistic communion reveals that God's being *is* this freedom insofar as it is this freedom as love that is given in Christ. Since the salvific experience is in Christ by the Holy Spirit, then the freedom of God is conceptualized in the form of the freedom of the Father to constitute the *way* or the *how* (*tropos hyparxeos*) of God's existence as Trinity.[88]

What emerges, then, in the latter half of the twentieth century is a theology of personhood in which the "person" is an event of irreducible uniqueness and freedom from the necessities of created nature. Lossky established the basic form of this theology of personhood within the horizon of the mystical ascent toward union with God, whereas Yannaras and Zizioulas amplified its meaning by situating personhood eucharistically—to *be* person is a eucharistic mode of being that is realized in the eucharistic assembly. Personhood, thus, is not a capacity or an achievement, but a mode of being realized in particular relations of love and freedom. Although there has been much debate over the patristic pedigree of this theological notion of person, a convincing argument has yet to be put forth that would refute the understanding of divine-human communion as a relational event of love of God and love of neighbor in which a human being—and

through the human, all of creation—is personalized, that is, constituted as irreducibly unique and *ecstatic*. In this sense, the contemporary Orthodox understanding of personhood resonates with the
deepest impulses of patristic theology. Nor can one accuse contemporary Orthodox theologians of social trinitarianism because this understanding of personhood is grounded in the experience of God in
Christ by the power of the Holy Spirit; in other words, it is a bottom-
up not a top-down approach. From the perspective of divine-human
communion, personhood is the realization of the love of God and
love of neighbor, an ascetical coming to be within a eucharistic relationality in which the human being embodies freely the irreducible
uniqueness that has existed on the side of God from all eternity. If
much of modern human rights discourse is based on the presupposition that each human being as person possesses equal worth and dignity, that no human being is more worthy as human than any other
human being, that each is unique in relation to all others, then it is
through this theological understanding of personhood that Orthodox
must assess modern human rights language.

Personhood and Human Rights

Much of the Christian resistance to human rights language is that it is
inherently linked, so the argument goes, to an anthropology that is
antithetical to the Christian claim that humans were created to be in
communion with God. Human rights discourse is grounded in the
idea of the human as a self-enclosed enclave, a sovereign embodied
territory that cannot be violated by another human being nor one's
community or state. Human rights language encourages an extreme
form of hyper-individualism, in which the community is seen as a
threat to the freedom to live one's life as one chooses. In the sense that
human rights discourse is unhinged from any thick metaphysical description of being human, it is inherently atheistic, developed especially as a counter-anthropology to the once-dominant Christian
understanding of the human. Indeed, this kind of interpretation of

human rights discourse is hard to square with a view of the human as created to learn how to love.

There are at least two questions in the Christian resistance to human rights language that need to be addressed: (1) Is human rights discourse inherently atheistic? (2) Can Christian discourse, which argues for a definitive purpose to being human, reconcile itself with a human rights discourse that is often dismissive of or indifferent to theological anthropology?

On the question of the inherent atheism of human rights discourse, Brian Tierney has convincingly showed that human rights language existed prior to the Enlightenment, and argues that the Enlightenment inherited a discourse of natural rights that was developed in the medieval Christian West.[89] As mentioned earlier, John McGuckin has demonstrated the presence of the language of rights in the Byzantine tradition.[90] In fact, as Nicholas Wolterstorff points out, those Christians who argue that the language of rights is an invention of secular thought only perpetuate a narrative that, ironically, is the invention of certain secular thinkers.[91] Rather than dig deeper into Christian history to discover the origins of rights language, they respond by rejecting the notion of rights because it is embedded in a nontheological or bad theological wrapping. The logic, then, is that the language of rights, which emerged in discourse that is diametrically opposed to religion, is nonintegratable into theological anthropology. Historically, this view is inaccurate.

It is also inaccurate philosophically, as Nicholas Wolterstorff has recently attempted to demonstrate. Rights are structured so as to protect any action that may violate the uniqueness of a human being and, thus, the dignity and worth associated with that uniqueness. Wolterstorff elaborates on the link between the concept of rights language, the nonutilitarian worth of a human being, and the experience of "being wronged." According to Wolterstorff, the experience of being wronged is one in which one's nonutilitarian worth is not respected and recognized,[92] and "[t]hat significance, *wronging*, is the source of rights."[93] A right is a claim "to the good of being treated in a certain way,"[94] and, negatively, against another from being wronged in such a way as to devalue the holder of the right.[95] In this sense, rights are inherently social, since they are always over-and-against another human being. Wolterstorff argues that a "theory of rights needs the idea of a person's worth requiring that she be treated in certain ways." Against eudaimonism, he adds that there "is no room in this scheme for the worth of persons and human beings, and hence not for one's right against others to their treating one a certain way on account of one's worth."[96] Wolterstorff argues, then, that rights are natural, meaning that they inhere in the person because of the irreducible, nonutilitarian worth of the person, thereby grounding the claim for social normative relations between human beings. Michael Perry makes a similar argument in claiming that to "affirm the morality of human rights is to affirm that every human being has inherent dignity and is inviolable."[97]

Both Wolterstorff and Perry further argue that insofar as rights language is linked to the inherent, inviolable, nonutilitarian worth of a human being, such a notion of natural rights can only be grounded theistically, that is, there can be no secular grounding for natural rights. Perry argues that if the notion of human rights is intrinsic to the understanding of the worth of the human being, the question begged is why such a worth is attributable to each and every human being. The inevitable "why" question is raised in relation to claims about the equal worth of the human being, and for Perry, secular attempts inevitably fail to answer this question. That the notion of human rights is inescapably religious is illustrated apophatically for Perry in the failure of nontheistic versions to ground the nonutilitarian value of the human person. "The point," according to Perry, "is not that one cannot live one's life in accord with the fact (if it is a fact) that every human being has inherent dignity unless one believes in God. Many who do not believe in God manage to live their lives in truly saintly ways, and many who do believe in God are anything but saintly. The point is simply that it is open to serious question whether a secular worldview can bear the weight of the claim that we should— that we have conclusive reason to—live our lives in accord with the fact that every human being has inherent dignity."[98]

Wolterstorff is less apophatic in his assertion that natural rights are only grounded theistically. Such a theistic grounding, however, cannot be the notion of the image of God. What is needed "is some worth-imparting relation of human beings to God that does not in any way involve a reference to human capacities. I will argue that being loved by God is such a relation; being loved by God gives a human being great worth. . . . Being loved by God is an example of what I shall call *bestowed* worth."[99] In the constitution of this relation of love between God and human beings, God acquires rights of God's own in relation to human beings. God has the right both "to be worshipped" and "to our obedience to such commands as God may issue."[100]

There are points of affinity between Wolterstorff's understanding of bestowed worth of the human being by virtue of being loved by God and the contemporary Orthodox relational understanding of personhood that are worth drawing out. In particular, according to the logic of a relational personhood grounded in the principle of divine-human communion, a human being *is* person, and, thus, rendered irreducibly unique or, to use Wolterstorff's language, of inestimable value by virtue of being eternally loved by God. This eternal relation with God also constitutes the person as *ecstatic* in the sense that the person is free from a reductionism of the human to the categories of essence. Put another way, *ecstasy* is a freedom from sameness of essentialism. Irreducible uniqueness or value, thus, cannot be reduced to any natural capacity, or even to any common definition of being human, not simply because such identifications and definitions are inevitably arbitrary, but because they essentialize the human and render her nonunique.

An example might be helpful. Suppose a newly born baby was abandoned in the fields—is this baby a person?[101] Our visceral response would be to affirm that, indeed, the baby is a person; by not admitting that the baby is a person there would be no defense against the abandonment itself: we could never say that it is morally wrong. To say, however, that the baby is a person would also fail to recognize that the baby has been depersonalized and rendered a nonperson.

This depersonalization is not simply subjective, that is, from the perspective of the perpetrator of abandonment; the baby has been objectively depersonalized in the sense of being constituted in relations that render her nonunique, replaceable, with a forgettable narrative.

The situation of the abandoned baby is similar to the depersonalization suffered by the victims of the Nazis in concentration camps. Although not abandoned, the victims of the Nazis were in the midst of relations that constituted them as nonunique, forgettable, and replaceable. This reduction to the same is most evident in the elimination of names and the assignment of numbers to the prisoners. It also has a domino effect, insofar as the embodied existence of depersonalization makes it difficult, if not impossible, for prisoners to relate to other prisoners, even if they are family members, in ways that affirm personal uniqueness and irreducibility.[102] As a result of the depersonalization at the hands of the Nazis, some prisoners were reduced to an embodied state of existence where they could only look at other prisoners, including family members, either instrumentally or as obstacles toward their survival.

One more example: a person with Alzheimer's disease suffers from a degeneration of her memory of her own narrative; she can no longer piece together the elements of the narrative that is uniquely her own. Once this memory is completely gone, if the patient is not surrounded by other persons who can recall elements of this story, then there is only so much that a doctor can learn through DNA testing. Narrative is the only way in which the personal uniqueness of one's history can be conveyed, and for those who suffer from Alzheimer's, their only hope to be related to as the person in this narrative is from people who are included in the narrative itself. Although the patient can be provided with care, the personal uniqueness of the Alzheimer's patient depends on those who can recall the details of her story. Otherwise, the most the healthcare providers can do is offer care. Wolterstorff also draws on the example of a patient with Alzheimer's to illustrate his point about a dignity-based account of rights: that only a "worth-bestowing relation to God" can account for how such inviolable dignity is possessed even by "impaired human be-

ings" who are not capable of certain duties or responsible action in relation to God.[103]

What these examples make clear is that humans are not unique
qua humans, but can be in the midst of relations that constitute humans as nonpersons, and, hence, nonunique. There is no inherent
quality or capacity that defends against this possibility. The only hope
for the baby abandoned in the field or the Nazi victims is the existence
of something more than the relations that constitute them as nonpersons, a being-related-to as person in the midst of depersonalization.
The only hope for the baby to be rendered unique is not something
the baby possesses by simply being human, but a relation that is realized at the moment of its creation.

Although Wolterstorff does not use this language, there is nothing in his recent writing that would cause him to disagree with the
point that humans can effect relationships of depersonalization. He
would also seem to be in agreement with what is implied in the logic
of Orthodox understandings of personhood, which is that any hope
against depersonalization lies in a relationship to what is beyond the
human—to God. Wolterstorff, however, does move in a direction that
is not so clearly implied in the Orthodox relational notion of personhood, which is to claim that such a relation then gives the human
being, even one who cannot speak for herself, claims *against* other
human beings not to be treated in a certain way. Such a move, indeed,
seems like an unproblematic next step, so what possible objection
could the Orthodox have with the claim that the inherent dignity bestowed onto or the irreducible uniqueness rendered to the human
being grounds the human right to be treated in a certain way?

The main worry with rights language has already been implied in
the thought of some of the Orthodox thinkers surveyed: rights language does not adequately indicate all that is possible for the human
in relationship with God. Although Wolterstorff grounds rights discourse in a relationship with God, it is a form of discourse that inevitably keeps humans at a distance from each other and from God.
The language of deification, of the realization of love of God and
neighbor, is one that attempts to think the overcoming of distance

without abolishing difference. Wolterstorff could concede this point but still argue that one could make claims of rights against another human not to be wronged while still recognizing that the best possibility for humans is forms of relationships in which such claims are unnecessary. This is an important point: the discourses of deification and of rights are not mutually exclusive. To understand, however, the discourse of rights within the discourse of deification would require qualifications of Wolterstorff's theistically grounded claim to rights.

The first qualification relates to Wolterstorff's argument that God has the right "to be worshipped" and "to our obedience to such commands as God may issue."[104] If worship is a form of loving God, then understanding worship-as-love in terms of divine-human communion means that it does not make any sense to speak of God's rights toward us. God creates the not-God out of love for love; to say that God has a right to our love has the force of obligation, which is not loving God for God's sake. It is also difficult to conceptualize what obedience to love means: how does one will oneself to love? God has, indeed, issued the command to love God and neighbor, but the ascetical tradition discerned that the fulfillment of such a command cannot be willed. It is realized through practices as an embodied experience; it is a transfigured existence, not a willed obedience. Within this transfigured existence, where the human is the image by both seeing the world as God sees it and reflecting the love of God in the world, God is loved not *because* of anything, including the commandment, but for God's sake. Obedience takes the form of free necessity, where one cannot do otherwise than love God for God's sake and, by extension, one's neighbor. There is a necessity to this form of love that is paradoxically a freedom from being essentialized. An understanding of love in terms of deification sees it as a mode of being, a progression to the point where one loves God and neighbor for no reason whatsoever. God does not want us to love God *because* God loves us, or even *because* God created us, but simply for who God is—Truth, Goodness, and, perhaps most importantly, incomparable Beauty. St. Maximus the Confessor summarizes it nicely when he says, "Perfect love casts out the first fear from the soul which by possessing it no longer fears punishment."[105] This point is wonderfully echoed by Calvin, who cautions us against our projections on God: "Besides, this mind restrains itself from sinning, not out of dread of punishment alone; but, because it loves and reveres God as Father, it worships and adores him as Lord. *Even if there were no hell,* it would still shudder at offending him alone."[106]

There is also a tension between Wolterstorff's dignity-based understanding of rights and his claim that God has rights over-and-against human beings. If human beings have rights over-and-against other humans because of a dignity bestowed in-and-through a loving relationship with God, does this mean that God's claims to rights are a result of some bestowed dignity? Though he does not elaborate, even Wolterstorff would agree that God's dignity is not bestowed but is simply possessed by virtue of who God is; God self-bestows dignity, perhaps, through God's eternal love of God's self. That notwithstanding, within the perspective of divine-human communion, the idea of God's rights evokes visions of the distant, nominalistic God. When Wolterstorff defends justice as rights to goods grounded in the bestowed worth of a human being by God, the God-world relation that is implicit is one in which the human person is standing in relation over-and-against other persons and God; God is there, I am here, and the goal is to claim right standing before God and others. In an ontology of divine-human communion, notions of the God-world relation in terms of "here" and "there" simply do not make sense. In creating the human, God is simultaneously calling the human being to a relationship of love realized in freedom. There is no claim on God's part since God cannot be wronged. Whatever sin is committed in relationship to God does not wrong God but, simply, wrongs our own self and, inevitably, the other. God exists not over-and-against demanding obedience but offers God's life so that humans can overcome the wrong they do to themselves and to God's creation. Humans are called to engage in the practices that would allow for the iconic manifestation of God's life in creation, a presence that is nearer to us than we are to ourselves.

While refuting the idea that human rights language is inherently atheistic, Wolterstorff's evoking God's rights to be worshipped or to be treated a certain way implies a God-world relationship that does not cohere with an ontology of divine-human communion. What is obfuscated is the reality that humans must make claims against other humans not to be wronged only because humans are engaged in a perpetual struggle to learn how to love. The need for rights language in the absence of love does not mean that rights discourse is incompatible with the principle of divine-human communion; nor does it mean that love and justice are mutually exclusive. It does mean that rights language must be instituted out of fear that humans have not realized all that is made possible for them by God's love.

The difference between forms of human relations regulated by rights and the Christian ascetical struggle to realize the love commandment and, thus, to embody the presence of God can be amplified with several examples. In the case of homelessness, one could argue that every human being has a right to food and shelter; that is, that to be deprived of food and shelter, even when one is not able to work through joblessness, mental illness, alcoholism, is to be wronged. If one is a Christian, then it would be difficult to walk past a homeless person and not feel challenged that she must do something to help him. The thought process might be something like: "I am a Christian, I must love my neighbor, follow the example of the Good Samaritan, and help this homeless person." This Christian may then provide food, money, advice on locating a shelter, or simply some company, and, rightfully so, may feel good about what they have done. What I am suggesting, however, is that relating to the homeless person either "*because* he is homeless," or "*because* I am a Christian," or "*because* God commands me to do so," or "*because* the homeless person has a legitimate claim to a right from me to food and shelter," is always self-referential and, in this sense, an objectification of the homeless person. Put another way, humans are capable of walking by the homeless person and relating to him not *because* of anything, but simply by being moved to be with Joe or Jane on the steps of St. Paul's. In an ironic twist, when God is not mentioned as the reason for approaching the homeless person, the approach may actually be more godly.

In the case of the debate over the rights of prisoners, arguments are put forth that even those who have violated the laws of society have basic rights to food and shelter. In the United States, a vigorous debate is occurring over whether prisoners have the right to life; that is, whether some crimes deserve the penalty of death. The Christian ascetical struggle in relation to prisoners, however, would not deny these basic rights but attempts to relate to prisoners in ways that seem counterintuitive. Those who commit certain crimes are easily susceptible to vilification and monsterization. The Christian "command" to love the prisoner, the treatment of whom is a criterion of eschatological judgment (Mt 25), is not simply to fight for the rights of prisoners nor to engage in prison ministry, but involves finding oneself seeing the prisoner as not reducible to the crime committed. Such a seeing does not excuse the crime committed, but the ascetical struggle to love is to see the prisoner not merely as prisoner, not as one who is simply identified with the crime. In the Christian call to love there is a "more" to relating to the prisoner than simply securing rights.

What does all this imply for human rights talk? First, the relational understanding of personhood resonates with Wolterstorff's notion of *bestowed* worth in a human being. This bestowal of worth is not an inherent quality *within* the individual, but is a relational event of God's never-ending, faithful divine love to each human being. In the midst of depersonalization by others, through relations of annihilation, God's eternal and particular love "bestows" on each person an indestructible uniqueness, and, thus, an incomparable worth. As St. Paul affirms: "For I am persuaded that neither death nor life, nor angels nor principalities nor powers, nor things present nor things to come, nor height nor depth, nor any other created thing, shall be able to separate us from the love of God which is in Christ Jesus our Lord" (Rom 8:38–39). Sin, both social and individual, is the attempt to denigrate that worth, to render it nonunique. If not for being eternally loved by God, such attempts to denigrate the worth of the other could be definitive.

Does, however, the affirmation that each human is eternally loved by God lead to rights language? In his own linking of rights language to God, Wolterstorff has worked from the notion of justice as rights to the idea of God. He is not offering a proof of God as much as he is declaring that if one values rights language, then to be internally consistent one must affirm that the only way to ground rights language is through the concept of God. This theistic grounding of rights language minimally refutes claims by Yannaras, Guroian, and the Russian Orthodox Church that rights language per se emerges from a hyper-individualistic and atheistic anthropology. Wolterstorff's grounding of human rights language in the concept of God does lead him to make statements that do not resonate with an understanding of God in terms of divine-human communion. Only in the theological affirmation of sin can one conceivably talk about God's rights. What God has a right to is not our love for God but for conditions that would maximize one's growth in intimacy with God, which also has implications not simply for the individual but for the wider relations that are part of the individual's narrative. *Theosis* is an embodied experience, and all embodied experiences are socially conditioned. It is difficult to read about the emaciation of prisoners at the hands of the Nazis and imagine that such prisoners should be thinking about *theosis*. The realism of divine-human communion, however, can illuminate this situation, insofar as the situation manifests the Nazis creating social conditions that facilitate the presence of the demonic—the anti-God. God has a right against those who consciously or unconsciously engage in actions and practices, in and through which social conditions are created or perpetuated, that block the sacramental presence of God to the world. From this perspective, rights are linked with the tragic reality of the world's separation and distance from God.

To say that a human being as human is deserving of rights to goods because God loves this human being is then potentially to make normative a relation between humans that falls short of all that humans can be. If I love someone *because* God loves another human being, then I am not loving in the way God loves, which is simply by virtue of who the other is. Something similar can be said about grounding rights in worth or dignity: if someone grants me human rights on the worth or dignity of the person, then there is something diminishing of worth or dignity if someone bases their relationship to me on something other than simply who I am.

The understanding of love in terms of divine-human communion lies at the heart of the Orthodox resistance to language of human rights. Structuring relations between humans in terms of rights falls short of all that humans are created to be. Moreover, the notion of divine-human communion does not simply inform human-human relations but also relations between humans and non-humans. As Alexander Schmemann reminds us, "God's own creation, is symbolic, is *sacramental*."[107] By sacramental, Schmemann means creation has the capacity to mirror the presence of God; nature is already and always a graced reality.[108] This capacity, however, depends on how humans relate to creation. Humans have the capacity to relate to God in such a way so as to, according to John Zizioulas, "personalize creation,"[109] in other words, to relate to all living things in such a way so as to render them unique and irreplaceable. What makes the Orthodox nervous about rights language is that it seems to imply a theological anthropology, and thus, a way of structuring human relations that is not consistent with its nonnegotiable affirmation about the realism of divine-human communion, *theosis*.

Is, then, the Orthodox notion of divine-human communion, and all that it implies about relational notions of personhood, mutually exclusive with the language of human rights? The simple, but not necessarily obvious, answer is no. In fact, I would argue that it actually implies the rhetoric of human rights. As I have been arguing, the existence of political communities results from the failure of humans to realize their potential for deification. Put another way, the necessity for political communities is ultimately based, in part, on fear and sin. From this point of view, one cannot expect to sacramentalize in fullness the political, since the sacramentalization of a community is what Christians call church (not to be equated with its institutionalized form). Political communities are by their very nature deficiently sacramental, put in place because humans have fallen short of relating to each other as God relates to each one of them, but not necessarily completely devoid of God's presence. Christians, thus, should never expect a fully sacramentalized form of political community, one in which the community exists in relations of love and freedom that constitute persons as unique and irreducible. Such an understanding of community becomes the ideal by which to prophetically critique political communities that inevitably fall short of this ideal.

Orthodox need not stop, however, at prophetic critique; they can exercise judgments about which form of political community mirrors a sacramental community, even if such political communities inevitably are not fully sacramental. Now we can reintroduce rights talk: insofar as the language of human rights is meant to provide the normative structures of human relations whereby the human person is treated as a unique and irreducible human being, then Orthodox Christians can judge political communities structured around the normativity of human rights as mirroring sacramental communities in which humans are constituted as unique and irreducible. In one of the only places that Zizioulas reflects on the implications of his theology of personhood for political theology, he affirms that "pursuant to the idea of personhood as something relational . . . people all have the same value and same rights because they themselves represent unique and unrepeatable identities for those with whom they are in a personal relationship. Therefore, *the law is obligated to respect and protect everyone, regardless of one's characteristics, because every man bears a relational identity, and with that, is a unique and unrepeatable person.*"[110]

Zizioulas elaborates on the paradoxical fact that although the law should be designed to protect the uniqueness and freedom that is constitutive of personhood, it does so through the threat of coercion: "Personhood, by definition, abhors coercion and thirsts after freedom. The law, by its very nature, contains elements of coercion to the point of depriving liberty in order to—how paradoxical—secure freedom."[111] For Zizioulas, the realization of person as *ecstatic* freedom-as-uniqueness is an event of noncoercive relationships. *Theosis,* the realism of divine-human communion, *is* this event of freedom, which is not an infinite freedom of choice. The paradoxical character of the law only highlights the distinction between political community—the state—and the church as eucharistic event: "Constraint is in the nature of the state and . . . the Church is a place of freedom and is par excellence a place of persons, at least by definition."[112] If the law is premised on the necessity for coercion, then it is also premised on fear, which further distinguishes the state from the church, the latter being the realization of love. By extension, if the law is meant to protect human rights understood as the normative social relation in which one's claim to a good is protected based on one's inherent worth, it is necessary only because of fear that one, such as the homeless person or the prisoner, may be the recipient of an action in which one's worth is denigrated. In this sense, human rights language is integral to the common good specific to a political community; it is language, however, that is not useful when attempting to express the degree of communion with the divine possible for the created.

The latter notwithstanding, Orthodox can judge democracy as that form of governance that is most capable of preserving and maintaining human rights, even if that form of governance must allow for practices that would permit expressions, verbal and otherwise, that are contradictory to Orthodox beliefs, such as maximizing the conditions for the possibility of rejection of God and the affirmation of atheism, and even while knowing full well that the language of rights is not neutral and can lead to idolatrous forms of hyper-individualism. The kinds of rights that Orthodox should consistently affirm in a political community are those outlined by Perry: the right to life, the right to moral equality, and the right to religious freedom.[113] A Christian would also find herself working toward securing the treatment of others that share less of a consensus in the United States: the right to healthcare, to food and shelter, to employment, to an environment that is not polluted. It is these rights that Christians with an eye toward divine-human communion would advocate for in public discussions on the content of rights, because it is these rights that would structure relations in a political community such that human beings are treated as irreducibly unique.

If I am right up to this point, then the claim of the Russian Orthodox Church to rights within the cultural life of Russia, which justifies privileging the ROC over other religious groups, is not consistent with the Orthodox core principle of divine-human communion. Zizioulas himself states, echoing Bulgakov, without referring to the

ROC, that "it is inconceivable for the Church to even pretend to enforce its principles or beliefs through the coercive means which belong
to the state, or to request that the state exercise such means toward a
similar goal."[114] As I have already argued, the principle of divine-
human communion demands, ironically, that Christians promote a
space that maximizes the conditions for the possibility of rejecting
God, and not the more intuitive privileging of the Orthodox Church
because of its claim to the truth. To be consistent with all that Orthodoxy says about the human destiny for communion with God, the
ROC must work toward securing a space in which such a relationship
with God is free; thus, it must act so as to secure a space in which
rights to religious freedom, including atheism, are guaranteed, even if
this means diminishing its own role within Russian society. It is only
by taking such a risk that the Russian Orthodox Church respects the
very freedom that God has given all humans to reject God. To respect
the right to religious freedom is also to respect the right to moral
equality, insofar as it treats all human beings as equally as God treats
them with respect to one's relation with God.

The ROC is also not consistent in linking the dignity of the
human being with morality, implying that the dignity, value, or worth
of the human being is related to particular moral practices. Insofar
as the incomparable worth and, thus, uniqueness of the human being
is realized in an event of communion with God, and insofar as God's
love is eternal, humans are eternally constituted as unique. The movement toward divine-human communion is not an increase in human
dignity as much as it is a recognition of the dignity that is always-
already present. God loves us even when we are immoral; what im-
morality does is not so much diminish our worth as much as block
our awareness of it.

The ROC is correct in implying that there is no such thing as an
amoral public political space; however, it is on less secure ground in
claiming that the modern notion of human rights promotes a minimalist morality that boils down to no-harm to other human beings. It
assumes that the modern notion of human rights excludes religion
from discussions of the common good, which can also be called the

common morality. The content of human rights is not self-evident and is always part of the public discussion, which is essentially a discussion of the common good. For example, at one time the right to vote was not extended to women; now, to go back on such a right is unthinkable in the Western context. The content of human rights is always being contested, always subject to public debate. It's really not a question of whether religion can have a public role; the discussion within both political theology and philosophy has shifted toward the acceptance of such a role, notwithstanding the continued presence of detractors. The challenge for the Orthodox Churches is to discern the content of the good particular to a political community that it should support, which is consistent with but does not necessarily embody the good that is the fullness of the realism of divine-human communion. Otherwise put, the challenge for the Orthodox Churches is to discern their limits in the public realm and to resist the temptation to appeal to history for privileging the morality of the Orthodox tradition within the public sphere.

This discernment is, indeed, part of the ascetical struggle of all Christians no matter what space they inhabit—work, political, familial, or ecclesial. As I have argued throughout, the ascetical is not compartmentalized from the political, but, rather, the political is the space, a desert, for the ascetical movement. That movement is toward personhood, which is not an accomplishment as much as a realization of being eternally loved by God and, thus, being already constituted as eternally unique. Such a realization is *ecstatic* existence. This mode of being is realized in practices, and, in the political space, such practices include allowing others the freedom to express alternative beliefs, even rejection of God. They also include practices that would care for the underprivileged, especially when it comes to providing nutrition, healthcare, shelter, and work opportunities. It is in and through such practices that a Christian struggles to realize the divine more and more in her life. The practices, however, are not simply to care for the other, but to work toward structures of political community in which such care forms part of the fabric of the common good. In other words, Christians engaged in the struggle to learn how to love know full well that humans, especially the underprivileged but even the privileged, need protection against humans who not simply have not learned to love but tend toward the demonic. All this is to say that the Orthodox endorsement of human rights language does not simply result from a theoretical contrast between the ideal eucharistic form of community and the political community, but emerges as a practice within the Christian ascetical struggle to love.

The above endorsement of human rights seems half-hearted, but it must be conceded that the Orthodox resistance to human rights language contains a kernel of truth: there needs to be a greater recognition that human rights language cannot be so easily spliced onto Christian understandings of God and the human person, especially if the Christian God is one of incarnation and communion. The evocation of rights language is linked to a failure on the part of humans to relate to each other as God relates to each one of them. Without the recognition of this failure, then it implies a theological anthropology that is not consistent with the realism of divine-human communion and, thus, the sacramentality of all creation. Recognizing that political communities are necessitated in part because of sin and fear, Orthodox can, and indeed must, endorse human rights talk, since human rights structure relations in such a way that humans are treated *as* unique and irreplaceable, thus mirroring sacramental communities. In other words, human rights can be considered a practice that realizes uniqueness and irreducibility, even if to a lesser degree than what is possible.

Chapter Four

Divine-Human Communion
and the Common Good

The last two chapters engaged in an immanent critique of Orthodox and non-Orthodox Christian attacks against modern liberal democracy and the modern liberal notion of human rights. Taking for granted Orthodox understandings of a eucharistic ecclesiology and relational notions of personhood, I argued that these particular understandings of church and personhood, rooted in the realism of divine-human communion, do not lead to the type of wholesale condemnations of modern liberal democracy and human rights that seem self-evident to certain Orthodox and non-Orthodox Christian actors.

This chapter will continue this line of immanent critique but in dialogue primarily with non-Orthodox Christian political theology that has unabashedly proclaimed Christian presuppositions as the starting point for a Christian politics, declaring dead the age of Christian compromise with "public reason" advocates. Promising for Orthodox theology are those political theologies that take as their starting point not simply the God of Jesus Christ, but the extended claim that this God of Jesus Christ created the world for communion with God.

I will begin with Hauerwas, who, in spite of his protests to the contrary, drives a wedge between church and political community without a very developed understanding of church and without a sense of the ascetical nature of the relation between narrative, formation, and virtue. Milbank makes up what is lacking in Hauerwas by offering a thick, metaphysical understanding of the church in terms of divine-human communion, which he contrasts to a liberal democratic political community. What Hauerwas and Milbank share in common is a theoretical approach to the question of the compatibility of Christianity and liberal democracy. The logic is that if Christians make certain claims about what church is, what constitutes a Christian community, then the church cannot accept a liberal democratic state, together with all its ontological presuppositions, without compromise. Although this theological reflection on the nature of the church is necessary for political theology, both Hauerwas and Milbank do not give any sense of the necessity of the kinds of ascetical practices Christians must perform in order to realize all that they say church is. The church is the performance of Christian practices, primarily the Eucharist, but also other practices that are eucharistic in form. Christians, however, engage in practices not simply in relation to others who form part of the eucharistic community but to non-Christians as well, including atheists, in a political space. Christians do not stop performing ascetical practices once the liturgy is over. Both Hauerwas and Milbank fail to tell us what difference that makes for political theology.

The work of Graham Ward, Eric Gregory, and Charles Mathewes does focus attention on the relation between Christian practices and political theology through the lens of divine-human communion. All three thinkers, in different ways, argue that Christian practices in the political space would cultivate a liberal democratic polity. More strongly, they argue that, without a transcendent horizon, a liberal democratic polity would implode on itself. The move is away from a question of the theoretical compatibility of Christianity and liberal democracy, to a fuller account of the form of polity Christian civic involvement would foster.

Though I applaud this move to practices in imagining Christian political theology, I would argue that insufficient attention is given to the fact that Christians are engaged in an ascetical struggle to learn to love. Ward, Gregory, and Mathewes all give the impression that Christians will engage in practices of love whose purpose is to transform or foster a certain kind of political space. In a way, they make the same mistake that Hauerwas, Milbank, Cavanaugh, and others do when they speak of the church as this ideal community over and against the political community; Ward, Gregory, and Mathewes convey an impression that Christians will de facto engage in acts of charity. And yet, the political space has to be imagined as one in which no one can count on Christians being Christian; or, as one of many deserts in which Christians are learning to love. This point may seem minor, but I will demonstrate its importance for Christian political theology. In the end, I agree with the turn to practices, and hope to offer further nuances of this turn.

Through these thinkers I will also move toward the position that, while I think that a liberal democratic polity without some notion of the transcendent would be threatened by an ever-expanding possessive individualism and consumerism, which would thus threaten the liberal democratic notions of equality and freedom, the form of the transcendent necessary for a liberal democracy to be true to itself is some notion of the common good that need not be "theocratic," as Ward puts it.[1] Within the political space, Christian practices would prevent any enforced common theistic perspective hovering over a liberal democratic polity, but it would not be contradictory either to being a Christian or to the idea of a liberal democracy to argue for a substantive common good as the necessary condition for a liberal democracy. The push for a common good that is substantive yet revisable is ultimately what would emerge from Christian practices in the political space. Christian practices of divine-human communion would both inform and be guided by a good common to all that inhabit the political space. The notion of the common good is often associated with the natural law tradition. While I will agree that the notion of divine-human communion does not allow for a nature-grace split, I will also demonstrate how it does lead to a non–natural law affirmation of a common good internal to a political community, distinct from though not separate from the good of divine-human communion.

Stanley Hauerwas

Hauerwas's disdain for liberalism and its democratic forms is a piece of a broader critique against Christian theological ethics in the twentieth century. According to Hauerwas, Christians should just concentrate on being Christians: the "Church does not *have* a social ethic . . . but rather the church is a social ethic as it serves this or any society by first being the kind of community capable of nourishing its life by the memory of God's presence in Jesus Christ."[2] To align the church with any form of liberal democracy, for Hauerwas, is a betrayal of the nature of the church and of the Christian message. In a more general sense, Hauerwas claims that the Christian church should not be in the business of endorsing any particular form of state. As it works to be constituted as a distinctive community, "all we know as Christians is that government will exist—not what form it will or must take. . . . Every society has its strengths and weaknesses which change through time. How Christians relate to those strengths and weaknesses will and should also change through time."[3] Now, beyond simply knowing that government will exist, it seems very odd for a Christian not to be able to say that government *must* not take the form of Communist totalitarianism or fascist totalitarianism. In this apophatic approach, it would seem that the Christian is incrementally moving toward an affirmation that a political community *must* look something like a liberal democracy. Hauerwas, however, will have nothing of such an endorsement, as he has built a career upon Christian antiliberalism, which, as Jeffrey Stout has rightly noted, entails a rhetoric of antiliberal democracy.[4] If Hauerwas has also made a career on the disavowal of violence, then one wonders whether his "antiliberalism" serves this latter cause, since such rhetoric is often used as a form of violence by those who are antigay, anti-immigration, and pro-war. Hauerwas does not espouse any of these views, but his rhetoric and his "story" about democracy in America is clearly not necessarily forming the character and virtues he is promoting, which means he needs to think about the story he is telling.

Hauerwas also does not really take the time to nuance what he means by liberalism, but several key elements include an underlying anthropology defined in terms of freedom and autonomy, a marginalized role for religion within the public sphere, and a state structure that ultimately legitimizes itself through violence. Regarding the link between the state and violence, Hauerwas rejects the accusation that he is calling for an "indiscriminate rejection of the secular order," maintaining that "Christians must withdraw their support from a 'civic republicanism' only when that form (as well as any other form) of government and society resorts to violence in order to maintain internal order and external security. At that point and that point alone Christians must withhold their involvement with the state."[5] Does Hauerwas really believe that the state can exist without some form of violence? He seems to imply that it can when he argues, against those who "believe a disavowal of violence requires a withdrawal from politics," that "politics only begins with such a disavowal, for only then are we forced genuinely to listen to the other, thus beginning a conversation necessary for discovering goods in common. From my perspective, far from requiring a withdrawal from the political arena, pacificism demands strenuous political engagement."[6] If politics really does begin with the disavowal of violence, then it is a politics without a state; but, that would mean it is the church. By implication, Hauerwas seems to mean that any engagement in a politics within the framework of a particular state structure is not a real politics since it is linked to violence.

It would be difficult to argue or even envision a state or any form of government of a political community that does not legitimize itself through violence of some sort. One could argue that not all states employ violence in the same way or to the same degree; it tends toward the incredulous when one attempts to identify the violence in Pinochet's Chile with that initiated by Western democratic states in order to highlight the diametrical opposition between any state and the church.[7] Hauerwas, however, does not care much about the kind and degree of violence, but implies, simply, that no state can be envisioned without violence. The liberal state, especially, has its imperialistic and totalitarian tendencies, compelling Hauerwas to issue the remarkable and ridiculous warning to "never forget the most democratically elected leader of modern times was Adolf Hitler."[8] Democracy is often characterized as an "ideology," which by definition entails violence.[9] If no state can be envisioned without violence, then Hauerwas is correct in criticizing any easy alliance between Christianity and democracy, as implied, according to Hauerwas, in some forms of liberal Protestant thought. The church should exist in a stance of perpetual critique against any form of state. And, yet, it seems counterintuitive to say that the church cannot comment on one form of government versus another but is simply called to react to whatever form of government in relation to which it finds itself. The question then is: react for the sake of what? Hauerwas would say the "peaceable kingdom." If that is the answer, could not the church say that some forms of government image the peaceable kingdom more than others? Could it do so while still maintaining a stance of prophetic critique to the violence that seems to be inherent to the very notion of "state"?

The same set of questions can be posed to Hauerwas's other two overriding concerns with liberalism: an anthropology antithetical to Christian anthropology—"the last thing the church wants is a bunch of autonomous, free individuals";[10] and a marginalization of religion in public life. Hauerwas is correct that philosophical forms of liberalism seem to imply an anthropology that is at odds with what Christians claim about being human. But does this incompatibility rule out a hermeneutical retrievability? Rather than posing a hermeneutics of suspicion to philosophical liberalism, why not a hermeneutics of charity that would (a) retrieve elements of philosophical liberalism in relation to Christian theological claims and (b) see strands of philosophical liberalism's antireligious rhetoric as entailing a genuine concern for the human being? There seems to be both a criticism of Christendom by Hauerwas and a narrative of suspicion against the godless liberalism that is trying to eliminate religion without considering that Christendom's complacency needed a dose of godless liberalism, just as Athanasius needed Arius to clarify the Christian point about the incarnation (and, by extension, the Trinity). The question is whether an incarnational Christian view of the human being could integrate philosophical liberalism's emphasis on freedom, equality, and tolerance without betraying the Christian message of divine-human communion; and whether a Christian understanding of the church's relation to the state requires that the church sometimes be told by the state what do to. There is very little unpacking of the Christian affirmation of the incarnation for political theology in Hauerwas, even if there is no shortage of provocative insights and rhetorical flares. What Hauerwas lacks is found in Milbank, who arrives at Hauerwas's conclusion based on a participatory metaphysics rooted in the Christian claim about Christ as the embodied revelation of God's Logos.

John Milbank

In the Acknowledgments of his 1990 breakout book, *Theology and Social Theory,* John Milbank references Hauerwas as one of his main sources of inspiration.[11] One does not have to read far into *Theology and Social Theory* to notice the same vitriolic rhetoric against liberal democracy that is evident in Hauerwas.[12] A consistent drumbeat in Milbank and his Radical Orthodoxy (RO) counterparts has been that the very principles of liberalism are antithetical to a Christian worldview.[13] Whereas Hauerwas would frame the difference between liberalism and Christianity as a difference in presuppositions—thus leading to a different account of the human that generates different stories and different moral norms—Milbank would much more thickly frame the opposition in terms of a battle of mutually exclusive ontologies. The very hallmarks of liberalism, such as tolerance and human rights, are the result either of an ontology that is anti-Christian or of bad theology.

Two fundamental principles stand behind Milbank's rejection of the secular and, by extension, modern liberalism: a particular understanding of church and of the relation between nature and grace, both of which are grounded in a conceptualization of the trinitarian being of God as gift. Although he is not always clear on what he means by "church," it is not, for Milbank, necessarily reducible to an institutional structure; it is also not necessarily reducible to a congregation of believers: "it being understood that the Church, like grace, is everywhere."[14] Church, for Milbank, is creation manifesting its sacramental potential; it is creation realizing its purpose, which is communion with God. In this sense, the presence of church is much more amorphous; its borders are less discernible: "We are that body of Christ we can never yet see."[15] Although Milbank follows de Lubac in almost identifying the church with the Eucharist, an identification also present, as we have seen, in Orthodox eucharistic ecclesiology,[16] the church as Eucharist is not limited to the celebration of the liturgy; church as Eucharist must also manifest itself in political, cultural, and economic production (*poiesis*). The church as Eucharist, then, is not simply about people and nonhuman life forms (trees, for example) but also about the practices that humans must perform in relation to other humans and the nonhuman world, the results of which produce what we name political, cultural, and economic spheres. Milbank does not deny the necessity of the spheres, he just rejects their autonomous status: "participation can be extended also to language, history and culture: the whole realm of human *making*."[17]

What drives this logic of the church is an understanding of the relation of nature and grace.[18] Milbank rejects any notion of the relation of nature and grace in which the two are distinct though not separate. He follows de Lubac in rejecting the distinction and argues that nature is always-already participating in the grace of God from creation. In other words, if humans were created for communion with God, then one must claim that there is no such thing as a natural order distinct from the supernatural; the logic of divine-human communion demands that such a communion already exists from the moment of creation. Otherwise, there is no way to conceptualize such a communion other than as a violent imposition of the more powerful other—God. It is for this reason that Milbank claims that an ontology of participation is an ontology of peace, since it is a communion effected through love-as-freedom. Even if Milbank himself can be, ironically, rhetorically violent, at the heart of his concern is the Christian vision of communion with God, a vision with which one can, at least, sympathize.

It is as a result of his rejection of the nature-grace distinction that Milbank rejects any attempt to construct a political theology on the basis of the natural law. Milbank and company interpret Jacques Maritain's New Christendom model as a disaster for Christian political theology, especially in its justification of a political order that is distinct from the ecclesial. Such an understanding of the political order also justifies the secular and, in so doing, the underlying ontology of violence that lurks behind secular discourse and the practices that reinforce it.

Milbank would challenge the legitimacy of a democracy that is secular—in terms of the lack of a common theological perspective— by asserting that democracy needs a theological perspective if it is to realize its most cherished values of the inherent equality and dignity of each citizen; and, of course, the particular theological perspective Milbank has in mind is not simply any idea of the transcendent but one that imagines the transcendent in terms of participation. As Milbank argues, "the Church needs boldly to teach that the only justification for democracy is theological."[19] Without such a theological grounding, democracy becomes tyranny: "Transcendence must here be invoked, and indeed it is clear that only the notion of a Trinitarian God who is eternally relation and eternally the expression of unity in difference provides the adequate thought of a grounding for human association that would point us beyond the current mutual complicity of state terror with anarchic terror."[20] What is ambiguous is whether Milbank is really talking about a political order when he adds, "We have seen that *ecclesia* names a new sort of universal polity, primarily democratic, yet also monarchic, which was invented by Christianity."[21] In the end, democracy parodoxically does not work without a certain kind of hierarchy:

> Christianity does not inevitably encourage liberal democracy, yet it always should encourage another mode of democracy, linked to the idea of the infallible presence of the Holy Spirit in the whole body of the church and by extension humanity across all times and places (since all human society in some degree foreshadows *ecclesia* and in this way always mediates supernatural grace). Unlike liberal democracy, this Christian democracy has a hierarchic dimension: the transmission of the gift of truth across time, and the reservation of a nondemocratic educative sphere concerned with finding the truth, not ascertaining majority opinion. Without this sphere, democracy will not be able to debate about the truth, but will always be swayed by propaganda: mass representation will represent only itself, not the represented. Christian democracy, though, should also be Christian socialism—not the somewhat limited Christian democracy of so-called Christian-Democratic parties. Or, one can say, it should be "Christian social democracy," and one should add there can be Jewish and Islamic democracy also, and that in many parts of the world—France perhaps imminently—we shall need hybrids.[22]

It appears that Milbank's hope is for a "deified democracy,"[23] since "to eternalize democracy, and maintain its link with excellence rather than the mutual concessions of baseness, deification as the doctrine of the offer of equality with God is required."[24]

Milbank's democracy, then, is really the church. In what is a signature move for Milbank and other RO theologians, Milbank argues that democracies most cherished principles are only realizable within a certain theological framework, and, without such a theological framework, liberal democracy implodes. Milbank's democracy realizes the equality and inviolable dignity of its citizens, but without the concepts of contract, toleration, dialogue, and human rights. Moreover, although the reigning theological perspective is an ontology of peace, his democracy is not necessarily without violence:

> The Christian, though, can only abide by her commitment to all or nothing. . . . In a sense then, yes, Christianity has led to violence: first, because it is a universalizing religion; second, because it aims so high. . . . In a word, we cannot as human beings suppose that violence is entirely unavoidable, in so far as it runs the educative risks of redemption. . . .
>
> Christians do, indeed, believe perfect peace to be the ultimate ontological reality and so to be attainable. But in that case, peace names the *eschaton,* the final goal. . . .
>
> We therefore should not and even cannot be pacifists . . . we can only try to force force [*sic*] with reserve and with hopeful risk that distorted realities will come to repent. This is the best we can do; our scenario is apocalyptic, not utopian.[25]

Milbank, thus, is not against violence per se; he is more troubled by liberal democracies projecting themselves as inherently non-violent and only provoked to use violence by nondemocratic forces. Since the perfect peace is eschatological, and itself realized only through noncoercive persuasion, until that time coercion seems unavoidable. What Christians should aim for is a nonsecular Christian society framed by a theological perspective that affirms a Christian metaphysics of participation. Given the inevitability that not all will be persuaded by this *mythos,* noncoercion within such a society is unimaginable. One could conceivably reject God, but one would have to live in such a society as if the Christian God existed, or face the consequences. As Milbank puts it, "if Dostoyevsky's monasticization of all society is, in a sense, a correct aim (if this means trying to bring about a liturgical society), one can nevertheless see that the monasticization of the whole of society is much more difficult than the monasticization of a celibate few."[26] Hence the need for coercion.

In an ironic twist, Milbank's understanding of the political order looks very much like the neo-scholastic principle that the rejection of truth should not be allowed in a political order, which means the state is justified in enforcing such truth. The only difference is that Milbank bases this argument on the assumption that the logic of an ontology of participation cannot allow for a political order that does not acknowledge the truth of the created order, and, thus, about God. As a result of this logic, Milbank keeps eliding political community and the church; even if the fulfillment of the church is the eschaton, the present, including the political, is the church in process.

Milbank's logic is not the only possible logic that emerges from the principle of divine-human communion, as it is not necessarily the case that an ontology of participation affirming the realism of divine-human communion leads to the rejection of a distinct political order with a good internal to itself. Somewhat ironically, the Christian affirmation of the realism of divine-human communion leads to a natural law–like conclusion without the natural law or, at least, a particular understanding of the natural law. If we follow Milbank's moves from the nonfoundationalist-but-foundational principle of the realism of divine-human communion to a eucharistic understanding of the church, and if the church is an event of divine-human communion that realizes relations of love-as-freedom, then there can be no forced imposition of this communion, a point that Milbank seems to accept, albeit ambiguously, when he says, "the purpose of ecclesial coercion is peace, and this can only in the long-term be attained by non-coercive persuasion, because the free consent of will is necessary to this goal."[27] If there is no forced imposition of this communion, then the church coexists as a presence in the world in the midst of those who reject the church.

One could argue at this point that the very rejection of the church is the problem; it is a false theology that ultimately results in idolatry. Theologically, this makes sense, but it is also the case, theologically, that if God desires a communion as an event of love-as-freedom, then God creates the conditions for the possibility of the rejection of this communion. Paradoxically, although Christians must strive toward communion with God, Christians must also maximize the conditions for the possibility of freely rejecting God. God's sovereignty, God's dominion over creation, is, ironically, made more manifest in a context that reveals God's vulnerability to creation in the form of rejection.

In a context in which the conditions for the possibility of rejecting God are maximized, it is more likely to be the case that existing as a Christian has little to do with cultural, social, or political expectations; that existing as a Christian is less about ethnic identity and more about an actual relation with God structured through a particular tradition. As an example of the latter case, when attending a conference in Greece in the summer of 2004, before a professor of philosophy from the University of Athens began his talk, I asked a co-organizer of the conference if he was Orthodox. She affirmed that he was. He then spoke long enough to prompt a follow-up question from me: "Does he believe in God?" She said no. The philosophy professor clearly rejects God but must identify as Orthodox, given the cultural reality in Greece. Such a situation must be avoided by maximizing the possibility of freely rejecting God.

Christians, then, must envision the presence of a church coexisting with those who reject God. Such a coexistence, however, is by definition a form of community distinct from the church, since it contains members who reject God. Insofar as it is not church and it is constituted by members who reject God, this political community has a good internal to itself; but, insofar as the principle of divine-human communion demands the existence of such a community, that is, one in which the conditions for the possibility of rejection of God are maximized, then the good internal to the political community is not antithetical to that of the church, which is the fullness of divine-human communion, but in continuity with it. An example of a good internal to the political community is mutual respect of the dignity of all human beings, even toward humans who reject God, and even if such rejection is expressed with hostility. Such a good is, to some extent, nonsensical in a church, since the idea of church cannot contain the thought of hostile rejection of God. In church, ideally, humans are treated with a dignity that is irreducible because of the maximization of love that is divine-human communion, not, as with political communities, through the institution of structures that shape patterns of relationship in which dignity is respected through fear of punishment. The respect for human rights can also be understood as the realization of a good internal to a political community, but that does not make much sense within a community that is both striving for and is the realization of the love commandment. Thus, the logic of divine-human communion leads to the formation of a liberal democratic political community with a good internal to itself and whose content is, minimally, a pattern of relationships in which each human is treated as irreducibly unique. Such a good iconically mirrors the fullness of divine-human communion, and, in this sense, presences the divine, but not to the degree that *is* church.

To affirm the necessity of a community distinct from the church—constituted by the political, economic, and cultural spheres—is not to reinstate the nature-grace divide, nor is it a denial of the sovereignty of God. A form of political community that maximizes the conditions for the possibility of rejecting God logically flows from the Christian affirmation of the realism of divine-human communion. Such a community, then, must be secular in the sense that it does not enforce a common theological perspective on the participants of the community.[28] It is not secular in the sense of being antireligion, nor in the sense of the complete privatization of religion; it is secular only in the sense that a common theological perspective does not justify the form and movement of the political, cultural, or economic spheres of a political community. The rejection of a common theological perspective also does not mean that religion has no voice within public deliberations; religion simply cannot be the dominant voice.

One could argue that for religion to be one among many voices is to allow the godless secular state to tell religion what to do; that it only empowers further the godless secular state; that it is self-contradictory for a Christian to assume such a role since the object of a Christian's allegiance is an all-encompassing truth. The all-encompassing God, as I have argued, is such whether one recognizes it or not. God's all-encompassing nature is not only actualized in our recognition of God. If the worry is that the full truth of the Christian message would be mitigated in a political community that negates a common theological perspective, I would argue a negation of a common theological perspective in a political community *is* the full Christian message, if this message is understood in terms of divine-human communion. What is required of Christians is not to discern theologically how to reject the secular; more effort is needed to discern theologically what kind of voice Christians should be in a political community in which not all are Christians, including those who profess Christianity. Even if not the dominant voice, it is still a voice that emerges from existing as a Christian, especially one working toward communion with God.

The logic of the realism of divine-human communion, or a metaphysics of participation, then, does not lead to Milbank's ironically Gnostic-like dualism between the Christian *mythos* and the liberal *mythos*.[29] Notwithstanding an antireligious trajectory within the liberal tradition, and all that such a trajectory entails, the realism of divine-human communion demands a stance of hermeneutical charity. First, like any good heresy, modern liberalism awakened Christian thought to its inner contradiction; put more positively, it compelled Christian thought to coherence with its core principles. For example, it simply makes no sense to speak of the realism of divine-human communion and the creation of the human in the image of God and simultaneously to promote the subordination of women to men, in any form, as Christianity has done for centuries. Second, a participatory metaphysics does not allow for a spatialized mutual exclusivity within the created order, even at the level of thought. Although unable to accept certain principles linked to some forms of modern liberal thought, such as a nonrelational notion of an autonomous subject, a hermeneutics of charity allows for the retrievability of other principles of modern liberal thought, such as church-state separation, which would not have emerged within Christian thought if not for the challenge of the varieties of modern liberal theory. Here Solov'ev and Bulgakov are more consistent than Milbank and company, as they were able to identify antireligious forms of political, cultural, and economic *poiesis* as retrievable, and even manifesting to some degree the realism of divine-human communion for which creation was created.

In short, an ontology of the realism of divine-human communion does not allow for a hermeneutical position of mutually incompatible frameworks; it does not allow for violence of any kind, even rhetorical and intellectual violence.

The Turn to Practices

Recent writings in Christian political theology evince less of a concern with the clash of presuppositions between modern liberalism and Christianity, or with their mutually incompatible ontologies, and more of an attention to Christians in the midst of a situation that is characterized by some as postdemocratic, postsecular, and driven by a market capitalism whose globalizing ambitions are, ironically, eviscerating materiality even as it promotes overconsumption of the material. This turn is especially evident in the work of Graham Ward, Charles Mathewes, and Eric Gregory.[30]

Charles Mathewes's recent book "builds upon previous debates on religion's role in public life, but does not contribute to it. It assumes that those debates have by and large ended, and that what we may call the accommodationists won, and the 'public reason' advocates lost."[31] The past few decades, such political theorists, philosophers and theologians such as John Rawls, Michael Sandel, Charles Taylor, Nicholas Wolterstorff, Jeffrey Stout, Richard Rorty, Ronald Thiemann, David Hollenbach, and Robert Audi, to name a few, debated Rawls's notion of "public reason," contesting to what extent, if at all, particularistic religious arguments could enter discussions of public issues. Occurring simultaneously with these debates, and related to them, were discussions over whether theories of secularization are now defunct, especially given the recent surge in public religion. Mathewes speaks for many in declaring a clear winner in these debates: religion is public, and it is not going away. In hindsight, these debates appear to some as almost silly: "So, when we begin to examine the way in which a new confessionalism is once again entering into the public arena, we have to recall that its absence from the public arena is not old and the idea, held by Rawls and others, that this absence goes back to the seventeenth century is nonsense."[32] The focus, then, has turned from speculative theological accounts of the compatibility of Christianity and democracy, from "public theology" carved around Rawls's notion of public reason, to attention to Christian practices in a culture that, if not post-Christian, is at least not manifestly as Christian as it used to be. The starting point is unabashedly particularistic, following Hauerwas's and Milbank's lead, even if the conclusions are un-Hauerwasian and un-Milbankian. The particularistic starting point for Ward, Mathewes, and Gregory has something to do with divine-human communion, in the sense that the goal of Christian practices is communion with God.

The work of Ward has always been associated with RO and, by extension, Milbank, and it is evident that Ward shares much with Milbank. Like Milbank, Ward begins with a metaphysics of participation: all things fall analogically within the embrace of the one God, who acts to establish God's kingdom in the world. As a result, there can be no such thing as neutral or religious-free political zones: the church cannot be relegated to a sphere walled off from other spheres. Creation was created for unity in the *ecclesia,* which is nothing less than unity in the body of Christ, and such unity *is* the kingdom of God. There can be no other Christian mission than to act in the world so as to establish this kingdom. Political theology is reflection on this action: it "begins with the sovereignty of the one God and the operations of that sovereignty in and across time. A Christian action is political not because it takes place within the polis and is implicated in the struggle for the city's soul . . . but because the God who acts in history is political, for this God exercises authority, power, and judgment in order to establish a kingdom."[33]

As a result of this starting point, Ward, like Milbank, argues that theology cannot but critique and expose the emptiness of what amounts to secular ideologies and the practices that support such a discourse. Christian discipleship is political by "first unmasking the theological and metaphysical sources of current mythologies and revealing the distortions and perversions of their current secularized

ecclesia (congregation of a Church

forms. Then we need to reread and rewrite the Christian tradition back into contemporary culture."[34] Such a rereading and rewriting entails engaging in religious practices that "are concerned with changing the cultural imaginary—that is, rereading and rewriting what appears to be the case in ways that are both critical and constructive."[35] Ward's own rereading and rewriting of Christianity into the contemporary culture is evident in his critique of secular ideologies and postmaterialist capitalism, the practices that reinforce such discourses, and their anthropological presuppositions.

What separates Ward from Milbank is his implicit allowance for a political order that is distinct from *ecclesia* and that, thus, is not necessarily grounded in a *particular* theological perspective. In other words, Ward seems less concerned with reestablishing a manifestly visible "Christian" culture, and more with a Christian response to an increasingly thin democratic polity that is caused by an unregulated capitalist market with global aspirations.[36] Ward fears the thinning of democracy that is a result of the ideologies of secularization, which "undermines the possibility for democracy because it disregards the theological foundations of sovereignty,"[37] and globalization, which attempts to realize an immanent secular eschatology of democratic unity through borderless capitalistic exchange. For Ward, democracy and capitalism are not evil per se, but his own Christian critique judges the current form as being shaped by presuppositions incompatible with Christian understandings of materiality and the human person.

Like Milbank, Ward argues that there are no clear borders to the church; the church is present in and through authentic Christian practices.[38] He does not, however, see a contradiction in affirming the Christian mission to expand *ecclesia* in the world and seeing that mission as simultaneously promoting democratic polity until the eschatological fulfillment. Although Ward is not giving a Christian theological defense of democracy, his understanding of church realized in Christian practices in the world leads him to imply that such practices promote a democratic polity; they can ward off the thinning of democracy. What grounds this distinction of the democratic polity from *ecclesia* is an "eschatological remainder" that "views eschatology not as what is lacking in all the secular ideologies of the future but what is excessive and superabundant to them . . . [that] emphasizes the supernatural mystery of Christ-with-us in that his body is both present and incomplete. . . . The presence of Christ with us now is discerned in the Eucharist, within every act of faith, among the congregation of the faithful, and analogically in every identification of justice, peace, love, joy, and community."[39] Unlike the all-or-nothing apocalypticism of Milbank, Ward develops a political theology based on his notion of the eschatological remainder, which more charitably identifies the analogical points of contact with a Christian metaphysics of participation in the body of Christ, and reads the Christian political response to the current situation in light of those analogical points of contact. The eschatological remainder "announces a new and better politics, a new and better sovereignty that, in our present condition, can help to facilitate 'democracy as a "community of dispute."'"[40]

Although Ward seems to allow for a democratic polity distinct from *ecclesia,* he is less forgiving of such a polity being secular and liberal. The latter have led to the thinning of democracy in the form of unfettered freedoms and isolated individualism. Having argued that "all political accounts of the social were implicated in metaphysics," he adds, "These metaphysics could be either good (fostering human flourishing and the commonwealth) or bad (deleterious for, or reductive of, the human condition). Lacking a theological appeal or foundation, these metaphysics of the social I viewed as inadequate to resist a prevailing dehumanization and dematerialization."[41] A Christian politics of discipleship counters such dehumanization and dematerialization fostered by secular eschatologies. Here, however, Ward seems to slide back toward Milbank in implying that democratic aspirations need a grounding in the transcendent: "If the rejection of theocratic language came with the acceptance of liberal-democratic polity and secularism, then, in a time of postdemocracy and postsecularity, should we not revisit this form of polity?"[42] Christian theocratic language is about the kingdom of God, a "theopolitical" notion, which "announces the continuing double axis: absolute submission to

God, on the one hand, and equality with respect to all neighbors, on the other."[43] What Ward seems to imply is that there can be no account of the political that is not metaphysical; any account that is immanentist follows a logic that is dehumanizing and depoliticizing; only practices grounded in an account of the transcendent can realize democratic aspirations; Christians engaging in such practices are true democratic citizens insofar as such practices form one to respect the other even while contesting the other, which is a form of respect.

Although Ward throughout his work is not shy about asserting the truth of a Christian metaphysics of participation, and how this truth fulfills the deepest longings of secular eschatologies, whose inevitable end is implosion, unlike Milbank he does not elide democracy with *ecclesia*. He does, however, suggest that democracy as a community of dispute, and, hence, of respect for the other, can only be saved with reference to the transcendent. The content of this notion of the transcendent is undefined in Ward, but his general point is clear: an immanentist metaphysics and eschatology is, ironically and ultimately, antidemocratic and antimaterialist. A true Christian politics of discipleship is pro-democracy and pro-materiality; and, as Christians patiently work toward the realization of the kingdom of God and engage in practices that make present that kingdom in the world, always grounding all they say and do in particularistic presuppositions, on the question of polity they must also challenge the assumption that a polity must be based on immanentist assumptions. But as Ward asks, "If the rejection of theocratic language came with the acceptance of liberal-democratic polity and secularism, then, in a time of postdemocracy and postsecularity, should we not revisit this form of polity?"[44] The implication is that if we don't, we risk democracy collapsing in on its own internal contradictions. Democracy then is not *ecclesia,* but it is also not the devil; it occupies the analogical middle in which Christians can participate while knowing fully that the kingdom is yet to come.

A similar emphasis on Christian practices is evident in the recent work of Eric Gregory and Charles Mathewes, who are both concerned to rescue the implications of Augustine's theology for political thought from the Christian realist appropriation. For both Gregory and Mathewes, Augustine's political theology cannot be reduced simply to the legitimization of some form of the liberal "secular" state for the sake of containing sin. According to Gregory, Augustine's "political thought," which usually means portions of the *City of God*, has been appropriated to argue for three kinds of liberalism: realist liberalism, Rawlsian liberalism, and civic liberalism.[45] The dominant virtues of the first two types of liberalism are hope and justice, but what they have in common is an overemphasis of Augustine's pessimism about the human condition and, thus, about politics. Gregory aligns his own project with civic liberalism, and together with Mathewes, refocuses the discussion of Augustine's relevance for political theology on the virtue of love. Both Gregory and Mathewes attempt to bring the reader's attention to Augustine's theological anthropology and moral psychology, which sees the human person as always-already participating in the life of God and as created for communion with the God who is already at the center of human existence. Augustine's contribution to political theology is one-sided if it draws simply on Augustine's reflections on the human tendency toward sin; it needs to be balanced by what Augustine says about what humans are created to be. Love is, thus, at the center of being human, and if that is the case, then it cannot be quarantined to the *ecclesia* while justice is identified as the political virtue. All forms of Christian interaction have something do with love, even political engagement. If the struggle of the Christian is to rightly order our disordered loves, then political engagement is part of that *ascesis*. In short, a political theology that draws more widely from Augustine's theological anthropology, which understands the human as constituted in love and, thus, as one who loves either disorderly or rightly, would look something like Gregory's notion of civic liberalism, which is sympathetic to modern liberalism but cannot be identified with it.

For Mathewes, the problem is less about religion in public life and more about a monopoly of a certain type of religious voice in public life, one that is driven by an apocalyptic imagination. Those who have attempted to construct the high wall of separation between church and state and those reactionary religious voices that will not allow for the erection of such a high wall are two sides of the apocalyptic coin. If Milbank has accused secular liberalism of bad theology, Mathewes extends the critique of bad theology to the Milbankian critique of modern liberalism, which has lent support to an all-or-nothing religious voice in the public sphere: "What has actually happened in the last few decades is that those religious voices attuned to the complexity of religion in public life have effectively ceded the rhetorical high ground of thick discourses to extremist and often reactionary (whether right-wing or left-wing) voices. Culture, like nature, abhors a vacuum, and bad theology drives out good."[46] What is needed, then, is good theology that can produce a Christian engagement in the public sphere that does not result in apocalyptic polarizations: "Thoughtful secularists and sincere believers can agree that we need, not *less* religion in public, but *more,* of a richer kind—for such believers would be a welcome addition to civic discourse."[47]

The good theology that Mathewes is referring to is an Augustinian account that "sees love, and not struggle—and thus communion, and not alterity—at the heart of the universe. Such an account offers a love-centered ontology that can make more sense of our interest in and commitment to one another." Such an understanding of the universe yields to "a sacramental politics" that acknowledges that the deepest longings of humans is one for communion, and that "these longings reveal that politics is motivated by a desire that it cannot itself comprehend, the desire for communion."[48] There must be a realization, however, that "just as the self will be only eschatologically realized, so political community aches for a communion that will be realized only in the *koinonia* of the kingdom of God."[49] Implicit here is an understanding of the human person as moving toward or away what is at her center, which is God. If, along with Augustine, we realize that our deepest longing is for movement toward this center—communion—then all forms of engagement with the other are driven by and a reflection of this longing, even if the engagement with the other is distorted.

Politics then is driven by this longing for communion but is not identified with *ecclesia,* insofar as not all political engagement is between Christian believers. An Augustinian ontology of love helps Christians to realize that all politics is rooted in our desire for communion, whose fulfillment is only in the eschaton. This eschatological perspective does not allow for a diametrical opposition between the political and the kingdom of God; to the contrary, it demands that Christians see the political as part of their ascetical struggle to be in communion with God. The Christian is to practice "ascetical citizenship" in which the other is not tolerated but engaged, and in such engagement, is related to as uniquely and irreplaceably loved by God, regardless of their "presuppositions."

Although Mathewes does not want "to use faith to support our democratic culture,"[50] ascetical citizenship yields something like a civic republican form of democratic polity. Civic republicanism, according to Mathewes, is something in between liberalism and communitarianism: "For civic-republicans, political life is most valuable not for its institutional outcomes (as liberals assume) or its solidaristic social effects (as for communitarians), but rather for its more immanent rewards for citizens. . . . Christians can take from civic republicanism its affirmation of civic participation as the primary public good, its suspicion of all attempts at political closure, and its insistence that explicitly political structures are fundamentally secondary to and derivative of what politics is really about—namely, civic participation."[51] Participating in this civic republican form of democratic polity, a Christian needs to be wary of this form's own tendency toward immanentism that can lead to fanaticism and apocalypticism. If the eschatological is at the forefront, Christians need not be concerned with accommodation since civic interactions are an ascetical form to deepen faith.[52] It also precludes a closed understanding of politics, which aligns more with the Christian eschatological perspective of the already-but-still-to-be finished character of all our attempts to realize communion with our neighbor and with God. In the end, "Christians should see politics as endless but worth engaging in anyway, in order to help cultivate real human virtue and piety."[53]

What Mathewes offers beyond Ward and Gregory is the more explicit recognition that the political space is an arena of ascetical struggle for the Christian, an opportunity to move toward a deeper love of God and neighbor. Although they would not necessarily disagree with this ascetical component, it does not figure prominently in their writings. Ward often gives the impression that the Christian stands apart from other citizens in engaging in practices that sacramentally transfigure the world, mirroring Hauerwas's and Cavanaugh's juxtaposition of the church and the political community. Gregory rightly emphasizes Augustine's understanding of the human being as created to love for a fuller sense of Augustine's politics, but fails to elaborate on how love is ascetically realized. Mathewes offers a necessary corrective to these political theologies that focus on Christian practices.

More, however, could be said. From this ascetical perspective, it is remarkable how much Christian political theology of late is unascetical. In the face of attacks against Christianity, of blatant attempts to eradicate religion or exclude it completely from the public square, some Christians have developed a political theology that looks more like a battle plan for war and destruction. In the face of mutually exclusive worldviews, the goal is to outmaneuver the opponent, as there can only be one remaining at the top. I call these political theologies unascetical because, although they seem driven by a certain Christian logic, either of the revelation of God in Jesus Christ or of divine-human communion in Jesus Christ, they betray a tone of anger, resentment, and even hatred, which is especially evident in their belligerent, uncharitable, and often hyperbolic style. These latter styles seem to be strategies to create audiences so as to rhetorically outdo the opponents.

In what is one of the most preeminent texts on the Christian acquisition of the virtue of love, *The Four Hundred Chapters on Love*, Maximus the Confessor warns: "When you are insulted by someone or offended in any matter, then beware of angry thoughts, lest by distress they sever you from charity and place you in the region of hatred."[54] Maximus is consistent in identifying certain vices as obstacles to love, including not only avarice, lust, and gluttony, but fear, anger, and hatred. Recent Christian political theologies have not been reticent to identify the ills of liberal democracy with promoting an excessive possessive individualism, focusing on the appetitive vices; they are less honest about the fact that professed Christians are often motivated out of fear, anger, and hatred—vices usually provoked when threat is impending—and feel justified in acting on such motives because they possess the truth.

Politics is many things, but it is an arena where one is susceptible to identity violence, in other words, that all that one thought was true about the world and oneself is questioned in confronting an other who does not share this worldview. Such opposition is not only seen among the religious, but among Republicans and Democrats. An easy reaction to identity violence is to monsterize the other so as to easily justify one's counterattack of destruction. And, yet, it is this monsterization that Christians ascetically struggle to avoid. So, while I agree with Mathewes that civic engagement is an ascetical practice, for Christians to even arrive at that way of looking at politics—where one is really listening to the other, arguing with the other, and willing to accept the fact that the other has not been persuaded—is a mark of ascetical growth or, otherwise put, an advance in love. If Christian political theology is to emphasize Christian practices, then greater attention needs to be put on what prevents Christians from loving and how the political space can magnify those vices that prevent love. It is in the political space more than the *ecclesia* in which the Christian command to love is most challenged; thus, it is in the political space that Christians especially need to engage in the practices that make love possible. Against the urge to monsterize and project unto the other, the Christian will attempt to engage in practices exhibiting humility, patience, respect, temperance, courage, and discernment. Together with some spiritual mentor, the Christian will, ideally, attempt to discern the appropriate political response in specific situations. It is in the very specific practices that the Christian performs to try and resist every temptation at demonization, to try and root out fear, anger and hatred, that one clearly sees that the type of polity that Christians are fostering is one that looks like a liberal democracy.

A Non–Natural Law Defense of the Common Good

What is somewhat remarkable in recent political theology is the consensus that Christian political theology must be particularistic and reject any accommodation to notions of "public reason," a notion which of late has very little traction in the debate of religion's role in public life. The consensus seems to extend to the understanding of the Christian life as oriented toward a communion with God: Ward, Gregory, and Mathewes use, in one form or another, the word "deification," and in relating it to political theology they challenge the distinction between the mystical and the prophetic/political, and show that the mystical is the political. To speak about divine-human communion is not to refer to a human being with superhuman powers nor one who exists in the world in a quasi-dematerialized form. It is to affirm that materiality was created to bear the weight of God's presence, the markers of which are the form of relationships, which means that political engagement is a sphere of divine-human communion. If the political is a community of dispute, in which civic engagement involves not simply tolerating the other but seeing her as an irreducibly unique creation of God, the political community can be a "proleptic communion." What one sees, then, in Ward, Gregory, and Mathewes is an indirect Christian defense of democracy, one that contains elements of modern liberalism without the ontological baggage. The defense is less speculative or theoretical as it does not take the form "because Christians believe *this,* political community should look like *that.*" The focus is on Christian existence in the world created for divine-human communion; as Christians work toward tapping creation's sacramental potential, the political form of community that such work reinforces is democratic.

What Ward and Mathewes worry about, however, is a form of democracy that is grounded in immanentist ontological convictions, if not explicitly at least implicitly, since, as Mathewes argues, there is no existing without ontological commitments. Such a form of democracy fosters a solipsistic, enclave-like, nonrelational understanding of the individual, and fosters an idolatrous materialism fueled by a capitalist machine generating infinite desire. Such a democracy cannot bear the weight of its own inner contradictions. If, however, the deepest aspirations of democracy are to succeed only through engaging in practices that orient the self to what is beyond the self, and if neither Ward nor Mathewes are calling for the return of a manifestly Christian state and culture, then what form should this transcendent take? What does Ward mean by politics grounded in "theocratic language"? If it cannot be an explicit reference to a Christian metaphysics that frames a Christian state and culture and if the logic of divine-human communion demands the maximization of the conditions of the possibility for rejecting God, then a politics that is "theocratic" cannot, ironically, have God as its grounding. The only alternative is some notion of the "common good."

The notion of the "common good" is most often associated with Catholic natural law theory, and raises the specters of dividing nature and grace in attempting to theorize a political space that is universalist in scope without referring explicitly to the Christian understanding of divine-human communion. As I argued above, however, the Christian affirmation of a political community with a good internal to itself, and which is distinct from though not separate from *ecclesia,* emerges from the logic of divine-human communion. Such a good must be labeled the common good insofar as it is the good of the political community. This common good, for Christians, cannot be identified with the eschatological good of divine-human communion, though, as Mathewes argues, it is the realization of a "proleptic communion." As such, it is analogically related to the eschatological good of divine-human communion.

One could still argue that the notion of the common good does not necessarily fulfill Ward's and Mathewes's call for a democracy rooted in some notion of the transcendent or, to put it another way, does not escape immanentist commitments. Such a claim would depend on the perspective from which one assesses the common good. For Christians who affirm the principle of divine-human communion, there would be a recognition that the common good inherent to a democratic political community is grounded in the Christian conviction that God created the world for communion. Contrary to Hauerwas's claim, a Christian understanding of the common good need not be linked to a theory of natural law that ignores Christian presuppositions, nor is it necessarily a product of "public reason" that is imposed on Christians. The common good is one that Christians can claim as emerging from their own metaphysical commitments, even while simultaneously maintaining a prophetic distance: it is affirmed as a good necessary for a particular type of political community, which Christians would prophetically critique in their conviction that humans are possible for more than the common political good.

From the perspective of the Christian affirmation of divine-human communion, the notion of the common good would not be immanentist, even if affirmed by those who have different convictions about the divine, including denial of the divine. Such a notion of the common good would not be one that logically follows from natural law principles, but one that emerges through civic-engagement-as-dialogue.[55] In fact, such engagement *is* the common good, which means that the common good entails the unequivocal equality among all citizens as co-participants in the dialogue or the "community of dispute." If the dialogue-as-engagement is authentic, then it must also entail some form of freedom to be truthful in the dialogue, to speak without fear of punishment. The meaning, however, of such notions as equality and freedom are not necessarily given, and what constitutes the common good is, in part, a tentative, always contested, "increasingly adequate but always revisable understanding of the good life."[56] It is then conceivable that Christians could contribute to the common good an understanding of equality and freedom that is grounded in a relational notion of personhood rather than one that is relationless, autonomous, self-sufficient, and soliptistic. This is not sneaking religious convictions through the backdoor but, rather, communicating an understanding of what it means to be a person that resonates with other, non-Christian ontological commitments. As Hollenbach argues: "Such an appeal to religion in public life is not simply a ratification of secular values for reasons that are different than those proposed in secular discourse. It seeks to enrich and transform the vision of the human good that shapes our common life in a pluralistic society, without necessarily expecting a full-fledged religious conversion of members of that society."[57] It's a movement toward a natural law–like understanding of being human, but one that, by virtue of the diverse voices, is never reified or settled. It would be one that would always be tentative and contested, and, as such, subject to revision. It is also a notion that would allow a measure of acknowledgement of transcendence, of there being more than oneself, even if, paradoxically, it is a common good that is affirmed by those who deny the transcendent.

The single greatest challenge to Christians, especially Orthodox Christians, is to discern their own limits within a political community. Milbank is right in the sense that it is counterintuitive for one to be convinced of a particular understanding of the God-world relation and to settle for a good that appears less than divine-human communion. And, yet, that is exactly how Christians who have been convinced that they are created for divine-human communion are to be in the world. Christians must be aware that their aim in the political community is distinct though not separate from the ultimate aim. They must affirm a common good whose content is not identical with, though also not inconsistent with, their deepest convictions. For example, if civic-engagement-as-dialogue emerges from an embodied, historical, and materialist—that is, incarnational—Christian struggle toward communion with God, such an engagement must work toward, ironically, maximizing the conditions for the possibility of rejecting God; in fact, such engagement has such conditions as a presupposition. Christians would also have to resist such proclamations as the inherently Christian character of the United States of America: simply because demographically the U.S. began as a Christian nation does not mean it need always be. Similarly, a true Christian ascetical engagement would be in tune to the fear that public school prayer or religious symbols on public property may evoke in those who do not share such religious convictions. These are simple examples of how a Christian must accept certain restrictions within the public sphere that are not operative within a particular Christian community, and such restrictions are not imposed from the outside, but are logically entailed in the Christian principle of divine-human communion. A Christian can accept these restrictions positively even while apophatically realizing that the human can be more.

At the same time, Christians can positively shape the content of the common good in a way that would reinforce a democratic ethos of engagement. For example, they can argue that the notion of the common good in itself is not a threat to democracy, but necessary for its fulfillment. They can also argue that freedom and equality do not necessarily entail maximizing negative freedom. A Christian voice in the common good would ultimately move toward a communal notion of democracy without being communitarian, in other words, that democracy entails a commitment to certain communal values if it is to succeed. Such a commitment would mean a societal set of norms that would hold people and corporations accountable for the welfare of its citizens and not simply for maximizing self-interest. It would not allow, for example, the development of products that intentionally target teenagers without any care or concern for how they affect their well-being. It would also push public schools not to teach simply math, science, and so forth, but to incorporate programs that foster social bonds. At this point, the common retort is: who's to say? The simple answer is—no one group, institution, or citizen. As is commonplace in contemporary philosophy, it is a myth to think that the space of a democratic polity is morally neutral. Even the maximizing of self-interest is a moral position. It is not the case, however, that a morality maximizing self-interest, so long as it does not harm another citizen, is the only way to conceptualize the moral public space of democracy. Christians in their civic engagement on the content of the common good could not accept such a definition of the common good. Somewhat ironically, Milbank gives us some sense of what the common good would look like to Christians:

Today, then, we need to surpass liberal democracy and search again for the common good in ceaseless circulation and creative development, a search that may involve law, but more fundamentally involves charity beyond the law. . . . We should locate and form real groups pursuing real goods and exchanging real gifts among themselves and with each other according to measures judged to be intrinsically fair. We need to acknowledge the place and point of families, schools, localities, towns, associations for genuine production and trade (not the mere pursuit of profit), and transnational bodies. However, if we conceive this within immanence or theological voluntarism . . . then these groups will themselves be reduced to quasi-individual mutually contracting entities and we will be back in the empty liberal echo chamber.[58]

As I have argued, the common good by definition is a form of transcendence, even if affirmed on the ground of immanentist convictions, such as secular humanism. The greatest challenge for Christian participation in the debate on the common good is to always discern the difference between a political community and *ecclesia.*

Chapter Five

Truth-Telling, Political Forgiveness, and Free Speech

The previous chapters explored the implications of the principle of divine-human communion for Christian thinking on both the form of political community and the performance of Christian politics. Though still anchored in the principle of divine-human communion, this chapter will deal less with the form of political community and more with an issue that has received much attention of late: the role of forgiveness in politics. The debate about forgiveness in politics has something to do with democracy in the sense that its purpose is to effect a reconciliation among diverse peoples for the sake of these peoples occupying the same political space as equals. My concern is not with how forgiveness in politics facilitates democracy but on how the principle of divine-human communion can illuminate the attempts at political forgiveness.

The primary catalyst for this surge of interest in political forgiveness is, no doubt, the leading role Archbishop Desmond Tutu played in establishing the Truth and Reconciliation Commission (TRC) in post-apartheid South Africa. Tutu forcefully and persistently proclaimed that the only way to envision a virtually unthinkable future for a united South Africa that included both the oppressed and the oppressors, the majority black South Africans and the minority white Afrikaners, was through forgiveness.[1] The TRC was the institutional mechanism designed to mediate national forgiveness and reconciliation toward a democratic South Africa.

Despite this surge of interest, there has been relatively little theological reflection on forgiveness in politics in the past two decades.[2] Of the theological works that have been written on forgiveness, little, if any, attention has been given to the sacrament of confession that is practiced within the Roman Catholic and Orthodox traditions. Such lack of attention to this particular Christian practice is somewhat surprising, especially since it is ultimately tied to forgiveness. If, as I have been arguing in the previous chapters, an ascetics of divine-human communion is a politics, then the ascetical/sacramental practice of confession cannot be irrelevant to the debate about politics and forgiveness. My own angle, then, will be to illustrate what difference understanding forgiveness as an event of divine-human communion makes for thinking about political forgiveness. Before doing this, however, I must offer an interpretation of the Christian practice of confession that is less juridical and centered more on the act of truth-telling. What will initially seem like a digression is the necessary interpretive foundation for seeing what relevance the Christian ascetical/sacramental practice of confession has for current discussions on political forgiveness. I will end this chapter with some reflections on how the particular understanding of truth-telling I am offering in this chapter could inform a theological account of democratic free speech, one that focuses less on conscience and more on the capacity of truth-telling to form particular kinds of relationships.

Confession as Contractual

Although testimony to the confession of sins is present in the scriptures (for example, Ps 50/51 and James 5:16), the confession of sins as a liturgical practice and its identification as a sacrament devel-

oped over time within Christian history.[3] From a public act performed in the midst of the community, confession eventually became
a face-to-face encounter between the confessant and the spiritual
father, spiritual director, or priest. Over the course of time in the
Christian tradition a particular interpretation of the sacrament of
confession began to dominate—one that continues to hold our imagination today when we think about confession. This interpretation
often is referred to as the juridical and penitential understanding of
confession. This forensic understanding of confession reaches its
peak in the proliferation of the Penitentials in the Christian medieval
West.[4] This juridical, forensic understanding of confession also appears in the Christian East.[5]

The focus of such a legalistic understanding of confession is on
individual sins that preclude one's entrance into heaven. Sins were
catalogued according to type—venial and mortal—and penances were
constructed to correspond with the type and degree of severity of
the sin. Although pastoral in intent, confession within the framework
of the Penitentials resembled a sort of bargaining for what one could
give in exchange for erasing a particular debt, leading to the abuses
often associated with casuistry and the indulgences. The emphasis in
this particular understanding of confession is almost exclusively on
the act, which, if sinful, not only requires God's merciful forgiveness
but some sort of repayment to balance the scales of justice.

If one looks at the language of the Penitentials, there is a puzzling
tension that exists throughout the texts. Although the focus is on individual sins, the Penitentials also are replete with the language of
"healing." What the Penitentials do not seem to answer, however, is
why, in the act of authentic speaking, all one dreads to speak to a particular listener, say, a priest, actually leads to healing. One could argue
that truth-telling is required if the confessor is to administer the
proper penance tailored to the particular sins confessed. It would
make sense that if one were going to confession in order to fix the
sin, then the confessor could not help in this endeavor without knowing exactly the sin in question. Penances, however, were constructed
more to balance the effects of sin rather than to fix the sin. What is

also missing from this model is the transformative power of truth-telling; in other words, truth-telling is reduced to a precondition both for the advice/penance necessary to fix the sin and cancel its effects and for the conveying of forgiveness. There is no sense of the power of the speech act of truth-telling for the *experience* of forgiveness.

Truth-Telling as Communion

Grounded in the principle of divine-human communion, the emphasis in the sacrament of confession would be on the practice of truth-telling to a particular listener and not on the fulfillment of contractual conditions for forgiveness. The point of confession, or of any sacrament, is not a grace that is imputed to creation, nor is it something that boosts creation beyond its "natural" capacity. It is to experience God's very life that is present in and through created reality and, as such, is a presence that has visible material effects. Particular practices are sacramental insofar as there is a recognition that the divine is present in and through the practices. The capacity of such a presence to transform depends on the one performing the practice. The insight in naming confession as a sacrament is the recognition that such conversations, such forms of truth-telling, are more than small talk between two people. To identify this form of truth-telling as sacramental is to affirm the transformative power of such truth-telling. The transformation is such that it can only be identified as material realization of the divine presence—or, grace.

How, then, is truth-telling sacramental, that is, transformative of the created reality as the actualization of the divine presence within created reality? As a way of understanding how truth-telling in the sacrament of confession is sacramental, it would be helpful to analyze more general forms of truth-telling. All forms of truth-telling are revelatory, and some truths are more revelatory than others. When two people meet each other for the first time, usually nonthreatening but still revelatory information is exchanged, such as one's name, where one lives, one's profession.[6] If the information is mundane and nonthreatening, whatever is revealed allows for some kind of relationship to begin. One could say that some form of communication as revelation is conditional for a relationship between two people. The more one reveals conscious aspects of his narrative, the more the character of the relationship changes. We cannot really label a relationship as intimate if the only truths revealed are one's name and where one was born. Intimacy between two people is usually born when one's hopes, fears, and regrets are revealed. There is a reason why human beings fear the revelation of certain information, since some pieces of our story more than others have the power to affect how one is perceived by others. This phenomenology of truth-telling reveals how much humans are invested in what we project to others, and to ourselves, since it is often difficult to be truthful to ourselves about certain happenings in our lives; it is difficult to accept things one has done, that have been done to the confessant, or something with which the confessant is associated as truthful aspects of one's narrative. The fact that human beings fear to speak certain truths either to the self or to others manifests the power of some forms of truth-telling.

The power of truth-telling to effect a relationship of intimacy is implicit in the Christian claim of Jesus as the incarnate Word. As Logos, or Word of God, which was "with God" and "was God" (Jn 1:1), the person of Jesus is the revelation of all that God is. This spoken Word is irrevocable—God cannot take it back. In the person of Jesus, God reveals all that God is so as to effect a relationship of communion with the listener. But this relationship depends on how the listener reacts to the Word spoken. One can manipulate this Word to one's selfish advantage, or one can respond in such a way through practices that would actualize the potential of this spoken Word for a relationship of communion. Although Jesus did not "institute" the sacrament of confession, as has been taught, confession as a sacrament is implicit in the Christian affirmation of Jesus as the incarnate Word of God.

Truth-telling, then, is not neutral; once spoken, the truth is irrevocable and will affect the relationship either negatively or positively. Speaking truth is not simply stating a fact that does not have relational or affective consequences.[7] In discussing this project with a colleague, I imagined that it would be difficult for Sun-Kyung Cho to admit to anyone that she is the sister of Seung-Hui Cho, the Virginia Tech shooter. The colleague responded that it should not be difficult since telling such a truth is simply a fact. This example, however, makes it clear that telling the truth is not necessarily simply like stating a fact, such as "it is raining outside." Admitting to be a sister of a mass murderer is a kind of truth that is emotionally laden, in part because of the adverse affective effect it may have on particular forms of relations, be they work-related or more intimate friendships. A truth spoken can be manipulated against the person who spoke it, causing rupture in the relationship, and effecting an affective response in the truth-sayer that may range through sadness, anger, and fear of trusting. A truth is spoken often to create attention for the truth-sayer in the form of a response of pity. Truths, however, are also spoken for the sake of healing and for the sake of a relationship. Much depends, however, on the listener if the truth spoken is to have a healing effect, or if it is to effect a relationship of intimacy. If one speaks about the violence done to the self, such as rape, it is hard to imagine how a response to such a spoken truth that entails blaming the victim can in any way be healing; in fact, such a response would extend the violence in both time and space. How the spoken truth affects a relationship, and the kind of affectivity it provokes in the truth-sayer, will depend on how the listener responds.

The power of the spoken truth, both on the dynamics of the relationship and on the self of the truth-sayer, depends not simply on how the listener responds but on who the listener is, or the role of the listener. The kind of investment the listener has in the spoken truth depends on who the listener is to the truth-sayer. One could speak the truth anonymously on the internet; though there will be a listener to the spoken truth, the truth-sayer has no visible relationship to the listener, reducing the listener's power to affect the truth-sayer with the spoken truth. If the truth spoken is in the midst of a face-to-face encounter, then the truth-sayer must ultimately face the response of the listener and the affective effect that the listener's response may evoke. The type of affective effect will depend on who the listener is to the truth-sayer: one could say the exact same words to a parent, boss, psychotherapist, priest, or Jerry Springer, with the result being a different affective effect produced in the truth-sayer. Fear would accompany the speaking of certain truths, no matter to whom it is spoken, but how the spoken truth rebounds off the listener and affects the truth-sayer depends on the symbolic role the listener assumes for the listener. Not only does the emotional response of the truth-sayer in the midst of the truth-saying depend on the symbolic role of the listener, but the listener also may potentially affect what the truth-sayer desires. In short, spoken truth can affect the landscape of the self's emotions and desire, but this affective effect depends on both the response of and the symbolic role of the listener.

Several examples of truth-telling further illustrate the iconic role of the listener. As is well known, Alcoholics Anonymous (AA) is one of the most effective mechanisms for controlling the obsessive impulse for alcohol. Alcoholics will often say that alcoholism is a disease for which there is no cure; the most that one can achieve in AA is impulse control. It almost goes unnoticed that a particular kind of confession constitutes an essential condition for such impulse control, for a transformative affective effect. This impulse control, however, depends on the listener—a group of fellow alcoholics. Finally, the nature of the response of the group—a greeting, some sign of support, applause—further magnifies the iconic role of the listeners in AA. The AA experience does not quite fit Foucauldian categories. In one sense, Foucauldians might be suspicious of AA, since it categorizes alcoholism as a disease whose production of truth relies on an extracted confession. "I am an alcoholic" implies locating an essential truth behind the subject, revelation of something concealed, a reduction to an "isness." The classification of AA as a disease with no cure, however, suggests that truth-telling in AA does not identify an essential truth behind the human subject but, rather, reconfigures the balance of power within the affective landscape of the human subject. Confession to a specific listener in AA opens the human subject to a rearrangement of relations between conflicting desires and emotions; it enables a "way out," a freedom for different kinds of relations with other human beings.

An example of the polar opposite of the AA experience reflects further the importance of the iconic role of the listener for understanding the dynamics of power in acts of truth-telling. In August 2006, the *New York Times* ran a story entitled, "On the Web, Pedophiles Extend Their Reach." It reported on how the web is offering opportunities for the self-proclamation or confession of pedophilia. Pedophiles are finding groups of other pedophiles where they can speak of their impulses. Unlike AA, pedophiles find groups of pedophiles who, rather than holding a fellow pedophile accountable for this impulse, offer justifications and rationalizations. In the case of AA, fellow alcoholics reflect the implicit command: you need to control this impulse. In the case of pedophilia, fellow pedophiles convey the message: embrace it and don't be afraid to act on it. Such chilling online confessions follow: "My daughter and I have a healthy close relationship. . . . We have been in a 'consensual sexual relationship' almost two months now. . . . I am happy to find this site. . . . I thought having a sexual attraction to my daughter was bad. I now do not feel guilty or conflicted."[8]

Though achieving opposite results, the contrast between truth-telling in AA and the online confession between pedophiles reveals the iconic role of the listener in acts of truth-telling. This iconic role does not simply depend on the saying conveyed by the listener—advice, encouragement, acceptance. Both AA and online confessions of pedophiles evince that affective effect of the truth-telling of an alcoholic and a pedophile depends on to whom such a truth is spoken. In other words, for impulse control, an alcoholic confesses alcoholism to a group of self-professed alcoholics who consider alcoholism a disease; for guilt-free acceptance of impulse, a pedophile confesses to fellow self-accepting pedophiles. Indeed, it would be hard to imagine a pedophile getting such acceptance from other persons.

The link between truth-telling, truth, and power is vividly portrayed in Fyodor Dostoyevsky's *Crime and Punishment* between Raskolnikov and Sonya. I'm thinking in particular of the scene in part 5, when Raskolnikov desires to confess to Sonya that he killed Lizaveta, his former landlady. First of all, what should not go unnoticed is Dostoevsky's characteristically masterful description of the affectivity that surrounds this confession, before, during, and after the confession itself, both on the part of Raskolnikov and Sonya. Sonya embraces, both physically and metaphorically, Raskolnikov in all his brokenness, and this acceptance surprises Raskolnikov. "'So you won't leave me, Sonya?' he said; looking at her almost with hope. . . . 'No, no, never, not anywhere!' Sonya cried out. 'I'll follow you, I'll go wherever you go!'" Raskolnikov even acknowledges that once the words are spoken, Sonya has a certain power over him: he says, "This stupid triumph over me—what is it to you?" Raskolnikov tries to rationalize what he did, hoping secretly that Sonya will accept those rationalizations. But Sonya will have nothing of it. While communicating her love and acceptance of Raskolnikov, she stands firm in naming the truth of the situation to him: "And you killed, killed," she says, the whole time exhorting him to confess to the police and accept his suffering, even if that means her own separation from someone she loves. She says, "Accept suffering and redeem yourself by it, that's what you must do."[9] Sonya represents the truth of what he has confessed, but does so in such a way so as to enable a self-revelation as self-destruction for the reconstitution of self that entails a transformative affective effect, one that allows Raskolnikov to love, be loved, and allows others close to him to love. All this materializes at the end of the book:

> He always took her hand as if with loathing, always met her as if with vexation, was sometimes obstinately silent during the whole time of her visit. . . . But this time their hands did not separate; he glanced at her quickly and fleetingly, said nothing, and lowered his eyes to the ground. . . . How it happened he himself did not know, but suddenly it was as if something lifted him and flung him down at her feet. . . . She jumped and looked at him, trembling. But all at once, in that same moment, she understood, and for her there was no longer any doubt that he loved her, loved her infinitely, and that at last the moment had come. . . . But here begins a new account, the account of a man's gradual renewal, the account of his gradual

regeneration, his gradual transition from one world to another, his acquaintance with a new, hitherto completely unknown reality. It might make the subject of a new story—but our present story is ended.[10]

None of this transformation could have been enabled if confessed only to Porfiry, the examining magistrate; it could come about only if he confessed to Sonya. The particular affective effect depends on the uniqueness of the listener as potential iconic other.

It may appear on first read that Sonya calls upon Raskolnikov to confess because of concern for his immortality. The scene at the end of *Crime and Punishment* suggests that Dostoyevsky directs our attention away from the afterlife to the transformative potential of this life. Even if behind bars, Raskolnikov has never been freer as the recipient of the capacity to love and be loved. Raskolnikov has managed to reinvent himself through confession to Sonya, who iconically represents and speaks what Dostoyevsky sees as the Christian truth about God as love, that is, the truth of divine-human communion.

Psychoanalytic theory recognizes the symbolic role of the listener in the dynamic of transference and countertransference between the analyst and analysand. From a Lacanian perspective, the conversation between an analyst and an analysand occurs on the premise of a split between the conscious and unconscious self. Lacan identifies the conscious self with the ego, and further links the ego to the imaginary register. Breaking with ego psychology, the ego, according to Lacan, constructs false notions of coherence and completion, concealing the fundamental split within the subject. Analysis cuts through those ego constructions in order to reveal a deeper, unconscious structure constituting the subject. Relevant to our discussion is the role of the analyst; according to Lacan, the analyst must not relate to the analysand as an observing ego. To do so would only enable the analysand to replace one false ego construction with another, perhaps that of the analyst. In order to cut through false ego constructions, the analyst must assume the role of the Other of the unconscious. It is only as Other that the analyst can speak in such a way that penetrates beyond what the analysand says of himself on the level of the imaginary, that is, as ego, to the place of the unconscious, the Other. In Lacan's words, "It is therefore because of what the subject imputes the analyst to be (his being being elsewhere) that an interpretation may come back to the place from which it can bear upon the distribution of responses."[11] Interpreting "The Direction of the Treatment," Bruce Fink amplifies: "the analyst's overall strategy remains the same: to situate herself in the analysis not as an ego but as the Other."[12]

Theologically, there are several elements in the thought of Dionysius the Areopagite that may be useful for clarifying the dynamics of acts of truth-telling in the midst of a listener. The first is his description of the Christian life in terms of desire for and union with God. In the *Divine Names,* he tells us, "And so it is that all things must desire, must yearn for, must love, the Beautiful and the Good" (4.10).[13] But this created desire has as its source a prior desire of God for that which is other than God. Dionysius continues: "And we may be so bold as to claim also that the Cause of all things loves all things in the superabundance of his goodness, that because of this goodness he makes all things, brings all things to perfection, holds all things together, returns all things. The diving longing is Good seeking good for the sake of the Good," or as Bernard McGinn translates, "Divine Eros is the Good of the Good and for the sake of the Good" (4.10).[14] This mutual desire is mediated symbolically, according to Dionysius. In other words, symbols mediate the divine eros for creation, and in so doing, evoke a greater, deeper, and more inflamed desire for God. Notwithstanding the fact that all symbols are inadequate for mediating the divine presence, not all symbols mediate this presence in the same way or to the same degree. Dionysius asks, "Is it not closer to reality to say that God is life and goodness rather than that he is air or stone?" (*The Mystical Theology* 3).[15] This is not to say that a stone could not mediate the divine presence, but, Dionysius would argue, it could not to the degree possible in the contemplation on the conceptual symbols of "life" or "goodness." The path to an increased desire for God is a path through more appropriate symbols that have the capacity to evoke a greater and deeper desire for God. The link between desire and symbol, I would argue, is present throughout the entire Dionysian corpus.

What Dionysius helps us to see is that though all material objects have the capacity to mediate divine presence—the Good and the Beautiful—not all do so to the same degree. A living human being can mediate the divine presence in a way that the rock cannot. The final building block that may give us a clearer picture of the puzzle between confession and desire is the notion of the icon. According to Jean-Luc Marion, the icon is different from the idol. For Marion, the idol is the "gaze's landing place," such that "[t]he idol thus acts as a mirror, not as a portrait: a mirror that reflects the gaze's image, or more exactly, the image of its aim and of the scope of that aim. The idol, as a function of the gaze, reflects the gaze's scope."[16] As a result, Marion adds, "the idol consigns the divine to the measure of a human gaze."[17] In short, for Marion an idol is a concept of the divine whose meaning is determined or given by the subject's intentionality. By contrast, the icon, for Marion following Levinas, effects a reversal of intentionality. According to Marion, "the icon does not result from a vision but provokes one." He adds that "in the idol, the gaze of man is frozen in its mirror; in the icon, the gaze of man is lost in the invisible gaze that visibly envisages him. . . . What characterizes the material idol is precisely that the artist can consign to it the subjugating brilliance of a first visible; on the contrary, what characterizes the icon painted on wood does not come from the hand of a man but from the infinite depth that crosses it—or better, orients it following the intention of a gaze."[18] More recently, Marion associates the icon phenomenologically with the "saturated phenomenon," which "exerts its own gaze over that which meets it. The gazer takes the place of the gazed upon; the manifested phenomenon is reversed into a manifestation not only in and of itself, but strictly by and on the basis of itself."[19] For Marion, in and through the icon, the phenomenon gives itself to be received, and it is in such a reception that the receiver is constituted as an "I," as a subject, as the gifted.

What Marion helps us to conceptualize is that in the encounter between the truth-sayer and the listener, there exists the possibility for the confessee to be "gifted," to be subjectified, to receive an "I" in and through the gaze opened up through the presence of the listener as icon. The measure of this subjectification is the transformation of the landscape of one's emotions and desires. What Marion also helps us to see is that such a phenomenon may be "saturated," meaning, as I understand him, that it is such that it exceeds any human intentionality. No words, interpretation, or meanings would ever be adequate to the phenomenon itself. What's problematic in Marion is that he gives the impression that the subject encountering the icon as saturated phenomenon is simply passive.

In a recent book, *The Dwelling of the Light: Praying with Icons of Christ,* Rowan Williams reminds us that icons themselves are not simply given, but are "actions that seek to be open to God's action . . . in the hope not that you will produce a striking visual image but that your work will open a gateway for God."[20] He continues, "In the icon, what you see is human beings and situations as they are in the light of God's action. . . . And you need to look and pray with that in mind, to look patiently and not analytically, and allow yourself to be 'worked on'—perhaps we should say, allow yourself to be looked at by God, rather than just looking at something yourself."[21] He adds that reverence is given to icons not "because the icons are seen as magical objects but because in their presence you become aware that you are present to God and that God is working on you by his grace."[22] In this more theological account of icon, the subject is not simply a passive recipient. The "action" of the subject is as essential to constituting the icon as the icon is to constituting the subject as an "I." In some sense, the power of the icon to be that in and through which God acts depends on the action of the subject in relation to the icon.

In the act of truth-saying, then, the saying of the truth is not neutral because the listener is not neutral; the listener assumes a symbolic role to the truth-sayer that will affect the way in which the spoken truth will rebound back to the truth-sayer. Speaking a truth one fears to speak to a rock, anonymously on the internet, or in the privacy of one's room will have a different affective effect than when speaking face-to-face to another human being. Confessing that one is an alcoholic will rebound back to the truth-sayer in a way that is different if said to a nonalcoholic friend or to an alcoholic. The affective response produced in the truth-saying will depend on what the listener symbolizes to the truth-sayer. Again, the truth-sayer could speak the exact same truth to many different people who assume distinct symbolic roles to the truth-sayer and feel differently each time the truth is spoken.

Let us return to the sacrament of confession. What is being recognized theologically is that the human being as *image of God* is a potential conduit for the presence of God to the other. The speech act of truth-telling actualizes the power of this image in a particular way; all human beings are potential confessors and, as such, potentially iconic images of the presence of God. What is also being claimed is that those who assume some form of leadership role within the community potentially symbolize the presence of God in ways that are distinct from those human beings who do not assume such roles. Leaders of monastic communities, both male and female, as well as priests, by virtue of their position symbolize God in a way that is distinctive from other human beings. With that said, human beings do not assume a neutral role to other humans—they are friends, parents, partners, spouses, strangers, therapists, and so on. By virtue of their role in a community, priests or monastics, both abbots and abbesses,[23] those who usually hear confessions in the Orthodox tradition, cannot but symbolize God in ways that, minimally, are distinct from a friend, parent, or psychotherapist.

In the context of confession, the confessor is constituted as an icon in and through the speech act; the act of truth-telling invests the confessor with the power to be iconic, to be the one in and through whom God acts, in and through whom God bestows, in a word, grace. The transformation of the landscape of one's emotions and desires that occurs through acts of truth-telling are moments of God's grace, which should not be understood as magical acts. Rather, the grace given is a gifted—not in one's control—increase in desire for God evoked through a personal encounter with the good and the beautiful, that is, with the gaze of the personal God mediated through the confessor. Getting back to Dionysius, a stone cannot mediate such a personal encounter with a personal God as a human being can, and, all things being equal, not all humans can mediate such an encounter to the same degree and intensity. I would, however, qualify this statement. Much does depend on context and character. Given this, a rock can, in fact, mediate the divine goodness and beauty to a greater degree than a manipulative religious representative. Religious representatives can also define the space of the spoken word of confession in a way that does not fill it with goodness or beauty, but with their opposites. But in the midst of religious representatives who are aware of their symbolic power and assume it with responsibility and integrity, then the religious representatives by virtue of their role have the capacity to mediate a divine presence to a greater degree than a rock. In confession, much depends on the character of the listener, but, as Dionysius makes clear, certain symbols, by virtue of what or who they are, have the capacity to mediate the divine to a greater degree than others.

Forgiveness as Communion

The phenomenology of truth-telling to another human being reveals that the sacrament of confession as *sacrament* is more than simply an imputation of forgiveness based on a contractual obligation of confessing one's sin, an obligation established by Jesus's decree to the apostles. Identifying truth-telling to a priest as a sacrament is a recognition that speaking the truth of one's sins—of the wrongs one has committed, which one fears to speak and own as part of one's narrative—to a priest is more than a contractual obligation that maintains distance between the confessant, confessor, and God. What the truth-saying enables is an event of communion between the confessant and God mediated through the priest, to the degree to which the priest by virtue of his role within a community is able to do.[24] If, in fact, certain truths spoken enable communion between two human beings, then the same must be true when it comes to the human relation to God. This communion, however, cannot be symbolically mediated if one were to speak such truths in the privacy of one's room; since God is invisible, the kind of communion that speaking truth to God can effect must be iconically mediated through human beings and, in its intensity, through the religious representative of the community—the priest or monastic.

Truth-telling to a priest or monastic thus empowers him to function as an icon mediating forgiveness as an experience of communion between God and the confessant. The sacrament of confession is the opportunity to experience the always forgiving God as God's loving presence, as God's very life. If the sacrament of confession is seen within the framework of ascetical practices, then it is one practice among many that can potentially realize the presence of God as gift and grace; the speaking of truth is a practice that cuts through the false projections of ego to allow the true self to emerge. It is in truth that the self meets God, or where the self discovers the truth of God. Such a presence is not claimed or earned but noticed, most especially in terms of how one feels and what one desires. Forgiveness, then, is not simply a matter of cognitive certainty but an affective realization the measure of which is how one feels and desires in relation to oneself and to others. This experience of forgiveness is embodied insofar as it involves an affective response where one does not negate the fact that what one has done is a sin, but in which the sin is not allowed to corrode the sense of self in a pool of guilt, shame, and self-loathing. Forgiveness as communion is knowing that one is not reduced to the sin and is loved by God in spite of the sin, and that one's uniqueness in relation to God is not eviscerated because of the sin. A genuine communion with God cannot but affect the desires of the confessant; the measure of a true communion with God is what one desires and the capacity to resist impulses that would threaten communion with God. Confession, however, should not be interpreted as a magical formula: confess and witness the transformation. Such a realization of forgiveness can be mediated iconically through the priest or monastic in response to the truth-telling of one's sins. If it were not for the possibility of this iconic mediation, then all one has is the guarantee of

God's forgiveness without the experience of God's forgiveness as God's loving presence.

Theologically, such an understanding of the sacrament of confession that focuses on the communion enabled through truth-telling has several implications for the understanding of forgiveness. First, God's forgiveness is neither contractual nor imputed, but is the self-communication of God iconically realized through the human image, and intensely in the priest or monastic. The measure of forgiveness is not a checklist of conditions but the markers of communion, which are embodied—volitional, cognitive, and affective.[25] Any sin committed has need of God's forgiveness, and the iconic role of the priest or monastic is as close as one can possibly get to face-to-face with God. But coming face-to-face with God does not mean that the wrongdoer does not have to face the victim. The wrongdoer's felt need to ask the victim for forgiveness is a manifestation of some measure of communion with God insofar as the wrongdoer sees how he has wronged the victim; he must see the truth of the situation. The wrongdoer's asking of forgiveness is then the condition for the possibility for a different relationship between the wrongdoer and the victim, a relationship of communion. If the sin committed effected division and distance between two people, then forgiveness is the movement toward unity-in-difference, an overcoming of the effects of sin without negating the sin. In the end, communion between two people is simultaneously a communion with God and, thus, a presence of divine-human communion. Such a communion can only be actualized through certain practices, such as truth-telling, and iconically mediated.

Forgiveness, then, is a response to moral wrongdoing and not just a transformation of feeling, emotions, or desires on the part of the forgiver. As a response to the moral wrongdoing, its goal is transformation not simply of the wrongdoer but of "the moral transformation of human relationships and society," especially that between the wrongdoer and the victim.[26] Clarification is especially important here: it could be that the wrongdoer and the victim never had a relationship prior to the wrongdoing; it is also misleading when talking about forgiveness as communion to conclude that the victim is obligated to

forgive for the sake of communion. A relationship of communion between two people cannot be forced and is not a matter of obligation; it
is an event realized through practices. Although it seems impossible
to imagine communion resulting from certain forms of wrongdoing,
such as torture, not to imagine such a communion would be to on-
tologize sin and evil, to give them the last word. Notwithstanding the
essential need for recovery, by not seeing forgiveness as communion,
the focus would be only on the recovery of the victim; grace would be
exclusively about the victim's healing.[27] If sin inevitably effects a certain kind of relationship, even one of distance, division, and destruction, then the overcoming of sin must extend to the entirety of the
relationship. Communion is the antithesis of sin, and forgiveness as
communion not only declares that sin does not have the final word
but that the movement from sin could be communion. Again, clarity
is necessary so that there be no misunderstanding: to say that one
outcome of sin can be communion is not to say that sin is good, or
necessary, or desired; it is also not to imply that the victim has some
obligation to restore the relationship effected by sin. To talk about sin
and restoration in terms of obligation is to interpret the dynamic of
sin and forgiveness within a juridical framework. In the language of
divine-human communion, the effects of sin become part of the spiritual struggle of both the victim and the perpetrator. The outcome
of that spiritual struggle could be a relationship of communion between the perpetrator and the victim, which one might call the fullness of forgiveness. Forgiveness is a movement and a process that
involves the wrongdoer's and victim's relation to self as much as their
relation to each other.

Although forgiveness is a response to moral wrongdoing, it would
be a mistake to minimize or eliminate the affective component to the
event of forgiveness.[28] Part of the wrongdoing that forgiveness is addressing as process and spiritual struggle is the affectivity involved
and effected by sin. To stress the affective dimension of forgiveness is
not necessarily to reduce forgiveness to a solipsistic obsession with
the self. If there is to be a moral transformation in the relationship of
wrongdoer and victim that exists as communion-as-gift, then it is
hard to imagine such an event without an affective dimension. On the

part of the wrongdoer, there is indifference and callousness, possibly hatred, in relation to the victim that leads to the objectification of the victim, the complete and utter lack of consciousness of the humanity of the victim. On the part of the victim, sin effects a range of emotions and desires such as hatred, rage, anger, fear, mistrust, frustration, sadness, hopelessness, surrender, and anxiety. It can lead to destructive impulses as a way of repressing all the negative emotions that can accompany the being-sinned-against. The insidious injustice of sin is that it can damage and sunder the self's experience of all that is good, even though the victim is not to blame. The wrongdoing, then, that forgiveness addresses is the affectivity that shapes the relationship and both the wrongdoer's and victim's sense of self.

If forgiveness can be an event of communion, then forgiveness by the victim cannot simply be volitional or cognitive. To say that the conditions for forgiveness are met if the victim commits to foreswearing resentment is to reduce forgiveness to a particular act.[29] The inevitable question is that if the conditions for forgiveness on the part of the forgiver are met by the commitment to foreswear resentment, what does one call the eventual elimination of resentment— forgiveness plus? It is hard to imagine that one has truly forgiven the wrongdoer if one continues to harbor feelings of hatred, anger, and resentment toward the wrongdoer. One could cognitively know that forgiveness is an obligation, and then will oneself to forgive out of obligation, even will oneself to relate to the wrongdoer, but the hatred, anger, and resentment indicates that the victim still sees the wrongdoer *primarily* as the one who did this wrongdoing that is part of the victim's narrative. Forgiveness is not about forgetting that the wrongdoer did this wrongdoing, but is to see the wrongdoer as more than this wrongdoing, and only in this kind of seeing is a relation of communion possible. Again, it is misleading to ask if the victim is obligated to relate to the wrongdoer in this way; it is not a matter of obligation but about what's possible in the victim's spiritual struggle in relation to God and to the wrongdoer. What's possible is a communion with the wrongdoer that is simultaneously a manifestation of divine-human communion.

The problem with those, on the one hand, who strictly identify forgiveness with the victim's emotion and those, on the other hand, who reject this definition of forgiveness, is that they both forget the affectivity of the wrongdoer. The wrongdoer could be motivated to ask for forgiveness for a variety of reasons—to reduce the sentence for a crime, perhaps, or to avoid going to hell in the afterlife. In the Christian tradition, it is often claimed that forgiveness is granted only with true repentance. The latter, however, cannot be willed but must be realized or gifted, and the markers for repentance are the affectivity directed to the wrongdoing and the victim. The Orthodox monastic tradition speaks of the "tears of repentance," and there exist prayers throughout the Orthodox liturgical tradition that such tears be "given," implying that there cannot be true repentance without remorse, regret, and sadness. That emotional state of being usually entails a nonobjectification of the victim and a seeing of the effects of the wrongdoing on the victim. It may even involve an empathy on the part of the wrongdoer—an imaginary identification of all that the victim may be feeling and thinking. Although the event of forgiveness may mitigate remorse, regret, and sadness, it does not entail eliminating these feelings. On the part of the wrongdoer, to seek forgiveness and to be forgiven could entail a renewed sense of self-worth that does not reduce the wrongdoer to the wrongdoing, that grants the wrongdoer the capacity to be loved and to love, but this transformation can coexist with the regret that the wrongdoing ever happened, that it is a part of the wrongdoer's and the victim's narrative, even if the wrongdoing is what led to the transformation of the wrongdoer.

Although the effects of sin can be overcome, and sin does not have the final word, the event of sin is eternal in the sense that it is forever a part of one's unique story and narrative. Forgiveness, then, cannot mean forgetting a sin, as Miroslav Volf has argued, but a new kind of memory of the sin.[30] Even if the victim and the wrongdoer act *as if* the sin did not occur, this only means that the sin itself is remembered differently. Forgiveness is a new kind of memory of the past event, one that does not function as an obstacle for communion between two persons. While I understand that the argument that forgetting may be necessary to move on, psychoanalytic theory reminds us that this moving on is probably a result of repression more than forgetting. Repressed memory is not the basis for forgiveness as communion.

Insofar as forgiveness allows for a new kind of memory of the wrongdoing, it is *the* Christian response to evil. Forgiveness is not a theodicy in the sense of justifying the goodness of God in the midst of the presence of evil in the world. Forgiveness allows evil to exist as such without justification. For example, if an alcoholic were to kill a child, the death of that child would exist as an eternal absence in the life of the parent. Nothing could make up for that unique absence. Theodicy-like justifications for the goodness of God in spite of evil in the world have the tendency to mitigate the unique irredeemability of such an absence. Forgiveness as communion indicates that the Christian answer to evil is not a theodicy but a response. The fact that, in many situations, the dead are not present to forgive only points to an eschatological resolution that engenders hope without mitigating the unique irredeemability of the absence of those wronged. Failed forgiveness or impossible forgiveness does not detract from the claim that forgiveness is the only way to avoid the ontologizing of sin and evil.

Jacques Derrida is, then, correct in asserting that forgiveness is impossible, insofar as the target of forgiveness is what cannot be forgotten, redeemed, or undone.[31] Derrida's critique, however, proceeds on an understanding of Christian or religious forgiveness that does not assume divine-human communion. Derrida presumes a model in which there is the forgiver and the one being forgiven over-and-against each other. The forgiver forgives the wrongdoer either when the wrongdoer expresses remorse, in other words, conditionally, which is not real forgiveness but an economic exchange; or the forgiver forgives unconditionally, without any repentance from the wrongdoer. But, for Derrida, unconditional forgiveness is only possible if the wrongdoer continues to do violence against the victim, which the victim always forgives. The impossibility of forgiveness in Derridean terms presupposes that forgiveness is a relationship of distance between the wrongdoer and victim in which there is either a mutual or one-sided response to the act done against the victim. Understood in terms of an event of communion, the language of conditionality and unconditionality appears not to fit. The goal is not necessarily an exchange, but a state of being; affectivity is not exchanged or willed as much as recognized and, thus, gifted; the act is neither undone, forgotten, redeemed nor repaid, but no longer an obstacle for a certain kind of relationship. Derrida could retort that communion as event between persons is an exchange, but there is a difference between exchange and engaging in a set of practices that allows one to arrive at a state of being in relation to another that one simply recognizes is the case. In forgiveness as communion one, indeed, is to the other in a certain way, but one is not to the other only *because* the other is a certain way.

Forgiveness, then, is not a volitional act but an event grounded in a state of being. In the Orthodox tradition, if the goal is a divine-human communion that is realized in Christ and made possible through Christ in the Holy Spirit, and if the movement toward such a communion is through particular practices, then one of the markers of spiritual progress is a person's capacity to forgive. Movement toward divine-human communion is to become godlike and, as such, to be forgiving. One could say that forgiveness is a virtue acquired, or one of the virtues that one hopes to acquire, through the spiritual struggle to be in communion with God. Forgiveness is not simply a volitional act that one wills in spite of one's emotions and desires: forgiveness comes because one is forgiving, which entails a seeing of the wrongdoing in light of the larger whole, of seeing the wrongdoer as more than the wrongdoing, as seeing the self as not defined by the wrongdoing, as an emotional state that is not dictated by the wrongdoing, and as desiring a relationship of communion in spite of the sin. In the spiritual movement toward God, one does not wait to grant forgiveness in response to a wrongdoing; one struggles to *be* forgiving and, in so doing, to see the whole and all the particulars within it as God sees it. It's difficult to know if one really is forgiving until something happens to a person; even then, some wrongdoings are more easily forgiven than others. The wrongdoing itself could provoke the spiritual struggle to forgive in a way not possible without the wrongdoing. It is possible, however, to also form one's life in a way that one finds oneself forgiving in the face of a wrongdoing. This formation is cognitive insofar as forgiving is a knowing of the wrongdoing in a particular way; it is also affective insofar as it, again, involves both an emotional state of being not dictated by the wrongdoing and a desire for a relationship of communion with the wrongdoer.

Forgiveness and Politics

As an event of communion, forgiveness requires a face-to-face encounter. It is certainly possible for the victim to forgive the wrongdoer even absent the repentance of the wrongdoer, or if the wrongdoer has died, but without a face-to-face encounter, forgiveness cannot be all that it can be as communion. What the sacrament of confession makes clear, understood in terms of divine-human communion, is that truth-telling in a face-to-face encounter can actualize a communion between God and the self mediated iconically through the priest and monastic; in a similar way, truth-telling can potentially actualize a communion between two people in the face-to-face encounter. What face-to-face truth-telling empowers is the iconic capacity of the face, as well as of the person.

If communion is all that forgiveness can be, then it appears that forgiveness in politics is an oxymoron. Political forgiveness can mean many things: forgiveness of perpetrators of crimes for political reasons; forgiveness between groups within a particular nation at conflict with one another; forgiveness between nations for past conflicts. How can one speak of communion between nations, especially since the very category of "nation" is itself contestable? How can one speak of communion between groups if there is no face-to-face between groups? Is forgiveness as communion really actualized if the vehicle of forgiveness is the impersonal mechanism of a commission?

If forgiveness as communion involves the cognitive and affective states of being of both the forgiver and the forgiven, then such a forgiveness is impossible between nations or groups. And yet, there have been public expressions of sorrow, regret, and apology from groups to groups—from one nation to another, from institutions to ethnic groups, and from institutional churches to other churches, to name a few of the most recent expressions. Although I have argued that Griswold's discussion of forgiveness in terms of meeting conditions is misleading, he is correct in saying that such public expressions of apology from groups to other groups cannot meet the conditions of forgiveness. Such public expressions are better named something other than forgiveness, such as apology or "quasi-forgiveness,"[32] even if they have elements of forgiveness, or look like forgiveness in some form, such as reconciliation.

In some sense, understanding forgiveness in terms of communion highlights the distinctiveness of a political community as a kind of community not meant to facilitate communion.[33] However, instead of asserting that communion and political community are mutually exclusive, perhaps it's better to see the relation in terms of degree—some forms of political community mirror communion to a greater or lesser degree than others, with those that allow for a greater measure of truth-telling mirroring communion to a greater degree. It is difficult to imagine how nations or particular ethnic groups can forgive each other and do so in a way that would realize an event of communion.[34] With that said, I would say that understanding the relation between forgiveness, truth-telling, and communion can still be illuminative in the politics of reconciliation and peace.

First, I have been attempting to suggest that a dynamic between truth-telling, affectivity, and communion depends on the role of the symbolic other. In the area of ethnic conflict, it is remarkable how effective for reconciliation and peace an apology can be when given from one who unequivocally represents a particular ethnic or religious group.[35] This was demonstrated quite powerfully when Pope John Paul II visited Greece and apologized to the Archbishop of Athens and of all Greece, Christodoulos, for the Roman Catholic Church's role in the Fourth Crusade. I would argue that the moment had an affective impact enabled by the symbolic roles assumed by Christodoulos and John Paul II, which facilitated a movement toward communion between the two churches. This communion has palpable signs both in the visit of Archbishop Christodoulos to Rome and in the cooperation, even if informal, between the churches of Greece and Rome toward opposing European secularization. Since the visit of John Paul II, the official website of the Church of Greece has posted papal pronouncements of the relation of Christianity to Europe, recognizing a common cause between the two churches but also tacitly recognizing the influence of the papal voice on issues related to the relation between Christianity and Europe.

Without living it, it is difficult to describe the deep-rooted suspicion that Orthodox harbor toward the papacy in particular. First, the Orthodox have never forgotten the crusades, which means that much of their own identity is based on this opposition to the Roman Catholics who attempted through subterfuge to conquer the most important city in Orthodoxy and, in so doing, laid the foundations for the fall of the Byzantine Empire. One could say that the Orthodox should just get over something that happened about eight hundred years ago, but such an attitude does not get how events like the crusades can solidify group identities as that against which such an injustice occurred; it also ignores how events in history, both triumphant and tragic, constitute group identities and, by extension, personal identities. By virtue of being related to a group, a person is emotionally invested in the aspects of the group's narrative that are constitutive for this identity. It is real people within the group that feel real anger and rage at the pope and Roman Catholics for something for which the current pope and Roman Catholics bear no responsibility but are associated with by virtue of their position. Injustice has a symbolic history, and it is only through the symbolism of the papacy that the negative affective attitude toward Roman Catholics, which almost seems to entail what it means to be Orthodox, can end. Put another way, it is remarkable how an apology from the pope, the one who unequivocally represents all Roman Catholics, can affect the emotional attitude of individual Orthodox Christians in such a way that does not constitute communion, but enables a movement toward communion between Orthodox and Roman Catholics. In the midst of the truth-telling about the Roman Catholic Church's role in the crusades, the symbolic presence of leaders of these groups evokes an affective response that enables better relations between the groups. After such an apology, it is difficult for Orthodox to self-identify against the Roman Catholic Church on the basis of their role in the crusades. Instead of self-opposition against the other, a more positive self-identification is possible in relation to the other.

On more of an ethnic terrain, it is the case that individual Greeks and Turks get along fine, but there is still anger, resentment, and fear on the part of Greeks toward Turkish aggression. Even new generations of Greeks both within Greece and in the Diaspora, who were not direct victims of the Ottoman oppression, or the ethnic-cleansing of Greeks from Istanbul in the 1950s, still base their identity on that history. Every March 25, the anniversary for Greek Independence Day, Greek-Americans around the country march in parades, perform plays, and recite poems recalling Turkish oppression. Victimization by the Turks became central to the modern Greek identity. An apology from the prime minister of Turkey, one who symbolizes authoritatively all Turks, would further reconciliation and peace between Greece and Turkey because it would effect an affective response that an apology from an individual Turk—such as a public intellectual—could not evoke.

There can, thus, be no forgiveness as communion between groups, but public expressions of apologies by symbolic leaders of these groups for injustices committed centuries ago can have a powerful affective effect on the individual members of a group, symbolically represented by their own leader, in a way that would affect how individual members of these groups relate to each other in the future. In and through the symbols, the truth-telling penetrates into the very psyche and sense of identity of group members enabling different kinds of relationships. This is not forgiveness per se, but something like forgiveness in the sense of the dynamic between truth-telling, symbol, and affectivity.[36]

I also think that the dynamic between truth-telling, affectivity, and symbol can help illuminate the limited success of truth and reconciliation commissions. Even though there have been many different kinds of truth commissions, and, as Priscilla Hayner has shown, the success of such commissions varies, the impulse that reconciliation requires a spoken truth is correct.[37] Hayner has shown that there is no formula that speaking truth leads necessarily to reconciliation. What such commissions provide, I think, is a kind of symbolic space that allows for particular forms of truth-telling to lead to reconciliation; put another way, it allows for particular forms of truth-telling to move away affective obstacles to reconciliation. Hayner also shows that the establishment of such truth commissions makes possible moments of interpersonal forgiveness that I am characterizing as communion.

I think one of the more interesting avenues of exploration suggested by the dynamic of truth-telling, affectivity, and forgiveness is the relation between affectivity and narrative. I find it worth exploring how the simple recognition of a wrongdoing as part of a narrative, both the perpetrator's and the victim's, can result in dissipating affective roadblocks to reconciliation, or even communion. National and ethnic identities are often grounded on an event or events that are not recognized by the other responsible for the event, even if it is a centuries-old event. I wonder what impact recognition of that previously nonrecognized would have on such national and ethnic identities? Why would such recognition have the potential for a new narrative of reconciliation? In the end, the question that I have is whether there is a relation between truth-telling, narrative, forgiveness, affectivity, and communion.

And there are more questions that could be raised, such as what it means to talk about forgiveness and politics for generations of ethnic groups far removed from the actual event. I want to suggest that the understanding of forgiveness as an event of communion, one realized through the affective impact of a form of truth-telling to a symbolic other, means that to speak of forgiveness in politics would diminish all that forgiveness can be, since there can be no such communion in political community. The understanding of the dynamic between truth-telling, affectivity, narrative, symbol, forgiveness, and, finally, communion, can illuminate why forms of truth-telling can be effective in moving political communities toward reconciliation and peace, which are not the same as communion. It can also explain why those political communities that allow for the speaking of truth mirror communion to a greater degree than those political communities that stake their existence on the suppression of the truth.

Addendum: Reflections on Confession, Free Speech, and Democracy

An unquestioned axiom for democracy is free speech. Democracies have debated who gets and what counts as free speech, but the so-called "rule of the people" takes as axiomatic that the voice of the people will shape and influence government—that the people will in some way participate in governing. Discussions on free speech and democracy often speak of free speech as an inalienable human right that no governing body can restrict unless it serves the purpose of furthering democracy. Free speech, then, is not unlimited; libel and threats to murder someone do not count as free speech, for example. Usually the first warning signs of a threat to a democracy are restrictions on free speech by the government, and the first sign of an emerging democracy is the range of free speech that is allowed.

Free speech is almost always discussed in terms of a negative freedom: a person can speak freely without fear of punishment by the governing body. What receives little, if any, comment is how free speech structures the way citizens of a political community relate to each other. The effect of free speech on how citizens relate to each other is made clear by looking at political communities where free speech is not axiomatic, and possibly dangerous. The most obvious example is the lack of free speech in former Communist countries, most of which were policed by agencies, such as the KGB and the Stasi, who spied not simply in other countries or on foreigners in their home countries, but on their own citizens. As chillingly dramatized in the film *The Lives of Others,* this policing of speech created a situation where citizens feared to speak any truth to other citizens, but also to friends and to family members. Within such societies, the possibility for manipulating the spoken word against the truth-teller was maximized; there was limited possibility for relationships of trust and, hence, vulnerability and intimacy. In short, there was limited capacity for communion within such societies in which free speech was not simply suppressed but actively policed. It is difficult to imagine growing up in a society in which you are socialized not to trust anyone because you may not be sure if your brother, uncle, childhood friend, doctor, is a Stasi agent. Every listener symbolizes the terror of the state, evoking, ultimately, fear in speaking any kind of truth. Vulnerability and trust in the form of free speech could mean imprisonment, torture, and death.

Minimally, then, in a political community where free speech is allowed and not restricted on the basis of gender, race, ethnicity, or religious conviction, certain kinds of relationships are more possible than in KGB-like societies. There may be many reasons that one may not speak truthfully to a neighbor, friend, parent, sibling, doctor, but fear of imprisonment would not be one of them. In making such a claim, I am not naively overlooking the fact that in modern democracies there has always existed surveillance and policing of speech. Since the terrorist attacks on September 11, there has been a vigorous debate on the government's right to police speech and provoke speech through torture for the sake of protecting the democracy. The U.S. government's legitimization of policing speech that threatens the state looks strikingly and eerily similar to Communist justifications for policing speech. The difference between American democracy and Communist regimes is that the language of human rights and free speech are presupposed in American democracy, even if not clearly defined. American democracy has been and will continue to be a tradition of debate on the content of human rights and the norms of free speech. Within American democracy there exists a mechanism for subverting government restrictions of free speech that do not cohere with the logic of democratic principles. Government has to

justify restrictions on free speech in a way absent in Communist regimes, and in a way that manifestly serves to advance democratic
principles. Again, to claim that free speech exists to a greater degree
in democratic states than in Communist regimes is not to naively
mask the abuses of power within democratic states in relation to free
speech. In democratic regimes, however, to take but one example,
governments are parodied in a variety of forms in a way that is simply
unthinkable in Communist states. Democratic states have traditions
of contestation on the limits of free speech and, as such, allow for a
degree of free speech that enables relationships of trust and intimacy;
the capacity for the latter are, at the very least, mitigated in totalitarian
regimes.

The paradox of the United States is that although truthful speech
enables relationships of communion, American democracy has been
accused of excessive individualism and enabling enclaves of self-
interest. Although there is a communitarian form for understanding
democracy, talk of communitarian ideals as necessary for protecting
democratic individualism is often met with suspicion that a particular
value system is being imposed both culturally and politically. The defense of free speech as an individual right is, for the most part, unhinged from any effects that free speech has on relationships between
citizens. And, clearly, free speech does affect relationships between
citizens, even if it is not truthful speech. Free speech can manifest itself as hateful speech; for example, there still exist those who would
argue that the white race is the superior race. Although not punish-
able by law, such speech as free, even as truthful in the sense that the
speaker sincerely believes in this hierarchy of races, is alienating, and
possibly threatening to democracy if it persuades enough people. Less
manifestly hateful but still potentially alienating are divisive public issues. I may freely speak my judgment on the right to abortion within
a democratic polity that may alienate me from someone who has the
opposite view. This expression of free speech could degenerate into
projections of those who support abortion rights as supporters of a
culture of death and those who oppose abortion rights as religious
fanatics. Truthful speech often evokes projections of demonization of

the other insofar as those demonizations attempt to marginalize certain voices within a democratic polity. Finally, even though the assumption is that free speech is truthful speech, that is not always the case. Free speech can be intentionally deceitful speech, which can take a variety of forms, such as intentional exaggeration for the sake of persuasion.

It is clear then that free speech as either truthful or deceitful is potentially alienating; and yet, American democracy in particular has moments in its history when free speech as protest has succeeded in mitigating alienation and projections. As a result of truthful protest—speech that attempts to express truthfully the judgment that the structures within American society do not cohere with its founding principles—the landscape of relations surrounding gender, race, and sexuality is manifestly different than it has been previously within our society. Such difference is still not ideal, but the ways of relating to women, blacks, and LGBTs within the American cultural and political space have clearly changed over the past three decades. In the case of homosexuality, truthfully expressed protest in support of gay rights has allowed homosexuals to be more truthful about their own sexuality. Again, to make such a claim is not to admit that the struggle against sexism, racism, homophobia, ethnophobia, or religiophobia is finished or ever can be; all forms of difference are fuel for projections and domination. Free speech as truthfully expressed protest, however, has created a space for difference that mirrors to a greater degree what I have been calling communion. Free speech as truthfully expressed protest allows for a mitigation of the projections and deceitful speech that justify domination. And although truthful speech on divisive issues may be alienating, a space where free speech is allowed makes possible more personal one-on-one encounters where the expression of opposing views on a particular issue need not lead to alienation. One could imagine two people on the opposite poles of the abortion issue having a conversation where they learn that they ultimately share a common concern: the value of a particular human life. For some who support abortion rights, it is the value of the freedom of women who have for so long been denied that freedom; and for those who oppose abortion rights, it is the value of the unique and irre-placeably unborn human life. Such a conversation may not lead to agreement, but it can lead to understanding, even empathy. It can also reduce the chances of demonization.[38]

It would be a mistake to read these reflections as an uncritical panegyric to American democracy, or to democracy in general. Po-litical communities, however, manifest how speech is not neutral, how speech has the power to shape relationships, how that power de-pends on the listener who is symbolically charged. Free speech within a democratic space can be deceitful, hateful, and manipulating, lead-ing to relationships of demonization and alienation; but, unlike in to-talitarian regimes, democratic spaces also make possible free speech as truthful expression that can lead to relationships of difference that involve respect, mutuality, and friendship not previously imaginable. It can lead to spaces where people of difference can more truthfully express and embrace their difference, where being a particular gen-der, color, ethnicity, or religion, or truthfully expressing that one is gay, transsexual or transgender, is no longer a cultural and political hazard.

Conclusion

The Politics of Divine-Human Communion

Since the fall of Communism in the early 1990s, the world's focus has shifted to Islam. There has been much discussion on whether Islam is mutually exclusive with Western liberal democracy. While it seemed that a universal consensus existed, especially after Vatican II, on the compatibility between liberal democracy and Christianity, the post-Communist situation in Eastern Europe provoked some cracks in that consensus. Was Orthodox Christianity similar to Islam in being an obstacle to the implementation of democratic structures in Eastern Europe? Is Orthodox Christianity on the wrong side of the "clash of civilizations"? Added to this was a Western Christian voice emerging over the last few decades that, in one form or another, declared modern liberal democratic principles to be antithetical to Christian understandings of God, community, and the human being. Many of these Christian voices base this claim on the newly revived notion of *theosis*, or "deification," which is especially troubling in the Orthodox world, since those Orthodox who are reflexively anti-Western, who are fighting at all costs for an Orthodox hegemony in traditional Orthodox countries, but who lack the intellectual resources for a rigorous and consistent political theology beyond appeals to the past, can

195

now turn to the thought of, ironically, non-Christian theologians to support their ambivalence to liberal democracy.

The basic claim grounding Christian ambivalence toward modern liberal democracy is that the latter embodies claims about being human that are antithetical to those espoused by Christians. With those who express this ambivalence, I stand in agreement that any consistent Christian political theology must begin with the claim of what it means to be Christian. I have defined what it means to be Christian in terms of *theosis* or, as I prefer to translate it, divine-human communion. It has long been assumed, even by the Orthodox, that the mystical notion of *theosis* has nothing to do with politics, that divine-human communion can only be achieved by fleeing from the "world" to the desert, the monastery, or the forest. And, yet, if we further clarify divine-human communion in terms of fulfillment of the commandment to love God and neighbor, then it becomes clear that the calling to embody the divine presence more fully in the material creation is not simply to those who flee the world, but also to those who remain in the world. *Theosis* was never meant to institute a Gnostic either/or-ness between the divine and the material creation, but affirms material creation as the arena of the divine presence. *Theosis* also does not allow this Gnostic dualism to seep into the various structures that shape our communal spaces; it is not meant to signify an escape from material creation nor an escape from the various structures within which we relate to that material space. It is simply not the case that only those who isolate themselves from family, work, or politics are capable of divine-human communion; it is also a calling for those who either choose or have no other choice but to remain in those structures.

Humans, then, are called from their very birth to communion with God, and their entire lives can be interpreted as one continuous struggle to embody this communion or, otherwise put, to learn how to love. Augustine got this logic straight long ago that if God is love, then our love is simply an indication of God in us, and the marker of that is how we love the other. Love, however, is not automatic; it has nothing to do with being a soulmate. Humans perpetually struggle against those things that seem to get in the way of love—predispositions, fear, low self-esteem, false ego-projections, just to name a few. It may seem that out of love a parent pushes a child in a certain direction, when it is often the case that such a push masks a deep-rooted fear of failing as a parent. What seems like love is often self-referential.

I am of the opinion that the ascetical tradition, in both East and West, understood that fulfilling the love commandment requires ascetical discernment and practices. The best way to look at this tradition is as one of thinking on how to acquire the virtue of love, which is to grow in deeper communion with God. The central question of this ascetical tradition is: what are the practices that one needs to perform in relation to oneself and the other in order to make oneself more available to love both oneself and the other in the way that God does? There is an ascetics to divine-human communion, which is simultaneously the Christian attempt to learn how to love.

Insofar as this ascetics of divine-human communion is performed always in relation to the other, then politics must be reconceived as an ascetical practice. Admittedly, politics was never thought to be such within the ascetical tradition. The ascetical struggle to learn how to love is inescapably in relation to the other(s)—family, friends, and strangers. The encounter with the stranger is simultaneously a challenge and opportunity for the Christian to learn how to love. It's always in relation to the other that the Christian must perform practices that make one more available to be loving, to communing with the divine. Politics are the forms of practices that humans engage in when relating, in Christian language, to the stranger. The type of politics one engages in shapes the way in which one relates to the stranger. Christian relating to the stranger, in other words, Christian politics, must be a performance of practices that either emerge from or attempt to contribute to the Christian struggle to learn to love. There is simply not a space in which the Christian is not to think about the performance of practices that would instantiate the divine presence in the particular relational space in which the Christian is situated.

So much of what passes as Christian politics is counter to a politics of divine-human communion. Christians, as well as those of other religions, often think that since they possess the truth it gives them the authority to engage in a politics of bullying. The "possession" of absolute truth justifies all kinds of politics of demonization and destruction, and of restrictions of certain freedoms, such as religious freedoms. This politics of bullying is part of an ascetics of the demonic. What is ironic is that what often gets paraded as loyalty, fidelity, and commitment to the truth of God simply masks a deeper insecurity that all on which one has staked one's identity, all that one has thought to be true, could simply be wrong. It is using God for the sake of identity politics; it is idolatrous.

Maximus the Confessor warns the monks he is addressing that the vices that get in the way of love are, to name a few, anger, fear, and hatred. It is these very vices that also get in the way of a genuine Christian politics, which is simultaneously an ascetics of divine-human communion. A Christian must be rigorously and vigilantly self-reflexive to make sure that his Christian politics is not motivated by anger, fear, or hatred. A Christian politics must be humble, which does not mean that the Christian is a pushover; to be humble and to be firm in one's convictions is not oxymoronic. A Christian politics, as Mathewes rightly points out, engages the other by not trying to project onto the other, but by listening, conversing, and debating. A Christian politics as asceticism risks losing the debate, but waits patiently for the other to see the wisdom of the Christian vision of divine-human communion. In the end, the politics-as-asceticism that the Christian will perform will contribute to shaping a political space that looks something like a liberal democracy. By liberal democracy, I mean nothing more than a political space shaped by a common good that embodies the principles of equality and freedom, with the former including social and economic equalities, and the latter including religious freedom facilitated by church-state separation.

It is simply nonsense to think that by working for this kind of political space that the Christian is accepting the anthropological baggage of modern liberalism, acquiescing to the modern liberal marginalization of religion, or furthering the modern liberal story of the violence of religion. Those who argue for a mutual exclusivity between any form of liberal democracy and the Christian eucharistic vision of the church are inserting a Gnostic dualism into the Christian theo-political imagination that is simply not consistent with the logic of divine-human communion. While recognizing that the fullness of the Christian vision is a church that exists eucharistically, the Christian attempt to embody a eucharistic mode of being in the world recognizes that the political is not the ecclesial; that how a Christian exists in the world affects the form of the political space; that the political space serves a purpose distinct from but analogous to the eucharistic understanding of the ecclesial. The political space that structures relations in such a way that mirror a eucharistic understanding of the ecclesial, especially in terms of relations that realize the inviolable uniqueness of all human beings, is a liberal democracy. Since, however, the political is not the ecclesial, that political space must structure those relations through human rights language, and, without some notion of the common good, which is revisable and debatable, the principles of freedom and equality embedded in a liberal democracy will simply implode upon themselves.

· Although it does not operate according to a nature-grace divide, an ascetics of divine-human communion contributes to a non–natural law understanding of the common good. Indeed, contrary to some understandings, or, perhaps, misconceptions, of natural law, Christian ascetical practices are not simply about the salvation of our soul. They all have political ramifications, insofar as their practice cannot but affect the political space. Even the practices of truth-telling and forgiveness, which are not willed acts as much as they are modes of being, are ascetical practices that affect the political. While understanding forgiveness as an event of communion that is realized through the practice of truth-telling mitigates against any facile understanding of political forgiveness, it is clear that the attempt at forgiveness between nations or groups can facilitate communion-like relations between peoples. Face-to-face forgiveness in the political space between strangers shapes such a space in the form of a liberal democracy.

While I understand the caution behind Christians not easily aligning themselves with modern liberalism, and while I applaud the exhortation that Christians more boldly assert their Christian presuppositions, the vitriolic rhetoric against modern liberalism, which extends to liberal democracy, is dangerous, especially in the hands of an institutional church with real political and cultural power. It is interesting that two of the loudest voices in this antiliberalism rhetoric, Hauerwas and Milbank, come from churches that are institutionally weak. Christians, then, should never forget that the political is not the ecclesial, but they should also remember that the mystical is the political, and that an ascetics of divine-human communion shapes a political space that is liberal democratic.

Notes

Introduction

1. Although a dominant theme in the Orthodox Christian tradition, deification has played a formative role in the Catholic theological imagination. Attempts recently have been made to demonstrate its importance for the Protestant traditions as well. See Paul M. Collins, *Partaking in Divine Nature: Deification and Communion* (London: T&T Clark, 2010). See also Norman Russell, *The Doctrine of Deification in the Greek Patristic Tradition* (Oxford: Oxford University Press, 2004).

2. In its emphasis on a theology of Christian politics that foregrounds the Christian response to the command for neighborly love, the work of Luke Bretherton has affinities with what follows, even if our approaches are not identical. See especially Luke Bretherton, *Christianity and Contemporary Politics: The Conditions and Possibilities of Faithful Witness* (Oxford: Wiley-Blackwell, 2010).

3. See *Orthodox Constructions of the "West,"* eds. George Demacopoulos and Aristotle Papanikolaou (New York: Fordham University Press, forthcoming).

Chapter One. Orthodox Political Theology through the Centuries

1. Christopher Rowland, "Scripture: New Testament," in *The Blackwell Companion to Political Theology,* ed. Peter Scott and William T. Cavanaugh, 21–34 (Oxford: Blackwell, 2004).

2. One would be hard pressed to find any Christian identifying any sort of empire, Roman or American democratic, with the eschatological kingdom of God, in view of the fact that the latter was proclaimed as a future, end-of-history event. This fact did not stop Christians from identifying close

political analogues to the kingdom of God, such as Eusebius's account of the Roman Empire after Constantine's conversion, or present-day fundamentalist Christian reverence of American democracy.

3. W. H. C. Frend, *The Rise of Christianity* (Philadelphia: Fortress Press, 1984), 483.

4. Ecumenical Patriarch Bartholomew, *Speaking the Truth in Love: Theological and Spiritual Exhortations of Ecumenical Patriarch Bartholomew*, ed. John Chryssavgis (New York: Fordham University Press, 2010), esp. 176 and 355.

5. Norman Baynes, "The Byzantine State," in *Byzantine Studies and Other Essays*, 47–66 (London: Athlone Press, 1955).

6. Eusebius of Caesarea, *Life of Constantine*, in *From Irenaeus to Grotius: A Sourcebook in Christian Political Thought*, ed. Oliver O'Donovan and Joan Lockwood O'Donovan (Grand Rapids, MI: Eerdmans, 1999), 62.

7. *Ecclesiastical History*, trans. J. E. L. Oulton (Cambridge: Harvard University Press, 1932), 9.10.1–15. Elsewhere, Eusebius speaks of the removal of the generation of those who hate God, *to ton theomison genos* (10.1.7).

8. Eusebius, *Life of Constantine*, 58.

9. Garth Fowden, *Empire to Commonwealth: Consequences of Monotheism in Late Antiquity* (Princeton: Princeton University Press, 1993).

10. On Eusebius, see John Behr, *The Nicene Faith* (Crestwood, NY: St. Vladimir's Seminary Press, 2004), esp. 61–75; and Lewis Ayres, *Nicaea and Its Legacy: An Approach to Fourth-Century Trinitarian Theology* (Oxford: Oxford University Press, 2004), 58–61.

11. Eusebius, *Life of Constantine*, 60–61.

12. Ibid., 61.

13. Ibid., 62.

14. Ibid.

15. Ibid., 60.

16. Baynes, "The Byzantine State," 48.

17. John Chrystostom, "From the Twenty-Fourth Homily on Romans," in O'Donovan and O'Donovan, eds., *From Irenaeus to Grotius*, 92.

18. Ibid., 93.

19. John Chrysostom, "From the Fourth Homily on the Text '*I Saw the Lord....*,'" in O'Donovan and O'Donovan, eds., *From Irenaeus to Grotius*, 98.

20. Ibid.

21. The most thorough and comprehensive treatment of this theme in both the Post-Nicene and Ante-Nicene Christian theologians is given by Kenneth Alexo Jr., "Toward an Ecclesial Theory of Politics: An Interpretation of the Political Theology of the Greek Church Fathers" (PhD diss., Princeton

University, 2009). Alexo is especially critical of Francis Dvornik, *Early Christian and Byzantine Political Philosophy: Origins and Background* (Washington, DC: Dumbarton Oaks Center for Byzantine Studies, 1966).

22. Chrysostom, "From the Twenty-Fourth Homily on Romans," 94.

23. Ibid.

24. Alexo, "Toward an Ecclesial Theory of Politics."

25. Ibid., 47.

26. Ibid., 40.

27. On this, see ibid., 476–95.

28. On the diverse ways in which deification was understood in the Greek fathers, see the monumental work of Norman Russell, *The Doctrine of Deification in the Greek Patristic Tradition* (Oxford: Oxford University Press, 2004).

29. Runciman, *The Byzantine Theocracy* (Cambridge: Cambridge University Press, 1977) 46.

30. John Meyendorff, *The Byzantine Legacy in the Orthodox Church* (New York: St. Vladimir's Seminary Press, 1982), 48. See also Runciman, *The Byzantine Theocracy*, 46.

31. Meyendorff, *The Byzantine Legacy*, 49. See also Justinian, "Novella 6," in O'Donovan and O'Donovan, eds., *From Irenaeus to Grotius*, 194.

32. Meyendorff, *The Byzantine Legacy*, 49. See also Runciman, *The Byzantine Theocracy*, 46.

33. Runciman, *The Byzantine Theocracy*, 36.

34. Ibid., 146.

35. It was questioned by Augustine in *City of God*, but this text, and Augustine in general, had no influence upon political theology in the eastern part of the empire.

36. Elizabeth D. Digeser, *The Making of a Christian Empire: Lactantius and Rome* (Ithaca: Cornell University Press, 1999).

37. Paul J. Alexander, "Religious Persecution and Resistance in the Byzantine Empire of the Eighth and Ninth Centuries: Methods and Justifications," in *Religious and Political History and Thought in the Byzantine Empire*, 238–64 (London: Variorum Reprints, 1978).

38. Thornton Anderson, *Russian Political Thought: An Introduction* (Ithaca: Cornell University Press, 1967).

39. For this history, see S. V. Utechin, *Russian Political Thought: A Concise History* (New York: Praeger, 1963); Charles J. Halperin, *Russia and the Golden Horde: The Mongol Impact on Medieval Russian History* (Bloomington: Indiana University Press, 1985); Dimitry Pospielovsky, *The Orthodox*

Church in the History of Russia (Crestwood, NY: St. Vladimir's Seminary Press, 1998).

40. Utechin, *Russian Political Thought*, 15. See also Henrik Birnbaum, *Novgorod in Focus* (Columbus, OH: Slavica Publishers, 1996), and George P. Fedotov, *The Russian Religious Mind*, vol. 2, *The Middle Ages: The Thirteenth to the Fifteenth Centuries*, ed. John Meyendorff (Cambridge, MA: Harvard University Press, 1966).

41. Utechin, *Russian Political Thought*, 15.

42. Richard Pipes, *Russia under the Old Regime* (New York: Charles Scribner's Sons, 1974).

43. Ibid., 232.

44. See Nicolas Zernov, *The Russians and Their Church*, 3rd ed. (Crestwood, NY: St. Vladimir's Seminary Press, 1978).

45. Pospielovsky, *The Orthodox Church in the History of Russia*, 70–76.

46. Pipes, *Russia under the Old Regime*, 234. See also Anderson, *Russian Political Thought*, 111–18.

47. Pospielovsky, *The Orthodox Church in the History of Russia*, 110. See also, Utechin, *Russian Political Thought*, 37–44.

48. Donald Treadgold, "Russian Orthodoxy and Society," in *Russian Orthodoxy under the Old Regime*, ed. Robert L. Nichols and Theofanis George Stavrou, 21–43 (Minneapolis: University of Minnesota, 1978).

49. The dynamic was, minimally, three-way: between bishops and monks, who did not always agree, and the emperor.

50. Pipes, *Russia under the Old Regime*, 240–44.

51. Treadgold, "Russian Orthodoxy and Society," 30.

52. Gregory L. Freeze, "Church and Politics in Late Imperial Russia: Crisis and Radicalization of the Clergy," in *Russia under the Last Tsar: Opposition and Subversion, 1894–1917*, ed. Anna Geifman, 269–84 (Malden: Blackwell, 1999).

53. See especially Jennifer Hedda, *His Kingdom Come: Orthodox Pastorship and Social Activism in Revolutionary Russia* (Dekalb: Northern Illinois University Press, 2008), and George F. Putnam, *Russian Alternatives to Marxism: Christian Socialism and Idealistic Liberalism in Twentieth-Century Russia* (Knoxville: University of Tennessee Press, 1977). Also see Geir Flikke, *Democracy or Theocracy: Frank, Struve, Berdjaev, Bulgakov, and the 1905 Russian Revolution* (Oslo: Universitetet Oslo, Slavisk-baltisk avdeling, 1994), and Andrzej Walicki, *The Slavophile Controversy: History of a Conservative Utopia in Nineteenth-Century Russian Thought* (Notre Dame, IN: University of Notre Dame Press, 1985).

54. Freeze, "Church and Politics in Late Imperial Russia," 270.

55. For Solov'ev's writings on political themes, see his *Russia and the Universal Church,* trans. Herbert Rees (London: Geoffrey Bles, 1948); *Freedom, Faith, and Dogma: Essays by V. S. Soloviev on Christianity and Judaism,* ed. Vladimir Wozniuk (Albany: State University of New York Press, 2008); *The Philosophical Principles of Integral Knowledge,* trans. Valeria Z. Nollan (Grand Rapids, MI: Eerdmans, 2008); *Politics, Law, and Morality,* ed. Vladimir Wozniuk (New Haven: Yale University Press, 2000); *War, Progress, and the End of History: Three Conversations, Including a Short Story of the Anti-Christ,* trans. Alexander Bakshy (Hudson: Lindisfarne, 1990); *Lectures on Divine Humanity,* trans. Robert Zouboff, rev. and ed. Boris Jakim (Hudson: Lindisfarne Press, 1995); *The Justification of the Good: An Essay on Moral Philosophy,* trans. Nathalie Duddington, ed. Boris Jakim (Grand Rapids, MI: Eerdmans, 2005).

56. "On the other hand, it should be pointed out that 'Orthodox theology' is not synonymous with 'Eastern Christian thought'"; from the introduction to *The Cambridge Companion to Orthodox Christian Theology,* ed. Mary B. Cunningham and Elizabeth Theokritoff (Cambridge: Cambridge University Press, 2008), xvi.

57. On Solov'ev as a theologian, see Brandon Gallaher, "The Christological Focus of Vladimir Solov'ev's Sophiology," *Modern Theology* 25, no. 4 (2009): 617–46.

58. For more on Solov'ev, especially his "sophiology," see Paul Valliere, *Modern Russian Theology: Bukharev, Soloviev, Bulgakov; Orthodox Theology in a New Key* (Grand Rapids, MI: Eerdmans, 2000). See also his "Vladimir Soloviev (1853–1900)," in *The Teachings of Modern Christianity on Law, Politics and Human Nature,* vol. 1, ed. John Witte Jr. and Frank Alexander, 533–75 (New York: Columbia University Press, 2006).

59. The necessity for individual growth is clearly implied in Eusebius, who was not a determinist, but it is much less emphasized in his cosmic, evolutionary blurring of the empire and the church.

60. For Bulgakov's political views and activities between 1905 and 1917, see Cathering Evtuhov, *The Cross and the Sickle* (Ithica: Cornell University Press, 1997).

61. Sergius Bulgakov, "An Urgent Task," in *A Revolution of the Spirit: Crisis of Value in Russia, 1890–1924,* ed. Bernice Glatzer Rosenthal and Martha Bohachevsky-Chomiak, trans. Marian Schwartz (New York: Fordham University Press, 1990), 140.

62. Ibid., 138.

63. Ibid., 143.

64. Ibid., 143–44.

65. Ibid.

66. Ibid., 147.

67. Ibid., 144–45.

68. Putnam, *Russian Alternatives to Marxism*, 111.

69. Bulgakov, "An Urgent Task," 149.

70. Ibid., 150.

71. Ibid., 151–55.

72. Ibid., 155–56.

73. Ibid., 158.

74. Ibid., 158–59.

75. Sergius Bulgakov, *The Lamb of God*, trans. Boris Jakim (Grand Rapids, MI: Eerdmans, 2008; orig. pub., 1933); *The Comforter*, trans. Boris Jakim (Grand Rapids, MI: Eerdmans, 2004; orig. pub., 1936); *The Bride of the Lamb*, trans. Boris Jakim (Grand Rapids, MI: Eerdmans, 2002; orig. pub. 1945 [though finished in 1939]).

76. Sergei Bulgakov, *Philosophy of Economy: The World as Household*, trans. Catherine Evtuhov (New Haven: Yale University Press, 2000).

77. For Bulgakov on the Trinity, see Aristotle Papanikolaou, "Contemporary Orthodox Currents on the Trinity," in *Oxford Handbook on the Trinity*, ed. Gilles Emory, O.P., and Matthew Levering, 328–38 (Oxford: Oxford University Press, 2011).

78. Sergius Bulgakov, *The Orthodox Church*, rev. trans. Lydia Kesich (Crestwood, NY: St. Vladimir's Seminary Press, 1988), 162–64.

79. Sergius Bulgakov, "The Soul of Socialism," in *Sergii Bulgakov: Toward a Russian Political Theology*, ed. Rowan Williams (Edinburgh: T&T Clark, 1999), 256.

80. Ibid., 257.

81. Christine Hall, *"Pancosmic" Church: Specific Românesc Ecclesiological Themes in Nichifor Crainic's Writings between 1922–44* (Uppsala: Uppsala Universitet, 2008), 61.

82. Ibid.

83. See Mihail Neamtu, "Between the Gospel and the Nation: Dumitru Stăniloae's Ethno-Theology," *Archaeus* 10, no. 3 (2006): 7–44; and "Revisiting Orthodoxy and Nationalism," *Pro Ecclesia* 15, no. 2 (2006): 153–60. See also Lucian Turcescu, "Dumitru Stăniloae (1903–1993)," in *The Teachings of Modern Christianity on Law, Politics, and Human Nature*, vol. 1, ed. John Witte Jr. and Frank Alexander, 685–711 (New York: Columbia University Press, 2006).

84. For what follows on Crainic, I am indebted to Christine Hall's masterful study, *"Pancosmic" Church.*

85. For religion and nationalism in Greece, see Panteleimon Kalaitzidis, "The Temptation of Judas: Church and National Identities," *Greek Orthodox Theological Review* 47, nos. 1–4 (2002): 357–79. Also see Spyridoula Athanasopoulou-Kypriou, *Not Me: Essays on Political Theology in Relation to Issues of Race, Religion and Ideology* (Athens: Armos, 2011; in Greek).

86. For an overview of Orthodox theology, see Aristotle Papanikolaou, "Orthodoxy, Postmodernity, and Ecumenism: The Difference that Divine-Human Communion Makes," *Journal of Ecumenical Studies* 42, no. 4 (2007): 527–46.

87. For Guroian, see chap. 2 in this volume; for Yannaras, see chap. 4.

88. Sophia Kishkovsky, "Russian Patriarch, Praising World War II, Sidesteps Stalin's Legacy," http://www.huffingtonpost.com/2010/05/13/russian -patriarch-praisin_n_575634.html. See also Irena Papkova, *The Orthodox Church and Russian Politics* (Oxford: Oxford University Press, 2011), esp. chap. 2.

89. For discussion on the law, see John Witte Jr. and Michael Bourdeaux, eds., *Proselytism and Orthodoxy in Russia: The New War for Souls* (Maryknoll, NY: Orbis Books, 1999). See also Wallace L. Daniel, Peter L. Berger, and Christopher March, eds., *Perspectives on Church-State Relations in Russia* (Waco: Baylor University J. M. Dawson Institute of Church-State Studies, 2008). See also Papkova, *The Orthodox Church and Russian Politics,* chap. 3.

90. See Papkova, *The Orthodox Church and Russian Politics,* chap. 3.

91. Available at http://www.mospat.ru/en/documents. For an excellent analysis of both documents, see Papkova, *The Orthodox Church and Russian Politics,* chap. 2.

92. As reported in the *Moscow Times,* 8 June 1999.

93. See Lavinia Stan and Lucian Turcescu, *Religion and Politics in Post-Communist Romania* (Oxford: Oxford University Press, 2007), and "The Roman Orthodox Church and Democratization: Twenty Years Later," *International Journal for the Study of the Christian Church* 10, no. 2 (2010): 1–16.

94. See the work of Elizabeth Prodromou, "The Ambivalent Orthodox," *Journal of Democracy* 15, no. 2 (2004): 62–75, and "Orthodox Christianity and Pluralism: Moving beyond Ambivalence?" in *The Orthodox Churches in a Pluralistic World: An Ecumenical Conversation,* ed. Emmanuel Clapsis, 22–46 (Geneva: WCC Publications, 2004); and that of Effie Fokas, "Religion and Welfare in Greece: A New, or Renewed, Role for the Church?" in *Orthodox Christianity in Twenty-first-century Greece: The Role of Religion in*

Culture, Ethnicity, and Politics, ed. Victor Roudometof and Vasilios N. Makrides, 175–92 (Burlington: Ashgate Publishing Co., 2010), and "Religion in the Greek Public Sphere: Nuancing the Account," in *Journal of Modern Greek Studies* 27 (2009): 349–74. Also, Pedro Ramet, ed., *Eastern Christianity and Politics in the Twentieth Century* (Durham, NC: Duke University Press, 1987).

95. See the essays in Roudometof and Makrides, eds., *Orthodox Christianity in Twenty-first-century Greece.*

96. See "Greek Ban on 'Blasphemous' Book," available at http://news .bbc.co.uk/2/hi/europe/672736.stm.

97. For such responses see Michael A. Sells, *The Bridge Betrayed: Religion and Genocide in Bosnia* (Berkeley: University of California Press, 1996), and Paul Mojzes, ed., *Religion and War in Bosnia* (Atlanta: Scholars Press, 1998).

98. Both quotes are from Chris Hedges, "Church's Role in Serbia Protests May Block Reforms," *New York Times,* 3 February 1997, A3.

99. Carlotta Gall, "Serbian Orthodox Church Urges Milosevic and His Cabinet to Quit," *New York Times,* 16 June 1999, A1.

100. "His Holiness Patriarch Pavle Received Dr. Vojislav Kostunica," *St. Savvya Youth Press Service of the Serbian Orthodox Church,* 26 September 2000; "Serbian Patriarch Appeals to Army Chief to Recognize Kostunica," *Agence France Presse,* 6 October 2000. For the statement of support for Kostunica issued by the Synod of the Serbian Orthodox Church, visit www .orthodoxnews.com.

101. Bjelaja Branko, "Yugoslavia: Will Religious Education Be Compulsory in Schools?" *Keston News Service,* 5 December 2000.

102. Thomas Hopko, "Orthodoxy in Post-modern Pluralistic Societies," *Ecumenical Review* 51, no. 4 (1999): 364–71, at 364.

Chapter Two.   Eucharist or Democracy?

1. For this phrase by Henri de Lubac, who, together with Nicholas Afanasiev, was one of the pioneers of eucharistic ecclesiology, see Paul McPartlan, *The Eucharist Makes the Church: Henri de Lubac and John Zizioulas in Dialogue* (Edinburgh: T&T Clark, 1993), xv.

2. This section is based on my previously published article, "Byzantium, Orthodoxy, and Democracy," *Journal of the American Academy of Religion* 71, no. 1 (2003): 75–98. I thank Oxford University Press for permission to reprint portions of that article in this book.

3. For a more recently published discussion of American democracy, see Stanley Harakas, "A Theologian's Reflections on the First Amendment," in *Wholeness of Faith and Life: Orthodox Christian Ethics*, vol. 3, *Orthodox Social Ethics*, 106–40 (Brookline, MA: Holy Cross Orthodox Press).

4. Stanley Harakas, "Orthodox Church-State Theory and American Democracy," *Greek Orthodox Theological Review* 21, no. 4 (1976): 399–421, at 399.

5. Ibid.

6. Ibid., 411–19.

7. Ibid., 414.

8. Ibid., 415.

9. Ibid.

10. A not-so-insignificant fact, given the history of the relation of the Armenian people to the Byzantine Empire.

11. Vigen Guroian, *Incarnate Love: Essays in Orthodox Ethics* (Notre Dame, IN: University of Notre Dame Press, 1987), 147. For more on Guroian's understanding of the church's relation to the state and to culture, see "The Struggle for the Soul of the Church: American Reflections" and "Church and Armenian Nationhood: A Bonhoefferian Reflection on the National Church," in his *Ethics after Christendom* (Grand Rapids, MI: Eerdmans, 1994).

12. Guroian, *Incarnate Love*, 148.

13. Ibid., 147.

14. Not all Orthodox theologians understood the church in terms of the Eucharist; most notable among those theologians are Vladimir Lossky and Dumitru Staniloae.

15. For more details on what follows as a general outline of Zizioulas's theology, including references to Zizioulas's corpus, see Aristotle Papanikolaou, *Being with God: Trinity, Apophaticism, and Divine-Human Communion* (Notre Dame, IN: University of Notre Dame Press, 2006).

16. Guroian, *Incarnate Love*, 143.

17. Ibid., 147.

18. Ibid., 162.

19. Ibid., 159. One must ask Guroian how it is possible for a eucharistic community, as an icon of the eschatological community, not to be concerned about a "more just ethic of power." Even given Guroian's assumptions, if it is not concerned with relations of power in a political community, at the very least, as an eschatological community, then it must give witness to a more just configuration of power. Such a statement by Guroian gives the

impression that Orthodox thought is not concerned with justice. But this does not cohere with Guroian's own eucharistic presuppositions.

20. Ibid., 157.

21. Ibid., 156.

22. Ibid., 157.

23. Ibid., 143.

24. Ibid., 142.

25. Ibid., 159.

26. For a comparison of Zizioulas and de Lubac, see Paul McPartlan, *The Eucharist Makes the Church: Henri de Lubac and John Zizioulas in Dialogue* (Edinburgh: T&T Clark, 1993).

27. What follows is from William T. Cavanaugh, *Torture and Eucharist: Theology, Politics and the Body of Christ* (Oxford: Blackwell Publisher, 1998).

28. Ibid., 228.

29. Ibid., 165.

30. See William T. Cavanaugh, "'A Fire Strong Enough to Consume the House': The Wars of Religion and the Rise of the State," *Modern Theology* 11, no. 4 (1995): 397–420. See also his *The Myth of Religious Violence: Secular Ideology and the Roots of Modern Conflict* (Oxford: Oxford University Press, 2009).

31. Cavanaugh, *Torture and Eucharist*, 3.

32. Ibid., 56, where Cavanaugh does not distinguish between different forms of the modern nation-state, that is, democratic versus dictatorial.

33. Ibid., 4.

34. Ibid.

35. Ibid., 14.

36. I use the phrase "postimperialist" fully aware that there are those who would dispute this description of our present context. See Michael Hardt and Antonio Negri, *Empire* (Cambridge, MA: Harvard University Press, 2001). In my mind, however, there is a difference between what is manifestly imperialist and what is latently imperialist masked behind a seemingly anti-imperialist political theology.

37. Guroian, "The Americanization of Orthodoxy: Crisis and Challenge," in *Incarnate Love*. See also "Human Rights and Modern Western Faith: An Orthodox Christian Assessment," *Journal of Religious Ethics* 26, no. 2 (1999): 241–47.

38. See Harakas's review of *Incarnate Love* in the *Greek Orthodox Theological Review* 35, no. 1 (1990): 71–81.

39. Jeffrey Stout, "The Folly of Secularism," *Journal of the American Academy of Religion* 76, no. 3 (2008): 533–44. See also his *Democracy and Tradition* (Princeton: Princeton University Press, 2004).

40. Charles Taylor, *The Secular Age* (Cambridge, MA: Harvard University Press, 2009); José Casanova, *Public Religion in the Modern World* (Chicago: University of Chicago Press, 1994).

41. Casanova, *Public Religion,* 215.

42. Ronald Thiemann, *Religion in Public Life: A Dilemma for Democracy* (Washington, D.C.: Georgetown University Press, 1996), 150.

43. Richard Rorty, "Religion as Conversation-Stopper," *Common Knowledge* 3, no. 1 (1994): 1–6. Rorty later acknowledged that religious discourse per se is not a conversation stopper in "Religion in the Public Square: A Reconsideration," *Journal of Religious Ethics* 31, no. 1 (2003): 141–49.

44. For "public morality" and "common good" see Brian Stiltner, *Religion and the Common Good: Catholic Contributions to Building Community in a Liberal Society* (Lanham, MD: Rowman and Littlefield, 1999); also, David Hollenbach, *The Common Good and Christian Ethics* (Cambridge: Cambridge University Press, 2002).

45. Thiemann, *Religion in Public Life,* 221.

46. While no Orthodox theologian would deny the identification of the church with the body of Christ, not all theologians would strictly identify the church as the body of Christ with the eucharistic assembly. The two most notable theologians who do not develop such an ecclesiology are Vladimir Lossky and Dumitru Staniloae. For both theologians, while the church is the simultaneous presence of Christ and the Holy Spirit, it is in process; analogous to the individual ascetical struggle to *theosis,* the church as a community is moving by the power of the Holy Spirit to more fully image in itself the fullness of Christ. For more on this difference, see Aristotle Papanikolaou, "Integrating the Ascetical and the Eucharistic: Current Challenges in Orthodox Ecclesiology," *International Journal for the Study of the Christian Church* 11, no. 2 (2011): 1–15.

47. For an interpretation of Zizioulas's understanding of personhood and the Eucharist as unfree, see Nikolaos Loudovikos, "Person Instead of Grace and Dictated Otherness: John Zizioulas' Final Theological Position," *The Heythrop Journal* 52, no. 4 (2011): 684–99. For a rebuttal, see Alexis Torrance, "Person and Patristics in Orthodox Theology: Reassessing the Debate," *The Heythrop Journal* 52, no. 4 (2011): 700–707.

48. Maximus the Confessor, *The Four Hundred Chapters on Love,* in *Maximus the Confessor: Selected Writings,* trans. George C. Berthold (New York: Paulist Press, 1985), 1:16 (37).

49. Ibid., 4:84 (85).

50. Ibid., 1:29 (38).

Chapter Three.   Personhood and Human Rights

1. On debates within Islam, see Irene Oh, *The Rights of God: Islam, Human Rights, and Comparative Ethics* (Washington, D.C.: Georgetown University Press, 2007). See also Abdulaziz Sachedina, *The Islamic Roots of Democratic Pluralism* (Oxford: Oxford University Press, 2001).

2. A representative example is Mary Ann Glendon, *Human Rights Talk: The Impoverishment of Political Discourse* (New York: Free Press, 1991).

3. John Milbank, *Being and Reconciled: Ontology and Pardon* (London: Routledge, 2003), 97.

4. In developed form, see Christos Yannaras, "Human Rights and the Orthodox Church," in *The Orthodox Churches in a Pluralistic World*, ed. Emmanuel Clapsis, 83–89 (Geneva: WCC Publications, 2004). For more on Yannaras as part of the "Neo-Orthodox" movement of the twentieth century, and his "political hesychasm," see Daniel P. Payne, *The Revival of Political Hesychasm in Contemporary Orthodox Thought: The Political Hesychasm of John Romanides and Christos Yannaras* (Lanham, MD: Lexington Books, 2011).

5. For this view of history, see Christos Yannaras, *On the Absence and Unknowability of God: Heidegger and the Areopagite,* ed. Andrew Louth, trans. Haralambos Ventis (London: T&T Clark, 2005; orig. pub. in Greek, 1967); also, Christos Yannaras, *Orthodoxy and the West,* trans. Peter Chamberas and Norman Russell (Brookline, MA: Holy Cross Orthodox Press, 2006; orig. pub. in Greek, 1992). On Yannaras on Augustine, see George Demacopoulos and Aristotle Papanikolaou, *Orthodox Readings of Augustine* (Crestwood, NY: St. Vladimir's Seminary Press, 2008).

6. Yannaras, "Human Rights and the Orthodox Church," 84.

7. Ibid., 85.

8. Ibid.

9. Ibid., 86. On the development of Yannaras's understanding of "religion," see Basilio Petrà, "Christos Yannaras and the Idea of 'Dysis' (West)," in *Orthodox Constructions of the 'West,'* ed. George Demacopoulos and Aristotle Papanikolaou (New York: Fordham University Press, 2013).

10. Yannaras, "Human Rights and the Orthodox Church," 84.

11. Ibid., 86–87.

12. See also Christos Yannaras, *The Inhumanity of Human Rights* (Athens: Domos, 1998). For a critique of Yannaras on human rights, see Pantelis Kalaitzidis, *Orthodoxy and Modernity* (Athens: Indiktos, 2007 [in Greek]);

also Constantine Delekonstante, *Human Rights: Western Ideology or Ecumenical Ethos* (Thessalonika: Kyriakides, 1995 [in Greek]).

13. Vigen Guroian, "Human Rights and Modern Western Faith: An Orthodox Christian Assessment," *Journal of Religious Ethics* 26, no. 2 (1998): 241–47, at 243.

14. Ibid., 244–45.

15. Ibid., 245.

16. Available at www.mospat.ru/en/documents. For an excellent analysis of this document, see Alexander Agadjanian, "Liberal Individual and Christian Culture: Russian Orthodox Teaching on Human Rights in Social Theory Perspective," *Religion, State, and Society* 38, no. 2 (2010): 97–113.

17. For an example of church-state cooperation in Russia toward the Russian Dispora, see Daniel P. Payne, "Spiritual Security, the Russian Orthodox Church, and the Russian Foreign Ministry: Collaboration or Cooptation?" *Journal of Church and State* 52, no. 4 (2010): 712–27.

18. For Metropolitan Hilarion's views on human rights, I am indebted to the article by Antonios Kireopoulos, "Seeking Justice and Promoting Human Rights: Orthodox Theological Imperatives or Afterthoughts?" in *Philanthropy and Social Compassion in Eastern Orthodox Tradition,* ed. M. J. Pereira, Studies in Orthodox Theology 2, 227–47 (New York: Theotokos Press, 2010).

19. Hilarion Alfeyev, *Orthodox Witness Today* (Geneva: WCC Publications, 2006), 233.

20. Ibid., 236.

21. In the final stages of the preparation of this volume, Patriarch Kirill of the ROC intervened in the dispute over alleged fraudulent parliamentary elections that took place in December 2011. Kirill defended the protests against the election as a "'lawful negative reaction' against corruption." This intervention in defense of electoral human rights caught many by surprise, as the ROC has been perceived by many to have aligned itself with the Kremlin in order to advance its own agenda in Russia. See Sophia Kishkovsky, "Disputed Election Turns Church, a Kremlin Ally, into Its Critic," *The New York Times,* 29 December 2011, available through http://www.nytimes.com.

22. For the Orthodox pro–human rights voices, see Stanley Harakas, "Human Rights: An Eastern Orthodox Perspective," *Journal of Ecumenical Studies* 19 (1982): 13–24; and Anastasios Yannoulatos, *Facing the World: Orthodox Christian Essays on Global Concerns* (Crestwood, NY: St. Vladimir's Seminary Press, 2003), esp. 49–78.

23. See his book that is part of the Christian Jurisprudence Project for Emory University's Center for the Study of Law and Religion: John Mc-Guckin, *The Ascent of Christian Law: Byzantine and Patristic Formulations of a New Civilization* (Crestwood, NY: St. Vladimir's Seminary Press, 2012).

24. Ibid., chap. 9. See also his "The Issue of Human Rights in Byzantium and the Orthodox Christian Tradition," in *Christianity and Human Rights: An Introduction,* ed. John Witte Jr. and Frank S. Alexander, 173–90 (Cambridge: Cambridge University Press, 2011).

25. Yannoulatos, *Facing the World,* 49.

26. Ibid., 51.

27. Ibid., 52.

28. Ibid., 57.

29. Ibid., 75.

30. Ibid., 62.

31. For a similar argument that religious discourse can deepen the modern liberal notion of human rights, see John Witte Jr., *God's Joust, God's Justice: Law and Religion in the Western Tradition* (Grand Rapids, MI: Eerdmans, 2006), esp. 63–113.

32. Yannoulatos, *Facing the World,* 77.

33. Ibid., 22.

34. Ibid., 43.

35. Ibid., 76.

36. Though it was developed principally for this chapter, most of this section first appeared under the title "Personhood and Its Exponents in Twentieth-century Orthodox Theology," in *Cambridge Companion to Orthodox Christian Theology,* ed. Mary B. Cunningham and Elizabeth Theokritoff, 232–45 (Cambridge: Cambridge University Press, 2008). I thank Cambridge University Press for permission to reprint the article in its entirety for this book.

37. Michael Aksionov Meerson, *The Trinity of Love in Modern Russian Theology* (Quincy, IL: Franciscan Press, 1998), 174. In his *Modern Russian Theology: Bukharev, Soloviev, Bulgakov* (Grand Rapids, MI: Eerdmans, 2000), Paul Valliere cautions that Bulgakov's personalism must be understood within the framework of his sophiology.

38. Christos Yannaras, "Theology in Present-Day Greece," *St. Vladimir's Theological Quarterly* 16 (1972): 195–214, and *Orthodoxy and the West,* trans. Peter Chamberas and Norman Russell (Brookline, MA: Holy Cross Orthodox Press, 2006). Also, John Zizioulas, "The Ecumenical Dimensions of Orthodox Theological Education," in *Orthodox Theological Education for the Life and Witness of the Church,* 33–40 (Geneva: World Council of

Churches, 1978). In spring 1996, Christos Yannaras explained to me in a private conversation that "I [Yannaras] started with Lossky." For Lossky's influence on Yannaras and on Greek theologians in general, see Basilio Petrà, "Personalist Thought in Greek in the Twentieth Century: A First Tentative Synthesis," *Greek Orthodox Theological Review* 50 (2005): 1–48, and Yannaras, *Orthodoxy and the West*.

39. Some challenge to the centrality of this axiom for theology, and not necessarily its truth, is emerging in the Orthodox world, especially in the work of John Behr. See his *The Mystery of Christ: Life in Death* (Crestwood, NY: St. Validimir's Seminary Press, 2006).

40. Vladimir Lossky, "Apophasis and Trinitarian Theology," in *In the Image and Likeness of God,* ed. John H. Erickson and Thomas E. Bird, 13–30 (Crestwood, NY: St. Vladimir's Seminary Press, 1974), 14.

41. Ibid., 15.

42. For Lossky on antinomy, see "Theology of Light in Gregory Palamas," in Erickson and Bird, eds., *In the Image and Likeness,* 45–70, at 51–52, and "Apophasis and Trinitarian Theology," 26.

43. "Apophaticism is not necessarily a theology of ecstasy. It is, above all, an attitude of mind which refuses to form concepts about God. . . . The way of knowledge of God is necessarily the way of deification"; Vladimir Lossky, *The Mystical Theology of the Eastern Church* (Crestwood, NY: St. Vladimir's Seminary Press, 1976), 38–39.

44. Ibid., 64.

45. See Lossky, "Apophasis and Trinitarian Theology," 23–29.

46. On this distinction in Lossky, see *Mystical Theology,* 51–54; also, Vladimir Lossky, *Orthodox Theology: An Introduction,* trans. Ian and Ihita Kesarcodi-Watson (Crestwood, NY: St. Vladimir's Seminary Press, 1978), 40–41.

47. "It was a question of finding a distinction of terms which should express the unity of, and the differentiation within, the Godhead, without giving the pre-eminence either to the one or to the other"; Lossky, *Mystical Theology,* 50.

48. On Michel René Barnes's misreading of Lossky's use of de Régnon, see discussion in Aristotle Papanikolaou, *Being with God: Trinity, Apophaticism, and Divine-Human Communion* (Notre Dame, IN: University of Notre Dame Press, 2006), 181n101.

49. Vladimir Lossky, "The Procession of the Holy Spirit in Orthodox Trinitarian Doctrine," in Erickson and Bird, eds., *In the Image and Likeness,* 71–96, at 81.

50. Ibid., 83.

51. Vladimir Lossky, "The Theological Notion of Person," in Erickson and Bird, eds., *In the Image and Likeness,* 111–24, at 120. See also Lossky, *Mystical Theology,* 122–23.

52. See Lossky, *Orthodox Theology,* 46–47.

53. "The experience of personal relationship, the experience of *participation* in the *active* manifestation of the otherness of the other, *may be expressed,* but *is never exhausted* in verbal formulation"; Christos Yannaras, *On the Absence and Unknowability of God: Heidegger and the Areopagite,* ed. and with an introduction by Andrew Louth, trans. Haralambos Ventis (New York: T&T Clark International, 2005), 86.

54. Ibid., 99.

55. "Eros is the dynamics of ecstasy, which finds its consummation as personal reference to supreme Otherness"; Christos Yannaras, *Person and Eros,* trans. Norman Russell (Brookline, MA: Holy Cross Orthodox Press, 2007). See also his *Elements of Faith: An Introduction to Orthodox Theology,* trans. Keith Schram (New York: T&T Clark International, 1991), and his *Freedom of Morality,* trans. Elizabeth Briere (Crestwood, NY: St. Vladimir's Seminary Press, 1984).

56. In a private conversation in the summer of 1998 in London. Zizioulas was less receptive to my suggestion that in light of the fact of Yannaras's own confession of "beginning with Lossky" that perhaps he was indirectly influenced by Lossky through Yannaras.

57. John Zizioulas, "Communion and Otherness," in *Communion and Otherness,* ed. Paul McPartlan (New York: T&T Clark, 2006), 9. See also John Zizioulas, "The Being of God and the Being of Man [*Anthropos*]" in *The One and the Many: Studies on God, Man, the Church, and the World Today,* ed. Gregory Edwards, 17–40 (Alhambra: Sebastian Press, 2010; orig. pub. 1991).

58. John Zizioulas, "Human Capacity and Human Incapacity," in McPartlan, ed., *Communion and Otherness,* 206–49, at 212.

59. See ibid., 215–37.

60. Ibid., 215.

61. "When we say that 'this is by Mozart,' or 'this is by Rembrandt,' we are in both cases dealing with a personal world which has no equivalent anywhere"; Lossky, *The Mystical Theology,* 53.

62. Zizioulas, "Human Capacity and Human Incapacity," 216.

63. Ibid., 216. Zizioulas adds, "This is not an entirely negative statement. The tragedy lies in the fact that it is at once positive and negative: the artist exists for us only because he is absent. Had we not had his work (which points to his absence), he would not exist for us or for the world around, even

if we had heard of him or seen him; he *is* by *not being there* (an incidental actual presence of the artist next to us while we are looking at his work would add nothing to his real presence in and through his work, which remains a pointer to his absence)."

64. Ibid., 216.

65. "But in so far as the human person is a being whose particularity is established *also* by its boundaries (a body), personhood realises this presence as *absence*"; ibid., 219.

66. Ibid., 224.

67. Ibid., 227.

68. Ibid., 224. See also 228n31: "Christian theology . . . denies the possibility of pure ontology on the basis of the world as it is: and it affirms that there *is* a possibility of a pure ontology of this world, yet only on the basis of the fact that it *will* ultimately exist—of the fact, that is, that being is personal and depends on love." Also, "On Being a Person: Towards an Ontology of Personhood," in McPartlan, ed., *Communion and Otherness*, 99–112, at 103.

69. Zizioulas, "Human Capacity and Human Incapacity," 235.

70. Ibid., 225.

71. Though *Being as Communion* was originally published in 1985, the first chapter was published in 1977 in Greek.

72. John Zizioulas, *Being as Communion* (Crestwood, NY: St. Vladimir's Seminary Press, 1985), 50.

73. Ibid., 51.

74. Ibid., 50.

75. Ibid., 52.

76. Ibid. For more on Zizioulas's notion of tragedy, see his "Preserving God's Creation: Lecture Three," *King's Theological Review* 13 (1990): 1–5, at 2. It is thus not the case, as Miroslav Volf argues, that a human being as "an individual . . . cannot at the same time be a person in Zizioulas's sense"; *After Our Likeness: The Church as the Image of the Trinity* (Grand Rapids, MI: Eerdmans, 1998), 102. Human existence in its longing for personhood, expressed in the act of communion, manifests aspects or degrees of personhood, but such a longing is inherently tragic because it confronts death, which negates all uniqueness. It is not simply either personhood or individuality, but that within the horizon of created, finite existence, all human longing for communion can only lead, in the end, to individuality, as Zizioulas defines it, because of death. Zizioulas is simply arguing that given the limits of finitude the only way that such a drive can be fulfilled is through an eternal relationship of freedom and love with God.

77. Published in 1991.

78. Zizioulas, "On Being a Person," 100–101. For an analysis of the same question, which results in ontological conclusions different from Zizioulas, see Charles Taylor, *Sources of the Self: The Making of Modern Identity* (Cambridge, MA: Harvard University Press, 1989), esp. 27–32.

79. Zizioulas, "On Being a Person," 103.

80. Zizioulas, *Being as Communion*, 107; in a footnote Zizioulas adds that "this observation of M. Heidegger is of great importance for an ontology of the world *taken as it is*, i.e. without reference to a beyond."

81. For a succinct summary of Zizioulas's understanding of the identification of the church with the Eucharist, see *Being as Communion*, esp., 143–69.

82. For Zizioulas's pneumatology, see his "Implications ecclésiologiques de deux type de pneumatologie," in *Commmunio Sanctorum: Mélanges offerts à Jean-Jacques von Allmen*, 141–54 (Geneva: Labor et Fides, 1981). Also, *Being as Communion*, 123–40.

83. On Zizioulas's understanding of salvation in the *hypostasis* of Christ, see McPartlan, ed., *Communion and Otherness*, 13–112.

84. For Zizioulas's interpretation of the *hypostasis, prosopon,* and *ousia* in the Cappadocian fathers, see *Communion and Otherness* in its entirety, and *Being as Communion*, 27–122.

85. Zizioulas, *Communion and Otherness*, 9; emphasis in original.

86. Zizioulas, *Being as Communion*, 41.

87. Ibid., 43. Also, Zizioulas, *Communion and Otherness*, 113–54.

88. The clearest expression of Zizioulas's understanding of the distinction between *what* God is and the *way* in which God exists appears in his "The Being of God and the Being of Man [Anthropos]."

89. See Brian Tierney, *The Idea of Natural Rights: Studies on Natural Rights, Natural Law, and Church Law, 1150–1625* (Atlanta: Scholars Press, 1997). See also his essay, "Natural Law and Natural Rights," in *Christianity and Law: An Introduction*, ed. John Witte Jr. and Frank S. Alexander, 89–104 (Cambridge: Cambridge University Press, 2008). See also the essays in Witte Jr. and Alexander, eds., *Christianity and Human Rights*.

90. See his *The Ascent of Christian Law*.

91. See Nicholas Wolterstorff, "Modern Protestant Developments in Human Rights," in Witte Jr. and Alexander, eds., *Christianity and Human Rights*, 155–72, at 156. This article contains a survey of modern Protestant theological resistance to the language of rights.

92. Nicholas Wolterstorff, *Justice: Rights and Wrongs* (Princeton: Princeton University Press, 2008), 297. See also his contribution to the Christian Jurisprudence II Project for the Emory University Center for the Study of Law and Religion, *Justice in Love* (Grand Rapids, MI: Eerdmans, 2010), which was not released in time for me to consider for this book.

93. Ibid., 293.

94. Ibid., 263.

95. Ibid., 286.

96. Ibid., 179.

97. Michael Perry, *The Political Morality of Liberal Democracy* (Cambridge: Cambridge University Press, 2010). This book constitutes Perry's contribution to the Christian Jurisprudence Project of Emory University's Center for the Study of Law and Religion.

98. Ibid., chap. 2. Perry first started to make this claim in his *The Idea of Human Rights: Four Inquiries* (Oxford: Oxford University Press, 1998). See also his *Toward a Theory of Human Rights: Religion, Law, Courts* (Cambridge: Cambridge University Press, 2007).

99. Wolterstorff, *Justice: Rights and Wrongs*, 352–53.

100. Ibid., 248 and 281.

101. A practice not so uncommon among Russian peasants of the nineteenth century. Sarah Coakley in a personal conversation posed this example as a challenge to relational notions of personhood.

102. See Elie Wiesel, *Night* (New York: Hill and Wang, 2006).

103. Wolterstorff, "Modern Protestant Developments in Human Rights," 171.

104. Wolterstorff, *Justice: Rights and Wrongs*, 248 and 281.

105. Maximus the Confessor, *Four Hundred Chapters on Love*, in *Maximus the Confessor: Selected Writings*, trans. George C. Berthold (New York: Paulist Press, 1985): 1:82 (44).

106. John Calvin, *Institutes of the Christian Religion*, The Library of Christian Classics 20 (Philadephia: Westminster Press, 1960): 1.2.2 (43). Emphasis mine.

107. Alexander Schmemann, *The Eucharist* (Crestwood, NY: St. Vladimir's Seminary Press, 1987), 40.

108. For this reason, I don't think it makes sense for Orthodox Christians to talk about human rights in a natural law tradition that doesn't understand nature as graced.

109. Zizioulas adds, "The crucial point, therefore, in the survival of the world lies in the act or the event of its communion with God as totally other

than the world"; "Preserving God's Creation: Lecture One," *King's Theological Review* 12 (1989): 3.

110. John Zizioulas, "Law and Personhood in Orthodox Theology," in *The One and the Many: Studies on God, Man, the Church and the World Today,* 402–14 (Alhambra: Sebastian Press, 2010), 408. Emphasis in original.

111. Ibid., 411.

112. Ibid.

113. Perry, *The Political Morality of Liberal Democracy.*

114. Zizioulas, "Law and Personhood in Orthodox Theology," 411.

Chapter Four.   Divine-Human Communion and the Common Good

1. Linking the transcendent to the common good I think is the insight of Stanley Harakas, outlined in chap. 2, without, however, the model of *symphonia.*

2. Stanley Hauerwas, "Remembering as a Moral Task: The Challenge of the Holocaust," in *The Hauerwas Reader,* ed. John Berkman and Michael Cartwright, 327–47 (Durham: Duke University Press, 2001), 341.

3. Stanley Hauerwas, "Why the 'Sectarian Temptation' Is a Misrepresentation: A Response to James Gustafson," in Berkman and Cartwright, eds., *The Hauerwas Reader,* 90–110, at 102. "The Church does not exist to provide an ethos for democracy or any other form of social organization, but stands as a political alternative to every nation, witnessing to the kind of social life possible for those that have been formed by the story of Christ"; Stanley Hauerwas, "Reforming Christian Social Ethics: Ten Theses," in ibid., 111–15, at 114.

4. See *The Journal of the American Academy of Religion* 78, no. 2 (June 2010): 413–48, for an exchange between Cornel West, Richard Rorty, Stanley Hauerwas, and Jeffrey Stout on Stout's *Democracy and Tradition* (Princeton: Princeton University Press, 2004). The exchange is a transcript of the panel discussion that took place at the 2003 American Academy of Religion Annual Meeting in Atlanta and which remains one of the most memorable academic experiences in my (short) career. For a defense of Hauerwas against Stout and a critique of Stout, see William T. Cavanaugh, "A Politics of Vulnerability: Hauerwas and Democracy," in *Unsettling Arguments: A Festschrift on the Occasion of Stanley Hauerwas's Seventieth Birthday,* ed. Charles R. Pinches, Kelly S. Johnson, and Charles M. Collier, 89–111 (Eugene, OR: Cascade Books, 2010). It is clear from Cavanaugh's article that Hauerwas is un-

able or unwilling to allow for any Christian endorsement of a particular form of political governance, seeing such an endorsement, in the end, as capitulation to non-Christian "narratives."

5. Hauerwas, "Why the 'Sectarian Temptation' Is a Misrepresentation," 105.

6. Ibid.

7. As William Cavanaugh, Hauerwas's student, does in *Torture and Eucharist* (Oxford: Blackwell Publishers, 1998).

8. Stanley Hauerwas, "Christianity: It's Not a Religion, It's an Adventure," in Berkman and Cartwright, eds., *The Hauerwas Reader*, 522–38, at 527. It is difficult to know what Hauerwas means by "*most* democratically elected"—100 percent margin of victory?

9. Ibid. See also, "Remembering as a Moral Task: The Challenge of the Holocaust," in ibid., 327–47, at 338–39.

10. Stanley Hauerwas, "Abortion, Theologically Understood," in Berkman and Cartwright, eds., *The Hauerwas Reader*, 603–22, at 612.

11. John Milbank, *Theology and Social Theory: Beyond Secular Reason* (Cambridge, MA: Blackwell, 1990).

12. For a good review of Milbank's political theology, especially his rhetoric against liberal democracy, see Eric Gregory, *Politics and the Order of Love: An Augustinian Ethic of Democratic Citizenship* (Chicago: University of Chicago Press, 2008), 125–45.

13. For very good introductions to RO, including RO's understanding of Scotus, see James K. A. Smith, *Introducing Radical Orthodoxy: Mapping a Post-secular Theology* (Grand Rapids, MI: Baker Academic, 2004), and Steven Shakespeare, *Radical Orthodoxy* (London: SPCK, 2007). Though not a central part of the narrative, RO's take on Scotus's influence in the history of Western thought finds some tacit support in Charles Taylor, *The Secular Age* (Cambridge, MA: Harvard University Press), esp. 295, and more substantive support in Louis Dupré, *Passage to Modernity* (New Haven, CT: Yale University Press, 1993). For a skeptical position, see Stout, *Democracy and Tradition*, 100–107. For an excellent response to RO's critique of liberation theology, see Michael E. Lee, *Bearing the Weight of Salvation: The Soteriology of Ignacio Ellacuria* (New York: Herder & Herder, 2009).

14. John Milbank, *Being Reconciled* (London: Routledge, 2003), 138.

15. John Milbank, *The Word Made Strange: Theology, Language and Culture* (Oxford: Blackwell, 1997), 280.

16. See Paul McPartlan, *The Eucharist Makes the Church: Henri de Lubac and John Zizioulas in Dialogue* (Edinburgh: T&T Clark, 1993).

17. Milbank, *Being Reconciled*, ix.

18. Milbank's most succinct statement on the relation between nature and grace appears in his *The Suspended Middle: Henri de Lubac and the Debate Concerning the Supernatural* (Grand Rapids, MI: Eerdmans, 2005).

19. John Milbank, *The Future of Love: Essays in Political Theology* (Eugene, OR: Cascade Books, 2009), 245.

20. Ibid., 247.

21. Ibid., 256.

22. John Milbank, "The Gift of Ruling: Secularization and Political Authority," in *After Modernity? Secularity, Globalization, and the Reenchantment of the World*, ed. James K. A. Smith (Waco, TX: Baylor University Press, 2008), 35. Elsewhere he says, "Really, there is only one stance that rescues democracy: this, as already intimated, is our truly humble recognition that we are all equally recipients of divine gifts, without which we would not exist at all"; *Being Reconciled*, 108.

23. Milbank, *Being Reconciled*, 133.

24. Ibid., 132.

25. Ibid., 38 and 42–43.

26. Ibid., 40. Milbank seems to conveniently ignore Dostoyevsky's warning of the use of coercion in the narrative of "The Grand Inquisitor."

27. Milbank, *Theology and Social Theory*, 418.

28. I give here a theological justification for Stout's understanding of the "secular," from his *Democracy and Tradition*, 93–100.

29. On RO's inability to avoid dualism, see Shakespeare, *Radical Orthodoxy*, 127.

30. Charles Mathewes, *A Theology of Public Life* (Cambridge: Cambridge University Press, 2007); Graham Ward, *The Politics of Discipleship: Becoming Postmaterial Citizens* (Grand Rapids, MI: Baker Academic, 2009); Gregory, *Politics and the Order of Love*.

31. Mathewes, *A Theology of Public Life*, 3.

32. Ward, *The Politics of Discipleship*, 140–41.

33. Ibid., 167.

34. Ibid., 165.

35. Ibid., 164–65.

36. Ibid., 63–76.

37. Ibid., 57.

38. Ibid., 188.

39. Ibid., 170.

40. Ibid., 180. Quoting Giorgio Agamben, *Time that Remains: A Commentary on the Letter to the Romans*, trans. Patricia Dailey (Stanford, CA: Stanford University Press, 2005), 58.

41. Ward, *The Politics of Discipleship*, 262.

42. Ibid., 299.

43. Ibid., 298.

44. Ibid., 299.

45. Gregory, *Politics and the Order of Love*, 75–124.

46. Matthewes, *A Theology of Public Life*, 7.

47. Ibid., 8.

48. Mathewes's emphasis on the self's deepest longings for communion echoes Zizioulas's account of personhood. See especially John Zizioulas, *Communion and Otherness* (New York: T&T Clark, 2006).

49. Matthewes, *A Theology of Public Life*, 274.

50. Ibid., 23.

51. Ibid., 176 and 178–79.

52. Ibid., 179.

53. Ibid., 180.

54. Maximus the Confessor, *The Four Hundred Chapters on Love*, in *Maximus the Confessor: Selected Writings*, trans. George C. Berthold (New York: Paulist Press, 1985), 1:29 (38).

55. For a dialogical approach to the common good, see David Hollenbach, S.J., *The Global Face of Public Faith: Politics, Human Rights, and Christian Ethics* (Washington, D.C.: Georgetown University Press, 2003), 3–18. See also his *The Common Good and Christian Ethics* (Cambridge: Cambridge University Press, 2002).

56. Hollenbach, *The Global Face of Public Faith*, 117.

57. Ibid., 116.

58. Milbank, "The Gift of Ruling," 43.

Chapter Five.   Truth-Telling, Political Forgiveness, and Free Speech

1. Desmond Tutu, *No Future without Forgiveness* (London: Rider, 1999).

2. For theological accounts of forgiveness that include political forgiveness, see Anthony Bash, *Forgiveness and Christian Ethics* (Cambridge: Cambridge University Press, 2007), and L. Gregory Jones, *Embodying Forgiveness: A Theological Analysis* (Grand Rapids, MI: Eerdmans, 1995). For an

explicitly theological account of political reconciliation, see Ralk K. Wüsten-berg, *The Political Dimension of Reconciliation: A Theological Analysis of Ways of Dealing with Guilt During the Transition to Democracy in South Africa and (East) Germany* (Grand Rapids, MI: Eerdmans, 2009). For affinities with the understanding of forgiveness I will present in this chapter, see Carolyn A. Chau, "'What Could Possibly Be Given?' Towards an Exploration of *Kenosis* as Forgiveness—Continuing the Conversation between Hampson, Coakley, and Papanikolaou," *Modern Theology* 28, no. 1 (January 2012): 1–24.

3. For this development, see especially John Mahoney, *The Making of Moral Theology: A Study of the Roman Catholic Tradition* (Oxford: Oxford University Press, 1987). See also John T. McNeill, *A History of the Cure of Souls* (New York: Harper Torchbooks, 1951); John Chryssavgis, *Repentance and Confession* (Brookline, MA: Holy Cross Orthodox Press, 1990); and Kallistos Ware, "The Orthodox Experience of Repentance," in *The Inner Kingdom*, 43–48 (Crestwood, NY: St. Vladimir's Seminary Press, 2001).

4. Mahoney, *The Making of Moral Theology,* 1–36, and McNeill, *A History of the Cure of Souls,* 112–35.

5. See Christos Yannaras, *Orthodoxy and the West,* trans. Peter Chamberas and Norman Russell (Brookline, MA: Holy Cross Orthodox Press, 2006), 94–97.

6. Though it should be noted that, given the capabilities of modern technology, there is no such thing as nonrisky information. Also, depending on what part of the world one lives in, information like name and place of residence can be life-threatening.

7. By "affective consequences" or "affective effect," I mean that truth-telling has the power to transform the emotions or desires one experiences.

8. "On the Web, Pedophiles Extend Their Reach," *The New York Times,* 21 August 2006, available through http://www.nytimes.com.

9. Fyodor Dostoyevsky, *Crime and Punishment,* trans. Richard Pevear and Larissa Volokhonsky (New York: Alfred A. Knopf, 1993), 405–22.

10. Ibid., 549–51.

11. Jacques Lacan, "The Direction of the Treatment and the Principles of Its Power," in *Écrits,* trans. Bruce Fink (New York: W. W. Norton, 2006), 494 [591].

12. Bruce Fink, *Lacan to the Letter* (Minneapolis: University of Minnesota Press, 2004), 11. For further elaboration of the difference between transference on the imaginary axis and transference on the symbolic axis, see 5–11. See also Bruce Fink, *A Clinical Introduction to Lacanian Psychoanalysis* (Cambridge, MA: Harvard University Press, 1997), 1–71.

13. *Pseudo-Dionysius: The Complete Works*, trans. Colm Luibheid (Mahwah, NJ: Paulist Press, 1987), 79.

14. Ibid. For the McGinn translation, see *The Foundations of Mysticism*, vol. 1 of *The Presence of God: A History of Western Christian Mysticism* (New York: Crossroad, 1991), 167.

15. *Pseudo-Dionysius*, 140.

16. Jean-Luc Marion, *God without Being*, trans. Thomas A. Carlson (Chicago: University of Chicago Press, 1991), 12.

17. Ibid., 14.

18. Ibid, 19–21.

19. Jean-Luc Marion, *Being Given: Toward a Phenomenology of Givenness*, trans. Jeffrey L. Kosky (California: Stanford University Press, 2002), 232.

20. Rowan Williams, *The Dwelling of the Light: Praying with Icons of Christ* (Grand Rapids, MI: Eerdmans, 2003), xvii.

21. Ibid., xviii.

22. Ibid., xix.

23. It is widely known within the Orthodox tradition that abbesses hear confession, without being able to perform the ritual of confession.

24. This would continue to be valid if the Roman Catholic and Orthodox churches allowed the ordination of women to the priesthood.

25. Understanding in terms of a checklist of conditions—in other words, under certain conditions an act can be identified as forgiveness—is implicit in recent theological and philosophical accounts of forgiveness. For the theological account, see Bash, *Forgiveness and Christian Ethics*; for the philosophical account, see Charles L. Griswold, *Forgiveness: A Philosophical Exploration* (Cambridge: Cambridge University Press, 2007). Although both Bash and Griswold speak of forgiveness in terms of conditions, both recognize its existential effects. Griswold recognizes that forgiveness involves affectivity, in particular, resentment. On the part of the forgiver, however, all that is required is the will to forgo resentment, not the actual transformation of resentment.

26. Bash, *Forgiveness and Christian Ethics*, 177.

27. Here I am agreeing with Bash and Jesse Couenhoven, who argue that forgiveness cannot simply be about the victim, but must also be about transformation of the wrongdoer. For Couenhoven, see "Forgiveness and Restoration: A Theological Exploration," *Journal of Religion* 90, no. 2 (April 2010): 148–70.

28. As I believe L. Gregory Jones does in *Embodying Forgiveness*.

29. As Griswold contends in *Forgiveness: A Philosophical Exploration*.

30. Miroslav Volf, *Exclusion and Embrace: A Theological Exploration of Identity, Otherness, and Reconciliation* (Nashville: Abingdon Press, 1996), 131–40.

31. Jacques Derrida, *On Cosmopolitanism and Forgiveness*, trans. Michael Hughes (New York: Routledge, 2002); also, "To Forgive: The Unforgivable and the Imprescriptible," trans. Elizabeth Rottenberg, in *Questioning God*, ed. John D. Caputo, Mark Dooley, and Michael J. Scanlon, 21–51 (Bloomington: Indiana University Press, 2001). See also Mary-Jane Rubenstein, "Of Ghosts and Angels: Derrida, Kushner, and the Impossibility of Forgiveness," in *Journal of Cultural and Religious Theory* 9, no. 1 (Winter 2008): 79–95.

32. I thank Jesse Couenhoven for this phrase.

33. It is because of my understanding of forgiveness as communion that my position differs from Donald W. Shriver Jr., *An Ethic for Enemies: Forgiveness in Politics* (Oxford: Oxford University Press, 1995).

34. For a good sociological analysis of apology from the many to the many, see Nicholas Tavuchis, *Mea Culpa: A Sociology of Apology and Reconciliation* (Stanford, CA: Stanford University Press, 1991), esp. 97–117.

35. "Nothing opens the doors of confession so readily as the ability of their leaders to come first with the declaration 'I was wrong'"; Shriver, *An Ethic for Enemies*, 107.

36. Martha Minow argues that the therapeutic healing power that truth-telling can offer to a group whose members have suffered trauma is similar to the healing power of truth-telling for an individual who has suffered trauma. See her *Between Vengeance and Forgiveness: Facing History after Genocide and Mass Violence* (Boston: Beacon Press, 1998), esp. chaps. 4 and 6.

37. Priscilla Hayner, *Unspeakable Truths: Facing the Challenge of Truth Commissions* (New York: Routledge, 2002).

38. For such an example in the abortion debate, listen to the episode "Nemeses" of *This American Life*. Available at http://www.thisamericanlife.org/radio-archives/episode/453/nemeses.

Index

abortion, 93, 192, 193–94
Afanasiev, Nicholas, 60, 63, 105
Agamben, Giorgio, 89
Alcoholics Anonymous (AA), 169–70
Alexo, Kenneth, Jr., 202n21
American democracy, 37, 38, 42,
    51–52
American Revolution, 32
anger, 83–84
Arius, 137
Armenia, 47
Armenian Orthodox Church, 63, 73
art, 106–7
Athanasius of Alexandria, 23, 137
atheism, 44, 98, 127, 128, 132
    atheistic humanism, 33, 34, 40, 49,
        87, 88, 94–95
    Bulgakov on, 37, 39–40, 43
    and divine-human communion,
        142–44, 156, 159
    and individualism, 49, 51
    relationship to human rights, 114,
        115, 121–22, 124
    relationship to liberalism, 51, 87, 93
Audi, Robert, 146
Augustine, St., 89–90, 92
    City of God, 151, 203n35
    and liberalism, 150–51
    on love, 151, 152–53, 154
    rejection of essence/energies
        distinction, 10–11, 90
autonomy, 7, 67, 88, 92, 135, 136,
    145, 158

Badiou, Alain: *Ethics*, 89
Bash, Anthony: on forgiveness,
    225nn25, 27
*Basic Principles of Attitude to the Non-
    Orthodox*, 48
Basil the Great, 23, 24, 25
Behr, John: *The Mystery of Christ*,
    215n39
Bosnian War, 47, 50–51
Brazil, 75
Bretherton, Luke: *Christianity and
    Contemporary Politics*, 201n2
    (Introduction)
Buber, Martin, 105
Bulgakov, Sergius, 13, 33, 36–43, 127
    on atheism, 37, 39–40, 43
    on Christian community, 40
    Christian socialism of, 36–37, 40–41
    on clericalism, 39
    on democracy, 5, 37–38, 40, 41,
        42–43, 45, 53
    on divine-human communion, 53,
        145–46
    The Orthodox Church, 41–42
    on personhood, 99
    Philosophy of Economy, 41
    on separation of church and state, 38,
        42–43
    on social sciences, 39
    on *Sophia*, 41–42, 43
    on the Trinity, 99
    "An Urgent Task," 37, 41
Bulgaria, 44, 47

227

Aristotle Papanikolaou

is professor of theology at Fordham University. He is the author
of *Being With God: Trinity, Apophaticism, and Divine-Human
Communion* (University of Notre Dame Press, 2006).

CPSIA information can be obtained
at www.ICGtesting.com
Printed in the USA
FFOW04n0720100317
33180FF